BRAVE MEN OF WAR
Tales of Valour 1965

BRAVE MEN OF WAR
Tales of Valour 1965

Lt Col Rohit Agarwal (Retd)

BLOOMSBURY
NEW DELHI • LONDON • OXFORD • NEW YORK • SYDNEY

Copyright © 2015, Centre for Land Warfare Studies

First Published, 2015

BLOOMSBURY PUBLISHING INDIA PVT. LTD.
New Delhi   London   Oxford   New York   Sydney

ISBN: 978-93-85436-80-2

10 9 8 7 6 5 4 3 2

Published by Bloomsbury Publishing India Pvt. Ltd.
DDA Complex LSC, Building No. 4, 2nd Floor
Pocket 6 & 7, Sector C
Vasant Kunj, New Delhi 110070

Printed at Sanat Printers, Kundli, Haryana

The Centre for Land Warfare Studies (CLAWS), New Delhi, is an autonomous think tank dealing with contemporary issues of national security and conceptual aspects of land warfare, including conventional and sub-conventional conflicts and terrorism. CLAWS conducts research that is futuristic in outlook and policy-oriented in approach.

Centre for Land Warfare Studies
RPSO Complex, Parade Road, Delhi Cantt, New Delhi 110010
Tel: +91.11.25691308 Fax: +91.11.25692347
Email: landwarfare@gmail.com Website: www.claws.in

Dedicated
to all the brave men who fought the war
and whose names don't find mention
in these pages

Contents

Acknowledgements

I gratefully acknowledge the help and support provided by the veterans and serving personnel of the Indian Army in writing the accounts of our brave and gallant men. I am indebted to Gen Shankar Roychowdhury, PVSM (Retd), Brig DP Nayar (Retd), Col Kanwaljit Singh (Retd), Lt Gen AS Sandhu (Retd), Lt Gen BS Nagal (Retd), Brig Shamsher Singh (Retd), Maj Gen Dubey (Retd), Brig Kanwaljit Singh (Retd), Maj Abdul Hafiz (Retd), Maj Gen Bhatti (Retd), Maj Parminder Singh (Retd), Col Sukhinder Singh (Retd), Brig Ravi Malhotra (Retd), Col RP Joshi (Retd), Brig HS Choudhary (Retd), Brig Arvinder Singh Baicher (Retd), Col J S Bindra (Retd), Brig SS Sohal (Retd), Col DS Shekhawat (Retd), Col HK Jha (Retd), Col Vijay Kala, Maj Satish Khanna (Retd), Sub Maj Amar Singh (Retd), Ris Maj Daryao Singh (Retd), Sub Darshan Singh (Retd) and Sub Naranjan Singh (Retd).

A special thanks is due to HH Capt Amarinder Singh (Retd), 2 Sikh, Deputy Leader of the Opposition in Lok Sabha and former CM of Punjab, for very generously sharing his own research with me. His personal recollections of the war and about the prominent personalities helped fill in a lot of gaps in the narrations. I am also grateful to Mrs Nita Roy for permission to reprint three stories written by late Maj Bhaskar Roy, originally published in the Doon School Magazine.

I am deeply indebted to Maj Gen Shokin Chauhan, SM, VSM, ADG PI, for his support and encouragement, and The War History Cell of Adjutant General Branch for their tireless assistance. Col Gajendra Sankhlan (Retd) provided critical research inputs and invaluable help with the maps.

I would also like to acknowledge Lt Gen Balraj Nagal, PVSM, AVSM, SM (Retd), Director CLAWS, for writing the stories on Lt Col DE Hayde and Heroes of 3 Jat, being a former Colonel of the Regiment of the Jats. His continuous guidance and enablement made this book possible. I would also like to thank the former and current Deputy Directors of CLAWS, Brig Vivek Verma and Col Deepak Induraj, for their constant support. A special thanks to the former for relating his experiences at Point 13620, which form a part of the story 'Spirit of a Warrior'. Thanks are also due to Geetika Kasturi, the Publications Manager at CLAWS, for her patience and perseverance through the confusing number of files that went back and forth as this book was being written and edited

Last but not the least, my grateful acknowledgement to Mr Paul Kumar, Ms Jyoti Mehrotra and Raj Bilochan Prasad at Bloomsbury for their patient indulgence through the multiple, and at times, chaotic revisions and reiterations before the book could take its final shape.

Prologue

Wars fought by the armed forces of a nation are eternalised in the annals of its history. Famous Commanders who led their forces to victory are feted generation after generation, as are soldiers whose valour and bravery captured the imagination of historians. Tributes and respect are richly deserved, for the nation owes a debt of honour to them. The Second World War saw heroes like George S. Patton, Erwin Rommel, Georgy Zhukov and Bernard Montgomery epitomise brilliance, genius and military leadership, and many Indians won the Victoria Cross, including Lt Gen PS Bhagat.

Stories of countless others who fought bravely, often to their last breath and last drop of their blood, are either forgotten completely or reduced to footnotes in the larger volumes of recorded history or left in official citations. It's not that the nation's debt to them is any less, it's just that the footnotes in history books have only so much space. This book is an attempt to extract some of those stories from footnotes and citations, and give them a rightful place of their own.

These stories have been pieced together from official histories, war diaries, previously published books and accounts, and from conversation with many of those who participated in the war. Even after telling these stories, many more will still remain untold – mainly because there's no one left to narrate them fifty years down the line. It would, therefore, be in order to offer obeisance to every single warrior who fought in the 1965 Indo-Pakistan war, even if his name doesn't appear in these pages.

The sights, sounds, and stench of the battlefield can never be reproduced on paper. Nor can the adrenaline rush or the abject fear that soldiers feel when bullets are flying and shells are falling around them. An author can only hope to tell a story, and leave the readers' imagination to fill in the gap.

An Overview of the War

There is never a right time for war. Yet, 1965 was particularly unsuitable for India, since the army had suffered a debacle at the hands of China three years earlier and the nation was humiliated. Attempting to rise like a phoenix from the ashes of this defeat, the Indian Army was in a modernisation and force augmentation phase in 1965 when war was suddenly thrust upon than again. A belligerent and opportunistic Pakistan, arrogant in its overconfidence, assured of its supremacy in equipment and morale, was nevertheless taught a befitting lesson.

The 1965 Indo-Pakistan war was significant for the Indian Army in many ways. There were many firsts. While earlier post-independence wars were confined to far-flung mountainous regions, this was the first time that the heartlands of both India and Pakistan were the battle grounds. Fighting took place almost along the entire Western border, and involved the combat might of both the countries. It was the first time ever that tanks were used in large-scale battles in the subcontinent, and the first time anywhere after the Second World War.

Pakistan was apprehensive about the rapid modernisation being undertaken by India. When completed, it would erode the technological edge they had over their already numerically superior enemy. So they had to act to wrest Jammu and Kashmir from India before it was too late. An assumption of a low morale in the Indian Army after the defeat in 1962 and thus India's likely reluctance to expand the conflict beyond Kashmir formed a significant part of Pakistan's calculus. Another factor in their (mis)calculation was underestimating Prime Minister Lal Bahadur

Shastri's leadership and resolve. Following the footsteps of a towering leader like Pandit Jawaharlal Nehru, he was considered by Pakistan to be a lightweight. They learnt otherwise at their cost when the diminutive leader dealt firmly and decisively with the threat to national security posed by Pakistani designs.

The threat of war loomed ominously ever since Pakistan's tentative experiment in the Rann of Kutch in April 1965. Bolstered by the fact that the conflict had remained confined to the Rann, and that foreign powers were quick to intervene to mediate a ceasefire, Pakistan felt that a swift operation in Jammu and Kashmir could win that coveted prize at a low cost. Thus, they launched Operation Gibraltar, it had striking similarities with the modus operandi adopted by the country in 1947–48. Irregulars infiltrating across the then unfenced Cease Fire Line (CFL), led and bolstered by regular army personnel in mufti, made a quick dash for Srinagar, hoping to start an uprising and declare Jammu and Kashmir's independence before Indian forces had a chance to react.

Early detection by shepherds, the lukewarm response of the local population, and swift retaliatory action by the Indian Army foiled their plans completely. To block ingress routes and choke supplies to the infiltrators, Indian forces undertook limited offensive actions to capture vital areas as also improve their own positions. Significant amongst these was the heroic capture of the Haji Pir pass, which gave the Indian side another, shorter link to the valley and Srinagar.

Pakistan reacted to the loss of the strategically vital Haji Pir with Operation Grand Slam – an offensive into India's vulnerable Chhamb–Jaurian sector. While this move was not completely unanticipated, the Indian side was a little unsettled by the rapidity of the enemy advance and this led to temporary upsets. Fortunately, Pakistan failed to push through their initial advantage and its forces paused for almost a day while the command of the attacking force changed. This gave Indian forces the time to regain balance and organise defences.

Enemy inroads into this sector threatened to cut off the vital Jammu–Srinagar communication link. To deny Pakistan the freedom to use its reserve forces to reinforce their initial success, India decided to retaliate by striking at its heart. Operation Riddle was launched into Pakistan's Punjab, aimed at a rapid advance along multiple axes astride the Grand Trunk (GT) road and threaten Lahore, the most prestigious and vulnerable target in Pakistan.

The initial Indian advance met with unexpected success, but could not be exploited due to a breakdown in communication. However, the threat to Lahore had the desired reaction of stopping the Pakistan offensive in the Akhnoor sector in its tracks. While the three-pronged Indian offensive stalled after an initial success, Pakistan launched a massive counter-thrust towards the Indian heartland after recovering in the Kasur–Khem Karan sector.

The sugarcane fields of Punjab witnessed heavy fighting as the armoured might of the Pakistani army attempted to strike its way towards the Beas bridge on the GT road and Jandiala Guru east of Amritsar. The plan was audacious but the execution, fortunately for India, wasn't. The Pakistan offensive by armoured forces was blocked and destroyed just a few kilometres inside the International Boundary (IB). The destruction of the Pakistan offensive force was attributed to the valorous and resolute action by the Indian infantry and armoured forces, and the final situation where Pakistan tank crews fled, abandoning many serviceable Patton tanks; these were later collected in what became known as 'Patton Nagar'.

In the meanwhile, the Indian offensive had been launched across the border in the Sialkot sector. It managed to make better headway than its Pakistani counterpart, but the prize of Chawinda or the Marala–Ravi Link Canal remained elusive even as the UN brokered a ceasefire. The Tashkent Declaration of 10 January 1966 was the culmination of the peace process in which India and Pakistan agreed to return to positions held on 5 August 1965 and repatriate prisoners of war.

The war ended but both sides had not fully exhausted their

combat power at the end of hostilities. However, the casualty figures and also the size of territories occupied by the opposing sides give a clear indication that India had the upper hand. Indian forces suffered 2,862 killed, while the Pakistani forces lost 5,800 all ranks. India captured 1,920 sq km of Pakistani territory, while 540 sq km of Indian territory was under Pakistani control when a United Nations brokered ceasefire put an end to the war on 23 September. Any ambiguities about which side came out the better were put to rest by none other than a former Commander-in-Chief of Pakistan Army Lt Gen Gul Hassan Khan. Gen Khan, who was Pakistan's Director Military Operations during the war, writes in his memoirs (published in 1993):

> ... *we have deluded ourselves that we emerged victorious in our 1965 conflict with India. – far from it. All that we attained was to ensure that our adversary did not make any telling gains, and this is a feeble pretext to console ourselves.*

The fiercest battles were fought over pieces of land or hills which, won over through blood and toil, were finally handed back after the war. It is fortunate that the soldier is not given to reflect on the importance of the land he is fighting over. For the soldier, it is an objective to be captured, or defended. It is a task that is to be performed, even at the cost of his life, for the *izzat* (honour) of the unit and duty to the country as well as self-respect. 'In war, the soldier gets no reward but honour, that of the regiment, and if at all he knows why he is fighting, it is only because of the tug to that invisible thread.'[1]

India clearly proved its ascendancy over a better equipped Pakistani army. It also regained its glory and morale after the setback of the Chinese debacle of 1962. All lingering doubts were put to rest after a short span of six years, when India won a decisive victory in 1971, forcing the Pakistani armed forces in East Pakistan to formally surrender and create an independent country, Bangladesh.

---

[1] Brig Desmond E Hayde, *The Battle of Dograi*.

THE PRELUDE

Spirit of a Warrior
Major Baljit Singh Randhawa – Kargil, Point 13620

A small group of soldiers is winding its way up a steep track towards the Indian Army post nestled on top of a mountain near Kargil, known merely by the intriguing name of Point 13620, which is actually its height in feet. The soldiers are led by a young officer and following in their wake is a trail of mules. The men and mules are transporting supplies for the troops deployed at top, and the officer is on a tour to familiarise himself with all the posts in the area. It is a routine mission, the year is 1993 and the Kargil war is still six years away. The officer, Captain Verma of the artillery, suddenly becomes aware of a commotion at the end of the column.

The mules have taken advantage of a momentary lapse of attention by their handlers and wandered off the track, apparently lured by tufts of sparse grass that have survived the vagaries of winter snow. The soldiers and the civilian handlers watch in dismay as a series of explosions flash suddenly, killing the mules who now lie in pools of their own blood and flesh. Capt Verma recalls the stern warning the Adjutant of the Madras Battalion at the base had given him: 'Never wander off the track. There are mines scattered all over and the track is the only guaranteed safe path.' Anti-personnel mines – small plastic containers packed with deadly explosives and primed to blow up when stepped upon – are relics from the wars fought on this mountain. Laid by Pakistani soldiers who once defended it, they are often displaced by cycles of falling and melting snow.

Since the mules are beyond help, the party continues on its way to the top, the mood is sombre after the ghastly scene of destruction that the men have just witnessed. On reaching, they sit down to rest their weary limbs while the JCO, the Post Commander, welcomes the officer and offers him a much needed cup of tea. As they start talking, Capt Verma asks the Post Commander about the uncleared mines.

The JCO goes on to narrate a remarkable story that sounds like fairytale to Capt Verma. 'Sir, this post was with the Pakistanis in 1965, that's when they first laid these mines. Then we captured it. Maj Randhawa of 4th Battalion the Rajput Regiment (4 Rajput) lost his life capturing this post. Even today, we can feel his spirit with us at the post.'

The young captain is sceptical, but the JCO continues, 'Only a few days back, when one of the sentries was sleeping on night guard, he was slapped awake. When he looked around, there was no one. They say that Maj Randhawa doesn't let any sentry sleep on this post while on duty.' Seeing the disbelief on Capt Verma's face, the JCO explains, 'See, there is also a tradition that no officer is stationed on this post. They say that with Maj Randhawa's spirit here, no other officer is needed. And whenever an officer has tried to spend a night here, he has had to leave before the night was over. He either fell ill and had to be evacuated, or was called down for some urgent mission elsewhere.'

Even though the young Captain is not fully convinced by the JCO's tale, he is glad he's not scheduled to spend the night at the post. He completes his tour of the post and after a quick bite, begins his descent to Kargil. However, he makes up his mind to find out more about Maj Randhawa and the battle of Point 13620. What he learns in his quest is an amazing tale of valour and determination.

Pakistan had been testing India's patience right from the beginning of 1965. Its misadventure in the Rann of Kutch in

April that year was one such provocation. The on-going low-level conflict that it tried to sustain in Jammu and Kashmir was another reason. The volatile Cease Fire Line (CFL), now known as the Line of Control (LoC), was constantly being violated by Pakistan, and soon the frequency of the skirmishes was stepped up in 1965.

The Indian Army decided not to remain passive any more. In May, a decision was taken to launch a limited offensive action to display India's resolve to hit back as well as to deny Pakistan the ability to strike across the CFL with impunity. The stage for this engagement was formed by lofty mountain features, one of which was Point 13620, and the other an adjoining feature called Black Rocks. These were occupied by Pakistan and troops located here dominated the Indian positions, including the Brigade Headquarters at Kargil. Not only could the men in these positions keep a watch on all activities of the Indian troops, they could also checkand correct their long-range artillery fire from several kilometres behind. They could easily disrupt traffic on the vital Srinagar–Kargil–Leh road, which was the lifeline for the forward troops. Capturing these heights would serve the dual purpose of asserting India's stance against a belligerent opponent and to secure this vital line of communication.

The task of evicting the enemy from these two features was assigned to 4th Battalion the Rajput Regiment (4 Rajput), which was part of the 121 Independent Infantry Brigade Group located at Kargil. Lt Col Sudershan Singh, the Commanding Officer (CO) of 4 Rajput, was summoned to the Brigade Headquarters by Brigadier V.K. Ghai, the Brigade Commander, one May morning. 'I want you to evict the enemy from 13620 and Black Rocks,' Brig Ghai told him. 'I know the time is short, but that's also to our advantage as we will take the enemy completely by surprise.'

The attack was to commence on the night of 16 May, so the CO barely had three days to work out his plan and prepare the battalion for a task that was nothing short of gargantuan. In this short time, he had to reconnoitre the objective, formulate his plan, divide the task between his Company Commanders, and allow them time to carry out their own reconnaissance. Simultaneously, the myriad details that go into preparations for such an operation, like the coordination of the fire plan with the artillery, cleaning and preparation of weapons, making arrangements for battle loads – all had to be taken care of. Due to the porous nature of the CFL, and the consequent presence of suspected enemy agents within the village, ensuring that news of the impending operations did not leak out was also vital. This added to the complications because it meant that civilian porters and ponies usually employed to carry heavy loads to leave combatants free to fight unencumbered, could not be used to. The dilemma was resolved thanks to 9 Border Roads Task Force,[2] which provided the manpower to carry ammunition, rations, and stores to forward pickets.[3]

The best place to get a closer look at the objectives was the forward-most post of the Rajputs, called Post No 8. Colonel Sudershan Singh peered at Point 13620 through his binoculars from this post and studied the enemy defences on the top. It was a craggy, rocky feature and the climb steepened steadily, becoming almost vertical for the last few hundred metres. The crest where the enemy positions lay, rose almost like a pyramid from the surrounding rocks. On the top of this pyramid, Pakistanis had used rocks and stones to construct bunkers from which they could shoot without being exposed to fire themselves. They had also constructed a five-foot high stone perimeter wall around their position. He saw that the only way to approach the top was from a narrow 'spur'[4] that was jutting out towards the left from this paramedical feature.

---

[2] A unit under the Border Roads Organisation, which consists mainly of civilians and is tasked with constructing and maintaining roads in forward areas.

[3] S.N. Prasad and U.P. Thapliyal, *The India–Pakistan War of 1965: A History*, Dehradun, New Delhi, Natraj Publishers, p. 50.

[4] A lateral ridge descending from a hill or mountain is referred to as a spur. A feature may have one or more spurs emanating from its top. The area between spurs is called a 're-entrant'. It is virtually impossible to reach the top of a hill from a re-entrant, which is why the approaches lay along spurs.

The enemy would also be aware of the possible approach, and the defences would have been sited to ensure that maximum fire could be brought down on anyone attempting to move up this spur. Surprise would, therefore, be crucial to the success of the Rajput attack. Their only chance lay in being able to move as close to the top without alerting the enemy, thus minimising the time they would be exposed to gunfire. After carrying out his initial reconnaissance of the objective and making up his mind about the best approach to attack, the CO briefed his Company Commanders.

Maj (later Brig) D.P. Nayyar and Maj Baljit Singh Randhawa were commanding Alpha (A) Company and Bravo (B) Company respectively. Maj Randhawa and his company were given the job of capturing Point 13620, while Maj Nayyar was to capture Black Rocks (Map 1). Maj Bikram Singh Chattri with Charlie (C) Company was to be the reserve. Since the battalion was deployed to hold defences which could not be left unmanned, the fourth, Delta (D) Company was to stay back and do the job.

While the battalion was buzzing with feverish activity in preparation for the attack, the young officers who had been left out of the action were feeling a little short-changed. Capt (now Colonel [Retd]) Ranbir Singh and Capt Upkar Singh Ahluwalia separately approached the CO to request that they be allowed to take part in the attack. The CO denied Capt Ahluwalia's request since his D Company had the important task of holding the defences, which were spread over an area of 13 kilometres. After much insistence by an eager Capt Ranbir and with the support of the CO of the artillery regiment who was witness to his pleading, the CO agreed to let him accompany B Company, Ranbir's former group, as the leading Platoon Commander.

The young Maj Randhawa had seen action with the battalion in Gaza and had also taken part in the operations to liberate Goa. Popular amongst the officers and men alike, he was known to be a simple, hardworking officer who never said 'no' to anyone. Happy-go-lucky and physically very fit, he was happiest when playing hockey with the men or singing Punjabi folk songs with his fellow officers. He had recently been blessed with a baby boy. At the time, he was quite excited about the prospect of commanding a company in battle, and approached Maj Nayyar for advice. Not only was the A Company Commander senior, he had also commanded B Company during the Goa operations. Nayyar assured Randhawa, 'The Gujjar troops of B Company are the finest, and knowing you, I am sure you will lead them to victory and glory.'

On the night of 15 May, the assaulting companies moved under the cover of darkness into Post No. 8 from where the CO had carried out his recce. On the 16th morning, Maj Randhawa and his Platoon Commanders took turns to stealthily approach as close to the objective as they could, to get a better idea of what awaited them that night. From their hiding places, they could observe the enemy soldiers relaxing and smoking. 'Enjoy yourselves all you can now,' Maj Randhawa thought, 'We're coming to get you tonight.'

Maj Randhawa selected a feature called 'Crooked Finger' as the Forming Up Place (FUP) where his company would organise themselves for the final assault that night. The approach from the FUP to the final objective was almost vertical and extremely narrow. This meant that the assaulting troops would have to approach it along a narrow front, giving the enemy the opportunity to concentrate their fire. To add to their problems, the entire area was under snow. This was bound to make their progress up the steep climb even slower. Their ascent was to take them from about 10,000 feet to almost 14,000 feet – a steep climb over a distance of about one kilometre, with each man carrying 20 kgs of weapons and equipment, under enemy fire. At these altitudes just the act of putting one foot ahead of the other while walking along a flat surface is enough to make one pant for breath. Maj Randhawa knew it would take all of them every ounce of their determination and courage to capture their objective.

After getting a fair idea of what lay ahead for the night's operation, they returned to the picket, leaving behind troops under Lt Chattopadhyay to keep vigil at the FUP. The rest of the day was spent in restless anticipation of the impending battle, which often prevents soldiers from getting much required rest.

At 2000 hours sharp, Maj Randhawa and his company marched out of the picket. It was a moonlit night, not the most ideal situation for such an operation since their olive green uniforms could easily be picked up by an alert enemy against the pristine white backdrop of snow. Marching towards the FUP, Maj Randhawa noticed a furry black creature moving silently alongside the soldiers. It was Kalu, the adopted pet dog of the post who had decided to accompany his masters. Fearing his bark would give their positions away to the enemy, they tried to persuade Kalu to return, but to no avail. To his credit, there was not a whimper out of Kalu during the entire ascent.

The company was ready in the FUP and raring to go well before the appointed Hotel Hour ('H' Hour) Hour – 0230 hours. Not wanting to waste time, risk detection, and to allow the men to cool down Maj Randhawa decided to attack before the fixed time. At 0200 hours, with a silent prayer on their lips, B Company of 4 Rajput crossed the 'Start Line' (SL).[5] The silent prayer replaced the fierce battle cry which is the rule on such occasions because this was a 'silent attack'. As opposed to a 'noisy attack' where artillery batteries begin pounding enemy locations the moment the attack starts and troops charge at the objective yelling war cries, silence was important to maintain the element of surprise as long as possible. This would enable the attacking troops to negotiate as much of the steep climb as they could before the enemy is alerted to the attack on their positions.

The surprise was short-lived and after about 150 metres of the climb the enemy was alerted, probably by a vigilant sentry. All hell broke loose as the enemy opened up with all their weapons firing on the Rajput troops making their way up along the narrow

---

[5] The forward edge of the FUP is designated as the Start Line (SL). The Hotel Hour (or 'H' Hour) is the exact time assaulting troops are supposed to cross the SL. The exactitude is maintained to coordinate the attack with other assaulting troops and more importantly, with artillery fire support.

pathway. Hugging the ground and making skilful use of the timiest of covers provided by rocks, the brave men advanced against raining machine gun and mortar fire. Maj Randhawa moved from rock to rock, judging the pauses between machine gun fire to dash forward. He did not allow the attack to stall, urging his men forward and leading by personal example in utter disregard to his own safety.

Since the attack was now far from 'silent', rousing cries of 'Bol Bajrang Bali ki Jai!' (the Rajput war cry) motivated the men forward. By 0315 hours, the Rajputs had broken into the enemy defences, negotiating the perimeter wall and rushing forward to evict the enemy soldiers from their bunkers and trenches. Maj Randhawa was at the forefront, leading and guiding his men on. The rat-tat-tat of machine gun fire and periodic loud thumps of exploding grenades filled the air. The dust and smoke from the explosions reduced the already dim visibility, further obscuring the enemy bunkers at the objective.

The stone bunkers were interconnected by shallow communication trenches along which the enemy could crawl undetected and suddenly appear at another place to open fire. The Rajputs closed in towards the centre, clearing each bunker by rushing at it, firing indiscriminately, and then hurling grenades before entering and finishing off any men left alive inside. Each bunker that was cleared had to be held to prevent the enemy soldiers from crawling back.

Maj Randhawa saw Capt Ranbir was hit while storming a bunker, and blood was oozing from the side of his head. At once he said, 'Move back and take care of your wound,' but Capt Ranbir insisted on pressing on with his platoon.

By 0350 hours, Maj Randhawa realised that dawn was approaching fast. He needed to speed up the attack and clear the enemy position before that, because his troops caught in the open would become cannon fodder for the Pakistanis ensconced in the remaining bunkers. There was one particular bunker that was holding up the advance with accurate machine gun fire and

Maj Randhawa decided to tackle this himself. He dashed forward unmindful of the flying bullets, firing into the bunker as he entered it. As he did so, he came face-to-face with an enemy JCO, and both fired simultaneously. The JCO fell dead to Randhawa's bullets, but not before he had fired a burst at the Majors chest too.

Though badly wounded, Maj Randhawa knew that one last determined push lay between victory and defeat. He refused to be evacuated, continuing to push his men to move forward until finally, his body had taken all it could withstand and he fell unconscious. By then the CO had moved up to the objective, and he asked Capt Ranbir to take over command of the company and push the attack to its culmination. By 0415 hours, with daylight dangerously close, the enemy finally had enough and abandoned their positions for the safety of the reverse slope. The Rajputs chased them down the slope, and as the day of 17 May 1965 dawned, the prize of Point 13620 was in their hands. Maj Randhawa was posthumously awarded the Maha Vir Chakra (MVC) for his gallant actions.

Meanwhile, on the right flank, phase two of the assault had already been launched for the capture of the second objective, Black Rocks. A fierce battle was raging there as well. A Company, under Maj D.P. Nayyar, had negotiated an equally arduous climb along the jagged, partially snow-covered terrain of the Black Rocks feature to reach their FUP. Although they were to have waited for the capture of Point 13620 before commencing their attack, they heard the gunfire raging from there, which is why Maj Nayyar decided to take a calculated risk and launched his own attack right away. He reasoned that the element of surprise had been lost in any case, and nothing would be gained by waiting further.

During their recce of the objective, Maj Nayyar had found two more knolls behind Black Rocks itself, which had not been visible from the Indian positions. He had named them Peak 1 and Peak 2, and had factored into his plan the need to capture these two before attacking the top of Black Rocks. A Company now launched near simultaneous attacks – No. 1 Platoon under 2Lt Harbhagwant Singh on the first Peak and No. 2 Platoon under Sub Ranjit Singh on the second. After a brief but fierce battle, these two peaks were wrested from the enemy – and then No. 3 Platoon under Capt S.N. Bhatnagar went straight for Black Rocks.

Maj Nayyar was following closely behind this platoon and soon realised that the area between the two peaks and Black Rocks, which he referred to as the Bowl, was a virtual death trap. It was covered in knee-deep snow and served as a good 'killing ground' for the enemy sitting on top of Black Rocks. He therefore ordered Capt Bhatnagar to outflank Black Rocks from the left, while the enemy's heads were kept down by fire from the troops at Peak 1. Simultaneously, he called for artillery and mortar fire on Black Rocks. The outflanking force had to traverse over extremely tough ground, but the result was reward enough. The enemy was completely taken by surprise by troops suddenly appearing from an unexpected direction, and within no time Black Rocks was captured.

In this way, 4 Rajput successfully captured both its objectives, but the price of victory was costly. Casualties suffered by the battalion included one officer, one JCO, thirteen Other Ranks (ORs) killed and two officers, one JCO and fifty ORs wounded.

But the story of Point 13620 doesn't end here. The feature changed hands several times after Maj Randhawa and his company captured it. Hardly a month later, it was handed back to Pakistan after the United Nations (UN) intervened and Pakistan's assurance that there would be no more cease fire violations. In August 1965 it was once again captured by India, and again returned under the Tashkent Agreement of 1966. It was captured for the third time during the 1971 war, and having learnt a lesson, this time round it was retained by India. And that's how Capt Verma happened to visit the area in 1993.

OPERATION GIBRALTAR

The Uprising that Never Was

For Mohammad Din, a young shepherd from Dara Kassi village near Gulmarg, 5 August 1965 was like any other day. He had set out early one morning, leading his flock to one of the many grazing grounds a little distance from the village. Once there, he found his favourite spot under a tree where he could recline and spend time daydreaming, while keep an eye on the animals. He didn't want any of them to go wandering off too far and waste his time in gathering them when it was time to go home. His reverie was broken a few hours later when he saw two men wearing green salwar kameezes that looked more like uniforms, approaching. Tall, swarthy and armed with deadly looking rifles, they certainly didn't look like locals to Mohammad. A little scared, he was just contemplating flight when one of the two strangers called out and summoned him. 'What's your name?' the stranger asked the scared boy, who managed to stammer out the reply. 'Mohammad, have you seen any military units around?' Shaking his head in negation, Mohammad's suspicion about these men and their intentions grew. 'Can you find out where the nearest military unit is?' the other man asked. 'We'll give you Rs 400 if you can guide us to it.'

This was a princely sum for the poor shepherd, more than he had ever seen. But his instinct told him that there was something very wrong about these people. Gathering his courage and wits, Mohammad replied nervously, 'I don't know myself, but I can find out from others in the village. If you wait here, I'll come back after finding out and then you can give me the money.' To his relief, the strangers agreed, and he quickly rounded up his flock to beat a hasty retreat to his village. Leaving the animals there, he ran all the way to the nearest police station at Tangmarg and reported his encounter with the strangers.

This scene was being repeated with remarkable similarity a few hundred kilometres away near Mendhar with another young herdsman, Wazir Mohammad of Dhabrot village, being accosted by another group of strangers and being made a similar offer. Wazir, too, reported the suspicious strangers and did not fall prey to their monetary enticements. It was thus that reports of large-scale infiltration started trickling in from various parts of Jammu and Kashmir.

The formations at both the locations, 161 Infantry Brigade and 120 Infantry Brigade respectively, responded to this information by sending out strong patrols to hunt out the infiltrators. A patrol from the 7th Battalion the Bihar Regiment (7 Bihar) in the Gulmarg area chased the infiltrators, who managed to disappear into the dense forests, but left behind a substantial cache of weapons.

In Mendhar, Capt Chander Narain Singh of 2nd Battalion the Garhwal Regiment (2 Garhwal), who was attached to 120 Infantry Brigade headquarters, was sent out with an ad hoc platoon made up of brigade headquarter personnel to deal with the infiltrators. Possibly, the infiltrators had anticipated a contingency where their presence would be reported, because they had taken up strong defensive positions on a hill. When the patrol approached, it was met with strong machine gun and mortar fire, killing one of the soldiers.

Capt Chander ordered his patrol to take position and they fired back. He instructed the patrol to keep firing to keep the enemy pinned down and crawled towards one of the flanks. Taking aimed fire, he silenced one of the machine guns firing from the hill top. The volume of fire that continued raining on them convinced Capt Chander that the enemy position was too strong to brush aside during the daytime. He, therefore, prepared a plan to launch an attack when night fell, and briefed his patrol accordingly. When night came, Capt Chander led a daring charge up the hill despite the heavy fire that rained all around them. In one rush they progressed

Infiltrators being Rounded Up

Captured infiltrators in Kashmir ready to be transferred to prisons

halfway up and then paused to reorganise. Deploying half his patrol here to give covering fire, he led the other half to a flanking attack on the enemy position. The attack was successful, but Capt Chander was cut down by a machine gun burst as he approached the top. The enemy fled, leaving behind six dead and many more wounded, besides a huge quantity of arms, ammunition, and equipment. Capt Chander Narain Singh was awarded the MVC for this brave action.

News of sightings of and encounters with infiltrators kept coming in from different parts of the state the next few days. The full extent of Paksitan's nefarious designs was soon pieced together through the interrogation of prisoners from different areas, and

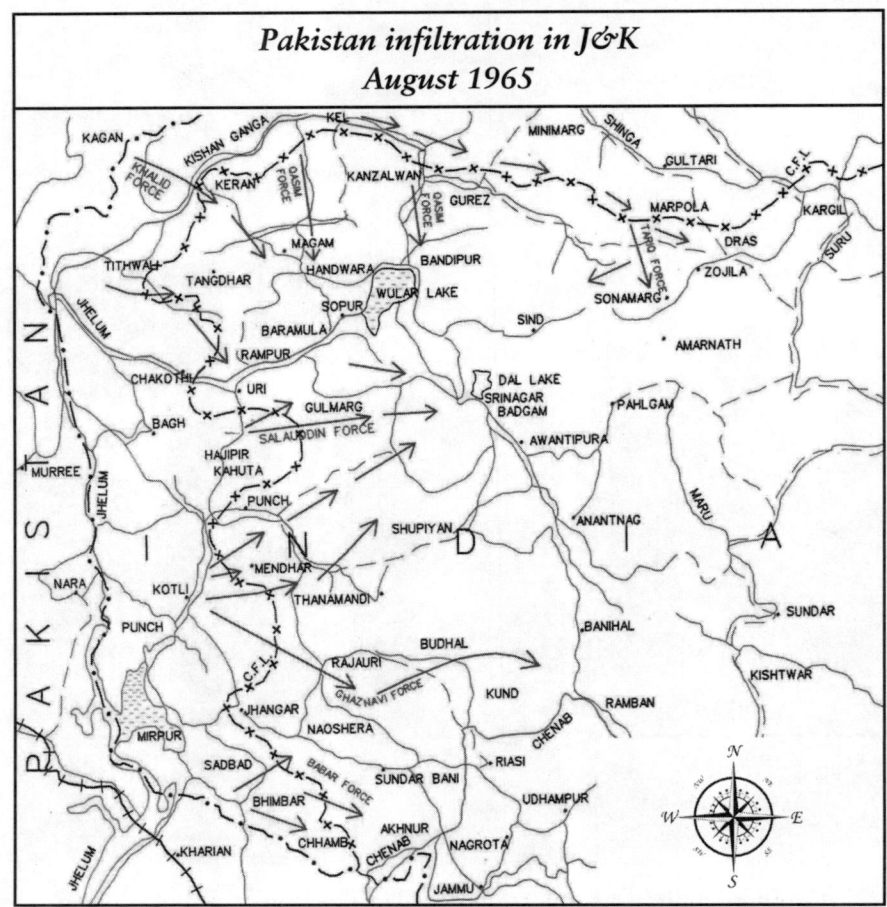

**Pakistan infiltration in J&K
August 1965**

units all over were put on high alert. Reports of large concentrations of raiders came in from Kalakot (near Rajouri), Magam (between Gulmarg and Srinagar), Haji Pir, Doda, and Chhamb. There were widespread instances of raids, sabotage, and skirmishes across the state. By 8 August, a large number of infiltrators had managed to sneak into the suburbs of Srinagar, and were dangerously close to the Srinagar airport. A company of 8 Jammu and Kashmir Militia and two troops of tanks from Central Indian Horse were deployed to protect the airfield.

The pattern of infiltration and inputs from prisoners indicated that the groups were crossing the Cease Fire Line (CFL) along selected locations and converging towards Srinagar from different directions. En route, they were taking every opportunity to raid isolated pickets and administrative dumps, and trying to disrupt communication by sabotaging bridges, telephone, and other communication lines. The Pakistani press and radio broadcasts had meanwhile started spewing out propaganda of how the people of Kashmir were rising up in revolt against India. Of course, on the ground the situation was completely different, as the reactions of the two shepherds, and also the ubiquitous hostility of the local populace towards the infiltrators, indicated.

On 11 August, Lt Gen Harbakhsh Singh landed in Srinagar to take stock of the situation himself. Capt Amarinder Singh, Member of Parliament and former Chief Minister of Punjab, who was the General's ADC at that time recalls that the situation was grim, and the need to build up additional troops in the valley urgent. Lt Gen Harbakhsh, therefore, ordered one company of 4 Sikh Light Infantry to be carried in his own aircraft. Also, 163 Infantry Brigade was moved from Leh to Srinagar.

On 13 August, the 8th Battalion the Kumaon Regiment (8 Kumaon) battalion base at Naugam came under heavy attack, supported by Bren guns, Brownings, rockets, and mortars. The enemy had achieved surprise, but the troops of the battalion reacted with alacrity and were returning fire after occupying their trenches within no time. The CO, Lt Col MV Gore, was personally controlling the battle, moving from trench, when he was hit by an enemy automatic burst and was killed instantaneously. The battalion second-in-command, Maj Gopal Singh was also wounded, but the battalion repulsed the attack with heavy injuries to the enemy.

Simultaneously with attacks and raids by the infiltrators deep inside, the Pakistani artillery had stepped up the frequency and ferocity of firing across all along the CFL. In the most severe of such shelling incidents, the Commander of 191 Infantry Brigade at Chhamb, Brig BF Masters was killed along with several officers of the brigade staff. This setback notwithstanding, the Indian forces had a firm upper hand against the infiltrators by now, and were undertaking aggressive actions to trace, chase, and decimate them from all across the state. The tide turned completely when the Indian forces decided to take the battle into the Pakistani side of the CFL as described in the next chapter.

HAJI PIR
OPERATION BAKSHI

The ceasefire at the end of hostilities in the 1947–48 Kashmir war left a sore thumb (literally and figuratively) sticking into the Indian side of the CFL. This was the Haji Pir bulge, which served as a convenient launch pad for Pakistani infiltrators. Before independence, the shortest route from Jammu to Srinagar ran via Poonch through Uri over the Haji Pir pass located in this bulge. According to legend, the Mughal emperor Shah Jahan was travelling from Rawalpindi to Srinagar and one night before his entourage was to cross this pass, he dreamt that the 'mazar'[1] of a great Pir (saint) was located on this pass. To his surprise, he found the mazar just as he had seen in his dream, and was the first person to pay respects there.[2] The loss of this pass meant the vehicles travelling from Poonch to Srinagar had to go by the longer route via Banihal pass (later tunnel), increasing the distance by 200 kilometres (km).

Pakistan set Operation Gibraltar into motion in the first week of August 1965 and reports of large-scale infiltrations started trickling in from different parts of Jammu and Kashmir. Lt Gen Harbakhsh Singh, the Army Commander (GOC-in-C) Western Command, had recommended a change in the deployment and strategy to deal with the Pakistani misadventure across the CFL even before the full magnitude of Operation Gibraltar was realised. His plan called for strong reserves to tackle infiltrators and simultaneously strengthen forward positions to prevent infiltration and thwart capture of important areas. He also proposed taking a limited offensive action across the CFL to capture areas which

---

[1] Tomb.
[2] Amarinder Singh, *Lest We Forget*, pp. 345–46.

served as launch pads for infiltration. The Haji Pir bulge was high on this list.

The magnitude of the infiltration operations was apparent as it unfolded between 5 and 8 August, and the Jammu and Kashmir government had some very anxious moments. On 8 August, the Chief Minister even recommended that the state be handed over to the army and martial law be imposed. Lt Gen Harbakhsh Singh strongly advised the Chief of the Army Staff (COAS) and in turn the government, against such a move. It would be playing right into Pakistan's hands by drawing international attention besides tying down urgently required troops. Instead, the strength of regular troops was reinforced by rushing additional battalions into the valley. The situation was soon stabilised by relentlessly hunting down the infiltrators.

By 11 August, matters had settled down enough for orders for the capture of the Haji Pir bulge to be given. The main task was allotted to 68 Infantry Brigade commanded by Brig (later Lt Gen) ZC (Zoru) Bakshi, a Second World War veteran who had fought in Burma. On 18 August, formal orders were issued for the operation, code-named 'Bakshi' after the 68 Infantry Brigade Commander. Simultaneously, Operation Faulad was to be launched from the direction of Poonch and link up with the attacking forces to complete the pincer that would seize the Haji Pir bulge, by clearing the enemy from the disused Poonch–Uri road.

Brig Bakshi's plan was to tackle the Haji Pir pass by launching his battalions along two approaches. 1 Para was to attack along the right (West) flank and capture three intermediate features, namely Sank, also known as Point 9591, Sar and Ledwali Gali, while 19 Punjab was to advance along the left (East) flank and capture Bedori, a prominent feature East of the Haji Pir pass. 4 Rajput would thereafter capture the pass itself (Map 2). But like the old saying goes, the 'first casualty in battle is the plan.'

Boldest Action Safest
Major Ranjeet Singh Dyal
– Haji Pir

Maj Ranjeet Singh Dyal had recently taken over as the Second-in-Command (2IC) of 1st Battalion the Parachute Regiment (1 Para), located in the Kashmir valley, after being posted in from 50 Para Brigade where he had been serving as the Brigade Major[3] (BM). The Commanding Officer (CO) of 1 Para, Lt Col Prabhjinder Singh, had also taken over command barely twenty days before the launch of Operation Bakshi to capture the Haji Pir bulge between Uri and Poonch by 68 Infantry Brigade. However, both officers knew the battalion and its men well. Over his almost twenty years of service, Maj Dyal had seen action in the Kashmir war of 1947–48 and in the North-Eastern Frontier Agency (NEFA) along with the battalion.

A die-hard soldier from a village called Tukar in Kurukshetra district, Maj Dyal belonged to a family with a tradition of illustrious military service. His brother was a recipient of the Indian Distinguished Service Medal (IDSM) before independence. Maj Dyal had studied at the King George Royal Military College, Jalandhar (which is now Chail Military School). A short, physically tough officer, Maj Dyal was known as a hard taskmaster who was loved by his troops for his fairness and sense of humour. Although the 2IC's role in operations of the battalion is often limited, Maj

---

[3] The Brigade Major used to be the senior staff officer in a brigade, looking after operations. The appointment is now held by a Lt Col and is called GSO 1.

Major Ranjeet Singh Dyal

Dyal was of a different mould. He requested the CO's permission to be on the forefront of the action. His request was readily agreed to, given the critical nature of the operations and the fact that the A Company Commander, Maj Harsh Yadav was away on leave and had not yet been recalled. All the other Company Commanders were outstanding but young officers with very little experience. The presence of a veteran like Maj Dyal at the forefront could (and did) make a great deal of difference in such fluid operations where the Commander was required to take instant decisions rather than wait for orders.

Operation Bakshi was to begin on the night of 24 August after 1 Para, which was deployed in Uri sector, was to be relieved by another battalion. However, heavy rains delayed the relief, which was why the operation itself was delayed by a day. It began on 25 August, and suspected enemy positions at Point 9591, Sawan Pathri and Agiwas, which lay on the approach to Sank, were engaged by a heavy artillery barrage before 1 Para rushed to capture them without resistance. Eager to make up for the delayed start of the operation, Maj Dyal decided to press on with a pre-dawn attack on the Sank feature with two companies, A and C.

He was taking a premeditated risk, since it meant that the fiercest fighting with the enemy at the actual objective was likely to take place in broad daylight rather than under the cover of darkness. The enemy would have the advantage of targeted fire at the assaulting troops from the safety of bunkers and trenches —but if the move succeeded, it would speed up the operation by a day and unnerve the enemy completely. Unfortunately, a determined enemy, assisted by daytime visibility stalled the attack along the barbed wire fences just ahead of the trenches. The fact that incessant rains of the previous days had made the steep slopes even more slippery aggravated their difficulties. The time now was 0930 hours and the casualties were mounting. Maj Dyal evaluated the situation. Even a determined push up the slope in broad daylight had little chance of success. Pulling back meant admitting failure, even if temporarily. Instead of allowing more of his men to fall just to save his own reputation, Maj Dyal decided to pull back for the time being. Bold actions don't always succeed, and a good Commander knows exactly when to push and when to bide his time.

The men of 1 Para broke contact with the enemy and fell back to their previously captured objective. They spent the day observing enemy positions on Sank and preparing for the next attack. Maj Dyal was restless, waiting for nightfall so that he could recommence the operation. To take his mind off his mounting impatience, he went around both the company locations and talked to the men. Joking with them, he ensured that their morale remained high for the second consecutive night attack.

At 2230 hours on 26 August, 1 Para attacked Sank again, this time with the other two companies, that is, B and D, but still under the overall command of Maj Dyal. The enemy was expecting this and the failure of the attack the previous night had emboldened them. They rushed out of their trenches, opening fire with their rifles and machine guns. But the relentless attackers pressed on, unmindful of the bullets flying all around them. Maj Dyal was in the thick of fighting, goading the men onwards and shouting expletives at the enemy. Slowly but surely, they began pushing the enemy back. Each inch of ground was contested, and the going was extremely slow. By 0430 hours the 1 Paras were within 450 metres of the enemy positions. Maj Dyal took stock of the situation and realised that a couple of bunkers firing Medium Machine Guns (MMGs) and Light Machine Guns (LMGs) were holding up their advance. He rallied one of the platoons and in a daring attack directly on the enemy bunkers, the automatics impeding their progress were silenced. Finding the attackers so close to their own positions and seeing their automatic weapons being put out of action was too much for the Pakistanis. They withdrew, abandoning their defences and leaving behind sixteen dead.

By the morning of 27 August, Sank was in the hands of 1 Para. But there was no time for Maj Dyal and his men to rest and savour the victory. Knowing Pakistan's propensity for counter-attacking lost positions quickly, he ordered B and C Companies to secure features around Sank where the enemy could be regrouping. This action was completed by the evening. From Lediwali Gali, one of the positions they had captured as part of this consolidation, Maj Dyal peered at the Haji Pir pass[4] through his binoculars. To occupy a pass, the troops have to physically deploy on the shoulders, so that they can monitor the road and fire on any enemy movement toward it. Maj Dyal carefully scrutinised both the shoulders and realised that there did not seem to be much enemy activity on either of them. While he could make out bunkers and signs of deployment, the number of troops did not appear to be too many.

The Haji Pir Pass

The 1 Paras had succeeded in capturing its initial objectives but matters had not been going as well on the other approach in the brigade. Bedori, being very strongly held by Pakistanis, remained uncaptured despite repeated attacks by 19 Punjab. This had put Brig Bakshi in a dilemma as the assault on the Haji Pir

---

[4] A pass is essentially the low-lying gap between two high features, called its shoulders, through which a road or a path passes.

pass itself was, according to his plan, dependent on the capture of this vital feature. Maj Dyal volunteered for this task, despite the fact that he and his companies had fought continuously for two nights. Both Brig Bakshi and he knew that a further delay in launching operations would afford enough time for the Pakistanis to reinforce the pass, making the already difficult task almost impossible to achieve.

Thus, when his observation from Lediwali Gali brought Maj Dyal to the conclusion that the pass was currently lightly held, he pressed his CO for permission to commence his operations right away rather than wait for nightfall. This proposal meant substantially changing the overall brigade and, in effect, the divisional plan for the entire operation. Attempting to capture Haji Pir while Bedori was still in enemy hands was risky, to say the least. But if the gambit paid off, it would speed up the capture of the entire Haji Pir bulge.

Maj Dyal waited impatiently while Brig Bakshi sought clearance from the Divisional Headquarters for the altered plan. His mixed column of A and D Companies was champing at the bit, waiting for the go ahead to take the prize that seemed within their reach.

They finally got their clearance and at 1500 hours Maj Dyal, along with Maj Vaswani and D Company, began the descent from Lediwali Gali. They moved towards the nala that flowed between it and the Haji Pir pass, which was known as Hyderabad Nala. The rains, which had been holding up for a while, started again, making their descent over the slippery clayey surface extremely tricky. That they were in full view of the enemy located on the Haji Pir pass added to the risk. It did not take the Pakistanis on the Haji Pir pass long to spot this column perilously slithering down in full view and they opened fire with an MMG and 81mm mortars, the only weapons in their arsenal which would be effective at that range. Undeterred, the paratroopers made their way through the mud and slush with sheer grit and determination.

A column of Pakistani irregulars withdrawing from the adjoining features that 1 Para had occupied also spotted them and joined in firing at them from a much closer distance. Not wanting to either delay his operations by halting to deal with this new threat or give away the progress of his main column through the sound of their firing, Major Dyal detached a platoon under Sub Arjun Singh to deal with the retreating column while the rest of the paratroopers continued.

Darkness had descended by the time the column reached Hyderabad Nala, and the rain continued to make their movement slow and miserable. They braced themselves for the steep climb, which promised to be even more strenuous than the descent, without gravity to help them along their way. And negotiating the climb after dark meant that they could not even see where they were going to get a good foothold on the slippery mountainside.

Since they had to be prepared for a lengthy fight without possible supplies, they had carried extra ammunition, mortar rounds, and communications equipment apart from their weapons and personal loads, which made the going slower still. Maj Dyal was leading, setting the demanding pace for his column. A couple of hours into the climb, he stopped suddenly as he could smell smoke from a wood fire. They cautiously approached seemingly abandoned mud hut from which the smoke was rising. He ordered the hut to be surrounded, and accompanied by one section, barged in. They found twenty-two Pathans from Pakistan's Azad Kashmir forces, who were retreating from their position and had taken shelter from the rain in the hut. They surrendered without a fight, and were gainfully employed to carry their heavy loads further.

Despite being relieved of the extra burden, the steep climb along the mountain face with no track to ease their passage, was laborous and exhausting. At several places, the troops had to crawl on all fours to avoid slipping. After climbing for the better part of the night, the column hit the old Poonch–Uri road by 0430 hours. The soldiers had been relentlessly in action for the past three days, and for this entire period had gone without a hot meal, surviving on 'shakkar paras' and puris, the staple 'self-containment' diet of the jawans. By now, even these meagre rations were running perilously low.

Maj Dyal knew that the soldiers would need all their energy and alertness for the final assault on the enemy atop the shoulder of the pass. Therefore, he decided to give his men a well-deserved rest before the final push. The relieved men sank to the ground and huddled into the scanty protection of their rain capes to rest their aching limbs. The brief rest worked like magic to raise the morale and re-energise the troops and they resumed their march with renewed determination. They reached close to the pass itself by 0900 hours. The Pakistanis were surprised by their sudden appearance nearby. They had not expected them to traverse the distance between Lediwali Gali and the pass overnight through incessant rain and had completely lowered their guard. But it did not take them very long to regain their wits and start firing at the paratroopers.

Maj Dyal quickly sized up the enemy deployment. There was MMG fire coming from the western shoulder of the pass, and LMG and small arms fire from the pass itself. He led two platoons up the shoulder, and after a brief fight the Pakistanis ran. Rolling down from the shoulder on to the pass itself was a much easier task, despite the broad daylight, and the Pakistanis were completely routed. By 1000 hours on 28 August, Maj Dyal reported to the brigade that the Haji Pir pass had been captured.

There were celebrations all around in the Brigade Headquarters as they received the message of this incredible success against all odds. But Maj Dyal and his men still had work to do before they could celebrate their hard-fought victory. They surveyed the abandoned enemy defences and Maj Dyal ordered them to be re-sited to meet any threats of a counter-attack, which was likely to come from the opposite direction from where the defences were facing. Then, after detailing the sentries, the paratroopers finally took their well-deserved break.

The problem of food still remained. The weather ruled out air dropping of supplies, and it would take a while for the

Indian troops hoist the tricolour on Haji Pir Pass,
after the assault on 28 August 1965

The brave paratroopers at Haji Pir

Major Dyal receiving Gen Harbkhsh at Haji Pir

Mrs Indira Gandhi, then information and broadcasting minister
visiting Haji Pir

Maj Dyal receiving the MVC from the President of India

administrative elements to catch up. A solution was found by rounding up the goats that were fortuitously spotted grazing around the pass, ensuring that the soldiers could feast after the meagre fare of the past three days.

Naik Chokha Ram, the officers mess waiter who was accompanying the assault force, produced four different brands of whisky – each of the four officers in the column happened to have different preferences, well known to Chokha Ram. He didn't confide in the officers about the choice he had to make between carrying his blanket and the bottles – he eventually decided to sacrifice his blanket so that the officers he served could have a much needed drink after the battle!

Maj Dyal displayed immense moral courage and the willingness to put duty above everything else by undertaking this task at a great personal cost. This action turned the tide in Operation Bakshi. The capture of Bedori was completed on the 29th of August. The capture of the Haji Pir pass and the areas to the north closed infiltration routes into the Kashmir valley, sowing panic amongst the infiltrators and their urgency to withdraw to Pakistan Occupied Kashmir.

The casualties suffered by the 1 Paras during the operations included one officer, eighteen ORs killed and two officers, two JCOs and sixty-eight ORs wounded. Maj Dyal received the MVC for the outstanding leadership and personal courage he displayed during the entire operation. Shortly thereafter, he was promoted to the rank of Lt Col and appointed as the CO of 1 Para. He went on to become a Lt Gen and an Army Commander.

He continued to serve the nation even after retirement as the Lt Governor of Puducherry and the Andaman and Nicobar Islands. This brave soul fought his last battle with cancer, and finally succumbed on 29 January 2012.

Adversity to Victory
Lieutenant Colonel Sampuran Singh – Bedori

Brig Zoru Bakshi had tasked 19th Battalion of the Punjab Regiment (19 Punjab), operating to the left, that is, east of 1 Para, to capture the Bedori feature, which towered at a height of 12,355 feet. While 1 Para was preparing for its attack on the Sank feature, Lt Col Sampuran Singh, CO 19 Punjab, was leading his battalion on a 30-kilometre march from Uri to their Forward Assembly Area (FAA) for the attack. They reached the FAA on the evening of 24 August, and spent the night waiting.[5] The wait, caused by the delay in the launch of the attack by 1 Para to their right, was made miserable by the incessant rain fall. With barely any cover to protect them, the men had to rely solely on their capes, which were inadequate to keep them from soaking. In between preparing for the attack and reconnoitring the objective, Lt Col Sampuran Singh kept up the morale of his men by going around and talking to them. He could sense their impatience to get the signal to go ahead.

Col Sampuran Singh was a CO who was feared but also loved by the battalion. He was a tough, no-nonsense officer, yet one who had a rare sense of compassion for his men – one who could drive the men hard without remorse as he would share every bit of their

---

[5] The Forward Assembly Area is normally occupied by attacking forces only for a few hours, before moving out to the Forming Up Place (FUP) for the assault – by this time the troops are psychologically charged up for battle.

hardships with them. If the men were soaking in the rain, so was their CO, with little more than his own rain cape for shelter.

The battalion finally got the orders they had been waiting for at 1400 hours on 25 August. The rain continued to fall, making their progress time-consuming and difficult, but at least they were on their way now. The troops taking part in such attacks usually carry just enough supplies to help them fight and survive. The administrative elements are left behind, and would move up to replenish them immediately after the battle. But knowing early replenishment may not be possible in this terrain, they were required to be self-sufficient for the initial action. As a result, each soldier had to carry an extra load—ammunition, rations, and a sundry of stores that would help them survive and hold on after capturing the objective.

According to the plan, they had to first secure a feature called Point 8336 (Ring Contour)[6] before tackling their main objective, Bedori. Conventionally, such features ahead of the main enemy defences are lightly held, occupied by enemy forward elements such as Observation Posts (OPs), Listening Posts (LPs), or Protective Patrols (PPs). These troops do not usually fight pitched battles, but are instead tasked to provide an early warning of enemy approach, and if possible, interfere in their movement to cause a delay to give the main defences more time to prepare for the impending attack. Thus less resistance was expected on these initial objectives.

On their approach to the Ring Contour, the battalion had to cross the Hathlanga Nala. On the map, this nala was an insignificant, small stream not expected to cause any delay, but the heavy rains of the past few days had resulted in it swelling up considerably. When the leading troops reported this situation, Col Sampuran moved up to take a look for himself. He decided that he was not going to allow a mere nala to interfere with his plan, and ordered his men to wade across it. Despite their best precautions, three soldiers were swept away in the fast flow of the

---

[6] A common name assigned to many a hill feature because of the ring-like appearance of its contours on the map.

nala before the battalion managed to get on the other side. Once across, they secured their FUP by midnight and without further delay launched the attack on the Ring Contour. As anticipated, the feature was lightly held, and a determined attack by the Punjabis sent the enemy packing. By 0200 hours, they were in possession of their first objective.

Barely pausing to reorganise, Col Sampuran led his battalion forward to Bedori, mindful of the need to press in their attack before daylight broke. Purposefully, the Punjabis covered the intervening 2000 yards and launched their attack on Bedori by 0400 hours.

The Pakistani troops occupying Bedori had sufficient warning of the Punjabis' approach from the time they had captured the Ring Contour. They were well fortified in their rock-solid bunkers, sitting atop a steep climb along a razor-thin approach. The assaulting troops had barely started from their FUP when they were met with heavy machine gun fire from the Pakistani positions. Col Sampuran rallied his troops and tried to push forward several times, but the narrow, heavily mined approach, effectively covered by automatic fire, made progress impossible. There was no way to approach from a flank and every attempt to move forward met with deadly hail of bullets. By then the sun was well above the horizon, and the Pakistani machine gunners could now pick up and target individual soldiers making any attempt to move ahead. They tried valiantly for six hours before the assault was finally called off at 1000 hours, as it made no sense to continue rushing headlong into certain disaster.

The Brigade Commander, based on the reports on the progress of action, had decided that this particular approach to capture Bedori gave an overwhelming advantage to the enemy and was too well defended to succeed. He, therefore, decided to use an alternate approach, tackling Bedori from the north-east instead. 19 Punjab was accordingly ordered to fall back to Uri. The long 30-kilometre trek back to Uri by the men, who had been continuously on the move or in battle for over forty-eight hours, was bound to take a further toll on their morale. But Col Sampuran Singh spoke to the men and promised them that the battalion would get another chance to finish the task they had to leave unfinished that day.

Two more unsuccessful attempts were made to capture Bedori on 27 and 28 August by 4 Rajput and 7 Bihar. Remember that the 1 Paras had already captured the Haji Pir pass by 1000 hours on 28 August, and the enemy positions in this area had to be eliminated at any cost to consolidate this victory.

Col Sampuran was smarting from the failure to achieve his objective and wanted his men to redeem their honour. When he learnt about the subsequent failures to capture Bedori, he insisted that Brig Bakshi give his battalion another crack at it, assuring him that this time they would definitely succeed. The Brigade Commander agreed, and 19 Punjab was tasked to attack Bedori again on 29 August. His troops were also well rested by now, and were eager to have another go at the enemy and keep up the name of their battalion. The battalion was moved to the north-east side, and prepared for the attack.

Since he had already experienced the formidable defence of enemy bunkers in Bedori, Col Sampuran considered ways to attack these while minimising casualties among his own troops. Usually, enemy defences are 'softened' by artillery before the infantry carries out its physical assault. However, being strongly fortified, these bunkers were impervious to the artillery shells landing overhead or in the vicinity. Hitting upon an idea, Col Sampuran spoke to his affiliated Artillery Battery Commander Maj Oberoi, and requested for a 3.7-inch mountain gun to be brought forward to the assembly area. These guns are usually deployed a few kilometres behind the forward troops, and fire at a high trajectory. The shells thus fired land on top of the defences and around them. But now this gun was deployed much closer to the targeted defences, and asked to fire directly into the openings of the bunkers. The shells exploded either inside the bunkers or in front of them propelling deadly splinters inside. This unconventional use of a single gun proved more effective than the combined pounding by several batteries in destroying the bunkers as well as the Pakistani morale. Consequently, the few enemy bunkers that were directly visible on the north-eastern face of Bedori and ones which would have been the first to interfere with the battalion's move up the feature were silenced. The gun, however, could not target the bunkers spread on other parts of the feature and out of the line of sight of the gunners.

D Company led by Maj Verma was tasked to secure the FUP and C Company under Capt Parminder Singh was to attack and capture Bedori. Col Sampuran spoke to Capt Parminder, a tough wiry Sikh officer. In chaste Punjabi, as he was wont to when excited, Col Sampuran told him, '*Jatt da putta hai, chad janautte.*'[7] Capt Parminder in turn spoke to the troops of his C Company. They were all hardy Dogras from Jammu and Kangra, and were as proud of their martial traditions as the Jat Sikh himself. Sub Damodar Singh, his trusty company 2IC, a World War II veteran of Burma, assured him that the men would live up to every expectation.

C Company left the FUP at 0330 hours on 29 August, and the men began their slow ascent towards the prize that had eluded them the last time. This direction provided a better approach to the objective, and therefore the going was not as tough as it was the last time. Also, the mountain gun had done its job well, and the bunkers that would have interfered during the most difficult part of the assault had already been silenced. They advanced towards the objective without the overwhelming casualties that otherwise would have slowed the progress and made it expensive.

Closing in towards the top of Bedori, the Punjabis systematically liquidated the remaining Pakistani resistance from the bunkers that had not been affected by the artillery fire since they had been out of the line of sight. The Pakistani morale was intact but the resolute action by the Punjabis seemed to break their will to engage in battle. After fighting through the bunkers and trenches, often hand to hand, the Bedori feature was captured by 0600 hours.

---

[7] Loosely translated, 'You're a Jat Sikh, and so are fearless. Just go and climb on top.'

As generally happens in mountains, the inversion of temperature due to sunrise led to a light mist engulfing the top of Bedori. Capt Parminder was to fire predefined colour-coded flares from a Verey Light pistol to signal success in capturing the feature to the CO, who was following on their heels along with his mobile headquarters. The mist added to the fog of war by obscuring the flares and Col Sampuran, after waiting impatiently for a while, contacted the Company Commander on his radio. With a couple of the choicest expletives, he enquired why the feature had not been captured so far. An exultant Capt Parminder's reply, also in Punjabi, was '*Fateh kar litta*!'[8]

It was thus that the elusive prize, Bedori, was finally captured. More than patriotism, more than anything else, it's the 'name' of his battalion that exhorts a soldier to undertake the most difficult of tasks and even willingly lay down his life. 19 Punjab had not allowed this 'name' or 'izzat' to be undermined by ensuring they took the objective they had failed to seize earlier. It was a very gratified Col Sampuran who passed on the news of his battalion's success to the Brigade Commander.

Owing to his personal leadership during both the attacks and the resilience shown by him in turning defeat into victory, Col Sampuran Singh was awarded the MVC. He went on to rise to the rank of a Brigadier.

---

[8] 'We have captured it.'

OPERATION FAULAD
– THE LINK UP

Operation Bakshi was only one component of Gen Harbakhsh Singh's overall plan to capture the Haji Pir bulge, tackling only the Northern part of the bulge. On the Southern end, two massive features dominated the old Poonch–Uri road that ran through the Haji Pir pass. Known locally as Raja and Chand Tekri (also colloquially referred to as Rani since it was slightly less formidable than Raja), the two had been turned into virtual fortresses by Pakistani troops. According to Lt Gen Harbakhsh's estimate, the combined strength on these two features was a battalion less a company, supported by two 3.7-inch Howitzers (similar to the gun Lt Col Sampuran Singh used so effectively against the Bedori defences), two 81-millimetre mortars, eight .30 Browning machine guns and other automatic weapons. The enemy bunkers were well fortified, with overhead protection against artillery shelling. Obstacles like mines and barbed wire had been laid on the approaches to the defence, to deter and slow down assaulting infantry, so that they could easily be engaged by the enemy bunkers.

These two formidable positions served as key staging posts for infiltrators being pushed across the CFL by Pakistan. It was necessary to capture them to complete the task started by 1 Para and 19 Punjab, namely, the capture of the Haji Pir bulge, and deny infiltration bases to Pakistan. This task had been allotted by Lt Gen Harbakhsh to 93 Infantry Brigade (commanded by Brig Zora Singh) under 25 Infantry Division (commanded by Maj Gen Amreek Singh). When on 24 August, Lt Gen Harbakhsh flew in to Rajouri, Maj Gen Amreek informed him that he could not muster enough troops to attack Raja and Chand Tekri; hence the plan was to bypass these features in the link up with 68 Brigade. The implication of this move was that it would leave pockets of enemy troops sitting on dominant mountain features within the bulge, which would be a constant threat to any movement in the bulge by Indian troops. The deadline for the capture of Raja and Chand Tekri was, therefore, extended to 3 September, and the Army Commander agreed to allot one more battalion, 2 Sikh, to 93 Brigade for the operation.

On 1 September, Brig Zora Singh issued orders to his battalions tasked with the capture of Raja and Chand Tekri. The operation was to be undertaken on 2 and 3 September respectively, and was to take place in two phases. In Phase I, 3 Dogra would begin its attack at 2130 hours on 2 September and capture Raja, with 2 Sikh as its reserve, by 2359 hours. In Phase II, 2 Sikh would capture Chand Tekri by 1000 hours on 3 September. It would have 3 Dogra and one company 3 Rajputana Rifles (Raj Rif) in reserve (Map 3). The initial attack by 3 Dogra did not succeed and the plan was changed for 5 September with 2 Sikh tasked to capture the Raja post and 3 Dogra to capture Chand Tekri.

Raja Litta, Raja Ditta
Lieutenant Colonel NN Khanna
– Raja

By the time they arrived at Poonch to be a part of Operation Faulad, which was to capture the Pakistani posts of Raja and Point 7702 (Chand Tekri), the officers and men of 2nd Battalion the Sikh Regiment (2 Sikh) were probably getting a good idea of what a shuttlecock in a game of badminton feels like. The battalion had been moved from its permanent location and formation, 19 Infantry Brigade at Damana, Jammu, to 191 Infantry Brigade in Chhamb about a fortnight ago. After twelve action-packed days in Chhamb, it was on its way back to Damana when it was halted midway and asked to report to 93 Infantry Brigade in Poonch. But Lt Col N.N. Khanna, the CO of 2 Sikh, and the entire 'paltan[1]' took these changes in their stride. After all, there was a war on, and the battalion had a rich legacy of valour in operations. They certainly did not want to sit this one out back in Damana.

Sub Darshan Singh, who was a Sepoy (Sep) with C Company during the war, remembers Col Khanna as a 'tall, slim officer who was physically as fit as any of the young soldiers. What was particularly remarkable about him', continues the retired JCO, 'was the fact that even though he was the CO, he treated all of us as if he was an elder brother. He would chat with us informally, and treat us with a lot of respect.'

On his arrival at Poonch, Col Khanna reported to the Brigade

---

[1] Battalion as it is colloquially referred to.

Headquarters and was briefed about the impending operations. In the Brigade Commander's plan, 2 Sikh was to act as a reserve to 3rd Battalion the Dogra Regiment (3 Dogra) for the capture of Raja in phase one—its real task would come in phase two of the operation. Col Khanna was, therefore, not too perturbed about the fact that he did not get too much time to carry out his reconnaissance, though he had used the one day that he did get to thoroughly familiarise himself with the area. In fact, he also took his commanders down to the section level to some of the forward posts from where the objectives were clearly visible. From there, Col Khanna pointed out the different parts of the objective and divided them amongst the companies and platoons. Each Company and Platoon Commander could, therefore, take a look at the objective and orient himself for the impending task.

2 Sikh spent the night of 31 August marching in the wake of 3 Dogra towards one of the Indian posts (Post 405), to assemble for the attack. Both the COs joined their respective battalions that afternoon after attending orders by the Brigade Commander. After giving their own orders and taking care of the final preparations, the COs led their battalions to the chosen FAA by midnight.

According to the plan, 2 Sikh was to wait in the FAA while 3 Dogra attacked the Raja post. Once it was captured, they would pass through and form up at the post for the next phase, the capture of Chand Tekri. Following the plan, the battalion waited and watched as the Dogra attack built up. In the dark night, all they could make out was flashes and sounds of gunfire, interspersed with the fierce Dogra war cry. Shortly after the attack went in, Col Khanna was pleased to see the pre-arranged success signal being fired by 3 Dogra, indicating that they had captured Raja. He ordered his two forward companies to move up to Raja where they were to form up for their attack on Chand Tekri.

It was still dark when they started moving forward. The two leading Company Commanders, Capt Anup Dharni and Capt Surjit Singh, reported that they were being fired upon from Raja. This was unexpected as the Dogras were supposed to have already captured the feature. Could it be the retreating enemy taking pot shots at the advancing Sikh column? That didn't make sense, since logically, the Pakistanis would escape towards their own positions at Chand Tekri, not into the direction from where the attack had come. Col Khanna, who was just behind the two leading companies, was pondering over this when he was informed by his Adjutant Maj Sukhinder Singh that 3 Dogra was falling back to the FAA and that Raja had, in fact, not been captured.

As it emerged later, the attacking Dogra troops had mistaken a lower height short of the top of the Raja feature to be the actual objective. After occupying it, they had given the success signal, thrilled at this easy victory. But their exhilaration was short-lived as they soon came under very heavy enemy fire from the top of the Raja feature itself – their actual objective – where the enemy was still strongly entrenched. On the 'false crest' that the Dogras had occupied they were sitting ducks for the enemy. As a result they had to retreat towards their FUP, the direction from which the Sikhs were advancing. The firing on the Sikh troops was coming from Raja, which was still occupied by the enemy.

Word of this mix-up reached the Brigade Headquarters and both the battalions were asked to return to their assembly areas, and thereafter pull back to Poonch.

On 4 September, after both the battalions had returned to the base, the Brigade Commander called a conference to take stock of what had happened on that fateful night. The two Dogra Company Commanders described the formidability of the defences and intensity of the enemy fire at Raja, which had forced them to retreat. Col Khanna interjected, volunteering to capture Raja provided he was given two days and two nights to carry out a reconnaissance and prepare his battalion. Brig Zora readily agreed and it was decided that the Sikhs would attack on the night of 6 September. However, due to heavy pressure from the government to bring the infiltration situation under control at the earliest, the date was advanced by a day to 5 September on orders from the Army Headquarters.

The new brigade plan then formulated reversed the objectives, with 2 Sikh attacking Raja and 3 Dogra tackling Chand Tekri. Also, both the attacks were to take place simultaneously instead of being staggered as earlier planned.

Col Khanna carried out a detailed reconnaissance to study the objective before formulating his plan. He could make out on closer inspection that the Raja feature consisted of two heights, which he called 'Left Height' and 'Right Height'. It was actually only the Left Height that the Dogras had occupied, and mistakenly assumed that they had captured the entire feature. Both the heights were strongly held by the enemy and Col Khanna felt it would be better to attack both of them simultaneously. This would deny the enemy the opportunity to concentrate fire from both these heights on to one column and would also avoid a situation like the one faced by the Dogras earlier.

To aid his planning further, Col Khanna decided to send reconnaissance patrols to probe the enemy defences. In a daring venture across the CFL right up to the enemy positions, the patrols led by Capt Anup Dharni and Havaldar (Hav) Ujagar Singh stealthily closed in and took stock of the routes and obstacles. They even managed to draw enemy fire by throwing a stone in their direction, which gave them a good idea about where the enemy automatic weapons were deployed.

Thus, when Col Khanna gave his final orders for the capture of Raja, he was better informed and fully appreciated the difficulty of his battalion's task. In a bid to do as much as he could to ease their efforts, he had placed his solitary 106 mm recoilless (RCL) gun[2] under 2Lt Naubahar Chand on Post 406 overlooking the Raja defences. Just as Col Sampuran Singh had used the howitzer before the attack on Bedori, Col Khanna directed fire at the enemy bunkers directly from the front. So while the battalion moved forward from Poonch to occupy their assembly area, this solitary detachment pounded the enemy defences. The enemy brought

---

[2] This is a jeep-mounted light weight anti-tank weapon with a crew of four men.

down an artillery barrage on the detachment, but it continued to move quickly from one position to another and fire, managing to get direct hits on at least two of the enemy bunkers.

Surprise – best friend of the attacker – had already forsaken the Sikhs. The enemy artillery continued to shell them intermittently while they were in the assembly area, fortunately with little damage.

In a daring and unconventional move, Col Khanna had decided to attack with three companies simultaneously (Map 4). Typically, in mountain warfare, battalion attacks go in with one or at the most two companies 'up'. Col Khanna's gambit meant that he would be able to contact almost the entire length of the defences simultaneously, giving the enemy no scope for re-adjusting his firepower from unaddressed parts. It also meant subjecting the enemy to immense psychological pressure. The flip side was that there was the possibility of more casualties, and that he had just one company in reserve for contingencies. But as events proved later, his move paid the dividends he was hoping for.

The plan did not go exactly as envisaged though, as there were delays in reaching the FUP, which resulted in the launch of the attack itself being delayed by almost an hour. As it was getting close to break of dawn, Col Khanna decided that instead of waiting for all the three companies to reach their respective FUPs and commence the assault together, each company would start as soon as they were ready. Thus A Company was the first to charge at its objective while the other companies were still moving towards their FUPs.

The brave Sikhs of A Company made slow progress up the steep slope of their objective, subjected to extremely heavy enemy fire. The 'Khalsas' kept shouting to encourage each other as they advanced against the deadly hail of bullets, unmindful of the heavy casualties. B Company soon commenced its attack, but the Company Commander, Maj Kailash Kalley, was shot in the knee within a few minutes of the assault. D Company's attack also didn't fare too well.

The Sikhs were inching ahead using the time-tested 'fire and move' tactic – a part of the attacking force fired from behind a covered position at the enemy to keep his head down while the other half advanced to the next available cover. After taking cover, they in turn would begin shooting while the first group leap-frogged and took up cover ahead. The defences on Raja had been well prepared by the enemy, who had got ample time to do so. The stone bunkers had roofs made of thick tree trunks over which several feet of earth had been packed, making them virtually immune to shelling. The trenches were deep, and all the bunkers were connected with shoulder-high communication trenches. Mines had been laid around the outer perimeter, which was then fenced off with barbed wire. Col Khanna was following close in the wake of B Company and in the breaking daylight he could see that all the three companies were getting stalled. They had reached the strands of wire obstacles along the forward edge of the defences, which were impeding further progress. The heavy artillery shelling, which usually causes enough breaches in such obstacles to enable attacking troops to get through, had failed to have this effect.

There was a strong possibility that the attack could get completely stalled at this point unless a way was found to cross the wire obstacles. There are times in battle when tactics, rationality, and caution need to be thrown to the wind in favour of desperate bravado, and this was one such time. What Col Khanna did next was incredible. Taking off his jacket, he started waving it around his head and shouting encouragement to his companies, as he started advancing towards the wire obstacles. Exhorting his men to remember the Gurus who had thought nothing of laying down their lives for their cause, he kept moving forward unmindful of the bullets whizzing past him. He forced down one of the pickets by holding the barbed wire and rushed through the minefield to the closest enemy bunker. As he unclipped a grenade from his belt and threw it into the bunker, a bullet struck him on his arm.

The entire battalion was electrified on seeing their CO's daring actions. To a man they rose and attacked, pulling down the wire pickets wherever they came across them. The entire objective soon became a confused mass of bullets, bayonets, and fighting bodies as the Sikhs grappled with the defenders, chasing them out of their bunkers and foxholes. The stunned Pakistanis, who had been taking potshots from the safety of their bunkers, were not prepared for this sudden near-suicidal rush by the attackers. Some of them abandoned their positions and rushed out, trying to flee from the oncoming charge of Sikh troops. Col Khanna, who was in the thick of this melee, caught a burst of MMG fire from one of the Pakistani bunkers still holding out, grievously wounding him. He continued to stagger forward, waving his arms to encourage his men on. As he gradually began to lose consciousness due to heavy bleeding, his last act was to tell the soldiers administering first aid to him was not to put out the news that he had fallen, lest it demoralise the battalion.

For the next one hour, Raja was a scene of savage hand-to-hand fighting for which there are no words to describe, as all the three Sikh companies tackled the enemy with ferocity and determination. The instances of individual and collective gallantry that marked this remarkable action are too many be recounted with due justice in this short account. However, to name a few, there was Lance Naik (L/Nk) Chattar Singh, who dashed under heavy enemy fire to replenish ammunition for his section's LMG from the body of a dead crew member, and after ensuring covering fire from this very weapon, charged at an enemy LMG up the hill before he was cut down. L/Nk Hari Singh led a number of grenade assaults across the wire on to enemy bunkers before being shot. 2Lt Keshav Singh, who was the Intelligence Officer of the battalion, formed the men around him into an ad hoc section and led them to attack and capture an enemy bunker. Using this as a base, they went on to capture several more bunkers in the vicinity.

Whenever a Company, Platoon or Section Commander fell – and so many of them did – someone automatically took charge and kept the fight going. This initiative displayed by the junior

The Raja defences seen from the direction of Rani

Captured MMG position manned by 2 Sikh

leadership ensured that no one had to look around, waiting for orders.

Then – by 0700 hours – 2 Sikh was in possession of Raja. However, Col Khanna had meanwhile succumbed to his injuries even as he was being evacuated to the Regimental Aid Post. As someone mournfully observed, '*Raja litta, Raja ditta*' (We gained Raja but sacrificed our leader). Apart from the loss of their CO, the battalion suffered heavy casualties – two JCOs and thirty-seven ORs killed; three officers, three JCOs and ninety-six ORs wounded. Amongst the losses were almost all of the battalion's finest sportsmen – most of its hockey team besides several athletes and players who had represented the Services and Command teams.

Col Khanna was posthumously awarded the MVC for his exemplary leadership in battle. While talking about him there is noticeable catch in the voice of Sub Darshan Singh, who says, 'Even after fifty years, talking about Col Khanna brings a tear to my eyes. He was truly a Raja.'

President S. Radhakrishanan, presenting the Maha Vir Chakra to Smt Savitri Khanna, widow of Lt Col NN Khanna, Posthumously

Irrepresible
Sepoy Jarnail Singh
– Raja

The soldiers of 2 Sikh took pride in the fact that just as they had proved themselves on the battlefield many times over their 200-year history, their sportsmen had also consistently won laurels for them during peace time. One of the battalion's star sportsmen was Sep Jarnail Singh of C Company. Not only was he the best basketball player in the battalion, he had also played for the Services team. His tall 6-feet something body hid a simple soul who liked desi ghee, playing basketball, and had never disobeyed an order in his entire life.

Jarnail, like most soldiers of his battalion, had taken war in his stride. He saw it as just another 'match' with the enemy, which gave him the opportunity to do his best for his team, the Company, and the Battalion. Always the first to volunteer to carry the heaviest of loads, Jarnail was also popular in the Company for his melodious voice.

But it was this very talent that was causing much distress to his Platoon Commander now. The Company had moved at the head of the battalion column marching towards its FAA for the attack on Raja. Jarnail, in high spirits, had insisted on singing loudly throughout the long march. It may have been his elation at finally getting a chance to emulate all the heroes who were part of battalion folklore and prove himself in battle, or just plain excitement. Whatever the reason, Jarnail simply wouldn't stop singing despite several warnings by his Platoon Commander and the Company Senior JCO, Sub Gurcharan Singh. He would fall silent for a while when reproached, but soon afterwards his singing could be heard in the still of the night. The JCOs were worried that his voice would warn the enemy of their advance.

When they reached the FAA, with Jarnail subdued after several rebukes but still humming below his breath, the two JCOs discussed ways to deal with him. They came to a consensus and approached Company Commander Capt Anup Dharni with a recommendation that Jarnail should be left behind as part of the guard at the FAA. The Company Commander agreed, sharing their apprehension of premature discovery by the enemy if Jarnail broke into a song at the FUP. Jarnail was crestfallen, but to him orders were orders, and even the thought of remotely defying them did not occur to him. He watched despondently as his comrades were soon on their way towards the FUP, leaving him and rest of the FAA party behind.

Jarnail was forgotten for the next couple of hours as Capt Dharni and the JCOs found themselves in the thick of battle for the capture of Raja. After the heavy fighting, when the enemy was finally routed, Capt Dharni was the first to reach the command bunker on the very top of the Raja feature that was the enemy's headquarters, only to find it deserted. Looking around at the several enemy dead bodies that lay strewn on the ground, he spotted the body of the Pakistani Captain who had apparently been the Commander of this post. Approaching the body cautiously, Capt Dharni found his enemy counterpart lying dead face down, still clutching his pistol in his hand. Gingerly turning the body around, he found a bullet wound on the Pakistani officer's chest.

On further inspection, Capt Dharni realised that the location of the command post was such that it could not have been fired upon by the attacking troops from the lower slopes. Had the Pakistani Capt killed himself or had someone reached there before him? It was then that he spotted a body in an olive green uniform, lying in stark contrast with the khaki uniforms of the several Pakistani bodies that were scattered round. It was the body of the enthusiastic singer, Jarnail Singh, who for all practical purposes was supposed to be guarding their equipment in the FAA.

Anup surmised that Jarnail, unhappy at being denied the once-in-a-lifetime opportunity to prove himself in battle, had 'deserted' his position in the FAA. After C Company left the FAA, Jarnail had probably quietly joined the column of B Company and fought through the objective along with them. He was apparently the first man to reach the top of the Raja feature where the enemy headquarters was located. Whether this was by chance or Jarnail realised the importance of striking at the enemy command post; whether it was he who had killed the Pakistani Capt or if the officer was already dead when Jarnail reached – these are some questions that could never be answered.

But it was clear that Jarnail Singh, probably for the first time in his life, had disobeyed orders.

GRAND SLAM
CHHAMB

Frustrated at the failure of Operation Gibraltar and upset by Indian offensive actions in the Haji Pir bulge and other selected places, Pakistan upped the ante with a full-fledged offensive of divisions plus into the Chhamb–Jaurian sector of Jammu and Kashmir. Although reports of a Pakistani build up in this sector had reached Indian Commanders by the last week of August and the sector was assessed as the most vulnerable to a Pakistani attack, they did not really believe that Pakistan would risk a full-fledged war by such precipitate action.

Flat open terrain on the foothills marked this sector, and despite being criss-crossed by several rivers and nallas, it was suitable for tanks to negotiate (unlike anywhere in the Kashmir valley). Any Pakistani success in this sector could seriously jeopardise the Indian position in Kashmir. The Jammu–Rajouri–Punch road passed over the Akhnoor bridge located in this sector; therefore, the capture of this bridge by the Pakistanis would cut off the road, isolating Rajouri and Punch. Further, the enemy would then be uncomfortably close to Jammu, which they could threaten with their armoured division. If they succeeded in capturing Jammu, the rest of Kashmir would also be cut off from India, and automatically fall into their bag.

The Indian 191 Infantry Brigade Group, commanded by Brig Manmohan Singh, was responsible for the defence of this sector, with a frontage that was unusually large for a brigade to hold, even with the additional forces that were allotted to it.

The offensive commenced at 0330 hours on 1 September with heavy artillery bombardment for two to three hours on the defences of 6 Sikh Light Infantry (LI) and 3 Mahar (Map 5). The Indian defences were pulverized and 6 Sikh LI was attacked by armour with infantry following; the enemy armour bypassed the defences simultaneously. To the north of the battalion, the enemy armour exploited the gap and advanced towards Dewa and Mandiala. 3 Mahar to the north was also attacked. By the afternoon, the 6 Sikh LI defences had been surrounded but the delaying action by C Squadron of 20 Lancers had slowed the enemy's advance. The defences of 3 J&K Militia were also overrun, at Redhill and Greenhill.

The defence minister approved the use of air strikes in the afternoon at approximately 1645 hours and by 1700 hours, twenty-six aircraft from the Pathankot airbase were launched. These aircraft attacked the cauldron that existed, hitting enemy as well as their own forces, which lost ammunition vehicles of armour and artillery. The Pakistani Air Force (PAF) shot down four aircraft of the attacking force. 15 Kumaon defences were attacked in the afternoon and two companies captured. At night, the brigade cohesion of the defences was non-existent; therefore, the brigade less 3 Mahar and 6/5 Gorkha Rifles were asked to withdraw to Akhnoor, while 6 Sikh LI did not withdraw but trickled back in small groups. Pakistani troops crossed the Munnawar Tawi at night and established themselves East of the river by 2200 hours.

The situation was deteriorating fast, and on 2 September, the PAK strafed and rocketed Indian positions around Jaurian, causing heavy casualties and damage. XV Corps moved in troops and armour to stem the Pakistani onslaught, and ordered redeployment of forces with a view to defend Akhnoor at any cost. The newly raised headquarters (HQ) of 10 Infantry Division had reached the area on 28 August and was asked to take charge of the situation on 1 September.

At this stage, instead of resolutely pushing on to capitalise on the advantage they had seized by this lightning operation, the Pakistani forces paused. As it emerged, the reason was that Maj Gen Yahya Khan (who later became the military ruler of Pakistan and was at the helm during the 1971 war) took over from the

Commander of the Pakistani offensive forces, Maj Gen Akhtar Hussain Malik. So while the Pakistani forces waited for the new Commander to take stock and issue fresh orders, Indian defenders were able to deploy and fortify their defences in multiple layers.

When the Pakistani offensive resumed on 3 September, India were better prepared to face the attacks. They could beat back attacks on Jaurian, but withdrew from the position on the night of 4–5 September. Beyond this area, the Pakistani forces were blocked and slowly, the tide started turning.

Meanwhile, the Indian government gave the army permission to escalate the war into Pakistani territory by opening a new front in Punjab. The Indian XI Corps commenced the offensive by launching multiple attacks towards Lahore on 6 September. Another Indian offensive action was launched by the Indian I Corps, towards Sialkot on 8 September. Its heartland threatened, Pakistan had to pull out its armour rapidly from the Akhnoor sector to reinforce its sensitive areas in the Sialkot sector. The threat to Akhnoor thus petered out, with Pakistani forces trying to consolidate their gains and Indians launching a counter-offensive to regain lost territory. They succeeded in re-capturing several important areas before the ceasefire brought the fighting to an end on 23 September. Even after the ceasefire came into effect, Pakistan tried to make the most of the prevailing confusion by occupying some vacant posts, and Indian forces launched several attacks to evict forces these right up to October 1965.

Indomitable Spirit

Lieutenant Colonel GS Sangha – Chhamb

Lt Col G.S. Sangha belonged to a family which had a long and proud tradition of service in the army, which included his father, grandfather and several uncles. Originally commissioned into the Sikh Regiment, Col Sangha had later been transferred to an elite machine gun unit of the Mahar Regiment, which he rose to command. Shortly after he had taken over as the CO, the battalion was converted to regular infantry and designated as 3rd Battalion the Mahar Regiment (3 Mahar).

The battalion had completed its tenure of deployment along the CFL in Jaurian and had received its orders for the move to 7 Mountain Brigade in Ambala but events overtook the unit in the form of large-scale infiltration from across the border. They had already handed over their support weapons and vehicles to 2 Sikh, which had come in to relieve them.[1] When reports of the massive infiltration by Pakistan came in, the battalion was rushed in for anti-infiltration operations in the areas of Dewa–Chhamb–Jaurian without its heavy weapons and vehicles.

The battalion, operating under extremely difficult circumstances and often going without food for several days, chased, smoked out, and apprehended fourteen infiltrators, while killing four in

---

[1] When infantry units move from one formation to another on a permanent posting, they hand over all their heavy weapons and vehicles in situ to the relieving units, and take over the same at the new location from the unit they are replacing in turn.

the exchange of fire that took place. On 15 August, the Pakistani artillery carried out heavy shelling in their sector, helped by the daring flight of an Air Observation Post (OP). Brigadier BF Master, the Commander, was giving out orders for a planned offensive against the infiltrators from a vantage point near Dewa, and his entire party was caught in the heavy enemy shelling. Brig Master was killed, along with his staff officer. The heavy shelling had caused a temporary breakdown in communications. As a result, the Corps Headquarters had no information about the fate of forward troops. It was feared that the defences of the 3 Mahar had been overrun by the Pakistanis. But Col Sangha had personally rallied his men and got them to deploy at a feature called Mandiala Heights, and the battalion was soon fending off attacks in an attempt to stabilise the situation. Thus they could foil the attempts of the infiltrators moving towards Jaurian who had banked on the disarray caused among Indian troops by the shelling to provide them with an easy passage.

The movement of infiltrators further inland had been effectively blocked, but they had not fallen back to Pakistan. Instead, they had occupied strong positions on high features within Indian territory, and it was necessary to throw them out. These features included Lallialli, Post 707, Maira and Nathuan Tibba. On 17 August, B Company of 3 Mahar was dispatched by Col Sangha to attack the Pakistani infiltrators at Maira. After an ardous march of six miles under constant enemy shelling, the attack led by Capt AB Kulkarni evicted the enemy and captured this post. On 21 August, Col Sangha personally led the attack of C Company on Nathuan Tibba, and after a daring bayonet charge, the enemy was evicted with just two of the Maharis suffering injuries. The next day, B and C Companies expelled the enemy from Post 707, while A and D Companies captured Lallialli.

After successfully clearing the enemy from these features, the battalion was asked to hold the positions and prevent any further infiltration. One company of 3rd Battalion Jammu and Kashmir Militia (3 JAK Militia) was also placed under the command of Col

Sangha. The battalion was deployed in the area of Lalialli when the Pakistani offensive of 1 September commenced. The Mahar and JAK Militia positions had been under heavy artillery and mortar fire well before dawn. By early morning, they could hear the roar of tanks all round them. Soon the JAK Militia Company Commander reported tanks firing directly on his positions and shortly after that, communications with this company were snapped. Within no time, C Company also came under heavy tank fire. The enemy seemed to be advancing at an ominously fast pace.

A tank is perhaps the most menacing and deadly adversary that infantry troops defending a piece of ground can face. It has the capability of firing directly at defences using its main gun, which disgorge 20–30 kilograms of explosives and metal at close range. It also has secondary armaments, which are similar to the infantry's own MMGs. An infantry battalion has special anti-tank weapons to deal with tanks, such as jeep-mounted RCL rifles and shoulder-fired rocket launchers or anti-tank guided missiles. Smaller weapons such as rifles, grenades and machine guns have little effect on the tank's crew sitting safely inside layers of thick steel armour. The tanks can thus advance towards the infantry positions spewing deadly fire and can easily overrun and crush defences under their deadly tracks. The Maharis were safe from the latter because Col Sangha reorganised the defences to positions on heights where the tanks could not climb.

The battalion had nothing more than their rifles and machine guns to counter the steel monsters that seemed to move menacingly towards them, slowly encircling their positions. As mentioned earlier, the units' anti-tank weapons had already been handed over to 2 Sikh in preparation of the force's own move to Ambala. Col Sangha spoke to the Brigade Headquarters, informing them of the precariousness of their situation. He was assured of artillery and air support, and also that tanks would be sent to support them soon. His orders were clear: hold on to the positions at any cost. None of the promised support materialised, but the brave Mahari soldiers did manage to hold on against all odds, an achievement that speaks volumes about the leadership that must have motivated them to stand fast.

By the night of 1 September, the rest of the brigade had been ordered to pull back behind the Munnawar Tawi river, except 3 Mahar and 9th Battalion the Punjab Regiment (9 Punjab), who were ordered to hold their positions and delay the enemy's advance. Very soon, the battalion's communications with the brigade were also cut off. The army pamphlet on motivation lists 'fear of isolation' as one of the causes of panic. It would have been understandable if this fear had set into the hearts of the Mahari soldiers holding on to their positions, knowing that they were virtually cut off from the rest of their own forces, with enemy tanks and troops surrounding them. It was the personal leadership of Col Sangha that prevented panic from setting in.

The battalion continued to hold out against all odds, with virtually no external support. On 2 September, a strong enemy force, including tanks, attacked Lalialli supported by heavy artillery fire. A Company steadfastly refrained from firing until the enemy infantry came to within 250 yards of their post, and then opened up with a section of MMGs, a section of 3-inch mortars and small arms. The sudden volley of heavy fire from close range wreaked havoc among the enemy assaulting troops and they quickly withdrew, leaving behind eleven killed. The company suffered two killed, including the company second-in-command and two wounded in this action. Sub Dhondiba Londhe and Sep Babu Dhere were posthumously awarded the Sena Medal and Mention-in-dispatches, respectively, for this action.

At about 2000 hours the same day, the battalion having lost communication with the brigade, received orders to be under the command of 9 Punjab, delay the enemy as long as possible and then withdraw to Kalidhar. During the night, the Lalialli post came under renewed enemy attack. The post had run low on mortar ammunition. Without any artillery support it was impossible to hold on to the post. As such, A Company was withdrawn and later, the entire battalion formed a defence box resting on Ikhni Nala to the south and Ghora to the north.

The battalion repulsed several attempts by the enemy to dislodge them between 3 to 5 September, beating the attacks back with heavy casualties to the enemy. The Indian positions continued to be at the receiving end of enemy shelling throughout. But nothing could shake them. Communications with the brigade were re-established through 9 Punjab on 4 September, and the battalion received a personal message of congratulations from the General Officer Commanding (GOC) XV Corps. He also conveyed his compliments on the personal role played by Col Sangha in such difficult circumstances.

On 6 September, information reached the Maharis of the Indian offensive in Punjab. This was good news indeed, because, as

Indian defences in the Chhamb sector

Col Sangha explained to his men, the Pakistanis would now be forced to withdraw from this sector to reinforce their positions in Punjab. They were told to look out for withdrawing enemy columns, and cause as much damage as possible to them.

The battalion continued operating in the area till the end of the war. Their contribution in evicting the infiltrators from the Chhamb–Dewa–Jaurian sector and also in foiling Pakistan's aim of cutting off Akhnoor was remarkable. The heroic stand of the battalion, despite heavy shelling and no logistic support against the enemy's superior numbers, armour and fire support, behind the enemy lines was acclaimed. For the display of commendable leadership in the most adverse circumstances, Lt Col G.S. Sangha was awarded the Maha Vir Chakra.

Tough and Resolute

Lieutenant Colonel PK Nandagopal – Kalidhar

When he received orders recalling him to re-join his battalion, Lt Col Pagadala Kuppuswamy Nandagopal was on a long overdue and well-deserved stretch of leave in his home town, Kolar, famous for its goldmines. As he bid farewell to his family, he reassured them that he would be back as soon as the unfinished business with Pakistan was done. It was obvious that war was round the corner due to the situation created by the Pakistani infiltration in the Kashmir Valley. He was commanding 6th Battalion the Sikh Light Infantry (6 Sikh LI), a newly raised battalion deployed in the Chhamb sector under 191 Infantry Brigade. He arrived at the Brigade Headquarters at Akhnoor on 15 August, and found the entire staff in great consternation. News had just come in that the Brigade Tactical Headquarters located ahead at Dewa had come under heavy artillery shelling, and the Brigade Commander had been killed.

His own battalion was deployed nearby at Sakrana and Col Nandagopal rushed to take command of what seemed to be a desperate situation. He found the battalion posts had not been attacked, and informed the BM that they would stay and fight rather than withdraw to Troti, as was being contemplated by the brigade. Brigadier Manmohan Singh, the new Brigade Commander, approved this proposal when he joined the next day.

The battalion was thus steadfast in its posts at Moel, Paur, Burejal, and Dalla, located on the junction of the IB and the commencement point of the CFL and further north along the CFL, when Pakistanis unleashed Operation Grand Slam on 1 September. All the battalion posts, including the Battalion Headquarters, came under intense artillery shelling from 0345 hours onwards. Under the umbrella of this shelling, enemy tanks started closing up towards the posts, both from the direction of the IB as well as the CFL. The battalion's RCL guns, deployed at Burejal and Dalla, were knocked out after initially engaging the leading tanks. The tanks of C Squadron, 20 Lancers, were also contesting the enemy armour onslaught around the Burejal area, but the enemy's advance was along too wide a front to be stopped by just one squadron. Enemy squadrons to the north of Burejal had broken through and by 0630 hours almost all posts had been surrounded by Pakistani tanks. By 0730 hours, the tanks had cut off the post at Paur and assaulted it with the infantry, led by tanks. The Sikh LI troops at Burejal under Capt Ravi Kumar were bravely holding on, having beaten back several enemy raids by 1100 hours.

Post after post soon came under attack, and though the men fought back valiantly, the odds were heavily stacked against them. By 1400 hours, the enemy tanks had almost reached the Battalion Headquarters at Chhamb. One by one, communications with the forward posts was breaking down, and it seemed that the enemy's overwhelming force was beginning to show signs of succeeding. By about 1800 hours, a handful of survivors from the forward posts started trickling in at the Battalion Headquarters. The battalion, deployed in platoon-sized or smaller posts over a vast area, had been swamped by one full division and two armoured regiments of the enemy, taking a very heavy toll. One JCO and twenty-five ORs were killed; two officers, three JCOs, and thirty-eight ORs had been wounded. In addition, eight officers, nine JCOs, and 428 ORs were missing. This totalled to more than half the battalion's strength. Realising the untenability of their position, at 1900 hours the brigade ordered 6 Sikh LI to withdraw towards Akhnoor. Despite the disarray and confusion caused by the heavy losses, Col Nandagopal ensured that the withdrawal was orderly and without further casualties.

The next day, on 2 September, Col Nandagopal was at Jaurian to meet the Brigade Commander when he was wounded in strafing by enemy aircraft. He was evacuated to the hospital at Udhampur, but did not stay there for long. The very next day he returned to his unit. 'The wound can be taken care of at the battalion medical station,' he informed the doctors.

Having lost several soldiers, the battalion was given the relatively 'soft' task of guarding the Akhnoor bridge. The offensive by XI Corps in the Lahore sector had, in any case, taken the steam out of the Pakistani offensive. By 18 September, the unit's strength had been built up to almost full, with stragglers joining in and new reinforcements received from the Regimental Centre. Even though the cease fire came six days later, the battalion's work was not done yet.

Immediately after the cease fire, Pakistani troops rushed to establish new posts in any area they found unoccupied in a bid to increase their bargaining power by bringing more territories under their control. Point 3776 and Malla were two such posts, located on the Kalidhar Ridge in the hilly northern part of the sector. The presence of Pakistani troops on these features posed a threat to the Jammu–Naushera road and the Sunderbani plains.

On 28 September, the battalion, concentrated at Sunderbani, was tasked to capture these two important hill features as a preliminary to clearing the entire Kalidhar Ridge. The Kalidhar feature had a sheer cliff on the northern side, which faced the Indian troops and thus it was virtually impossible to launch an assault from this direction. The southern side was easier to climb, but this meant having to first outflank the enemy without detection to launch the attack from his rear. The approach to Point 3776 also lay from the southern side.

Col Nandagopal personally led two companies of his battalion – C Company under Maj JS Negi and D Company under Maj GS Virk – and captured both the features after a ferocious hand-to-hand fight. The enemy counter-attacked, but the battalion stood fast, beating off three counter-offensives, however suffering

A view of the Kalidhar Ridge

casualties in the bargain. They stabilised the situation but had to give up Point 3776.

On 3 October 1965, the battalion was ordered to re-occupy Point 3776, along with 11th Battalion the Mahar Regiment (11 Mahar). The attack was to be launched on 4 October, and 6 Sikh LI was to capture an initial objective called 'Twin Pimple'. The 11 Mahars were to then pass through and capture Point 3776 itself. Maj JS Negi led C Company for the attack on Twin Pimple, boldly approaching the objective under heavy enemy artillery shelling. They ran across the strips of land mines and assaulted the enemy on the Twin Pimple feature, making liberal use of their weapons and bayonets. The enemy soon fell back, vacating the feature but continued to bring down artillery fire. By 0615 hours, the objective had been captured. Col Nandagopal, who was just behind C Company, reached the objective and was just about to tell the Company Commander to reorganise and deploy when the enemy launched a counter-attack.

Col Nandagopal was calling for artillery fire to be brought down on the counter-attacking enemy when two Pakistani soldiers armed with sten guns suddenly appeared before him, shouting 'Hathiyar niche daal do!' (Throw down your weapons!). With no time to draw his pistol from its holster, the CO hit the soldier closer to him with a walking stick that he was carrying. The second soldier reacted by raising his sten gun and bringing it crashing down on the CO's head. Meanwhile Sep Budh Singh, who was accompanying the CO as his radio operator, pulled out his 'dah' (Burmese word of knife) and disposed off the enemy soldier with one deadly stroke. The first Pakistani soldier got to his feet and tried to run but was shot down. Col Nandagopal had a fortuitous escape, as they discovered that the soldier's sten guns were loaded and functioning. It was just fortunate that the Pakistani had reacted by striking him with the weapon rather than firing it. It had left a nasty gash on his forehead, which bled profusely, but after basic first aid, the CO insisted that other more serious casualties be attended to on priority.

Col Nandagopal and Sep Budh Singh at Kalidhar Ridge

The time now was 0715 hours, and Col Nandagopal radioed the success signal to the brigade, requesting them to send 11 Mahar through for the next phase of attack. He was informed that the battalion columns were still on the move, and that they were to go ahead and attempt to capture Point 3776 themselves. Despite his wounds, an exhausted Col Nandagopal led his depleted battalion in a final assault on Point 3776, which was finally cleared of the Pakistani intruders by mid-day on 5 October. The battalion had suffered two officers, two JCOs and thirty-four ORs killed and four officers, two JCOs and eighty-four ORs injured in the two days of heavy fighting.

For his personal leadership and gallantry, Col Nandagopal was awarded the Maha Vir Chakra. He later retired as a Brigadier and settled in Kolar. He remained actively involved in social service after retirement, particularly in the welfare of veterans. He was one of the decorated veterans who in 2012 surrendered his hard-won medals, including the MVC, to the Supreme Commander in support of the demand for One Rank One Pension. This brave heart passed away on 16 June 2014 at the age of ninety-one.

Unconventional
Naib Subedar Sarup Singh – Kalidhar

One of the units rushed to Jammu and Kashmir in the aftermath of the infiltration operations by Pakistan was 9 Punjab. It moved from its peace time location in Ambala to join the 191 Independent Infantry Brigade Group at Akhnoor. The men of the battalion were excited at the prospect of seeing action, and the *'langar gap'*[2] was that their new Brigade Commander was Brigadier MF Master. This enthused the men even more, as he was well known to every man in the battalion since he had commanded 9 Punjab in 1961–62. But on reaching Akhnoor they received the sad news that Brig Master had been killed in the artillery shelling of the Brigade Headquarters on the very day that the battalion embarked on its journey.

Immediately on reaching Akhnoor, the battalion was pushed forward to occupy positions in the foothills of the Pir Panjal Range. They took over positions on the Kalidhar Ridge feature on 1 September, and immediately began strengthening their defences. But as mentioned elsewhere in the book, Pakistan's Operation Grand Slam had already been set into motion by this date. Therefore, 9 Punjab did not have any time to settle down or strengthen its defences before they were at war. Initially, the Pakistani thrust was aimed at the southern part of the 191 Infantry Brigade sector, which was composed of plains where their tanks

---

[2] News on the grapevine.

could operate, while the Kalidhar Ridge formed the northern part of the brigade sector. But by 6 September, the battalion positions came under heavy artillery shelling.

The shelling continued on 7 September. That night the listening posts reported hearing quite a few enemy patrols in their vicinity. Some patrols sent out by the Punjabis could also make out heightened signs of enemy activity. It was obvious that the enemy was getting ready to attack their position, hence the increased patrolling to gather more information about their positions and defences.

C Company of 9 Punjab was located at a picket known simply as 702, and its Company Commander was Sub Dewan Singh, an experienced and wise JCO. Nb Sub Sarup Singh was one of the platoon commanders. Both the JCOs were quite certain that the enemy attack would come that night – the only question was when and from which direction.

The anticipated assault did come that night, and along with C Company, the enemy also attacked the neighbouring B Company. As a result, the companies could not reinforce each other. The attack was preceded by heavy artillery shelling and rocket fire. Sub Dewan Singh continued to rally his men despite being wounded, but the enemy had come perilously close by then.

Nb Sub Sarup Singh realised that the enemy had almost reached their defences and was negotiating the wire obstacles that protected their forward line. He knew that if they managed to break through this line, the Punjabis' position would become untenable. In a daring, almost crazy bid, he grabbed an LMG and ran towards the right of the company defences. Crossing the entire line of defences, he headed for the wire and took up a flanking position from where he could clearly make out the enemy. He opened enfilade fire with the LMG. Fire from a flank, or 'enfilade' fire, gives a weapon the advantage of firing along the longer axis of an approaching enemy, and is thus much more effective and lethal. Moving the LMG to sweep the attacking enemy column, he had the satisfaction of seeing them running helter-skelter trying to avoid the deadly hail of bullets cutting through their ranks. He continued firing, replacing magazine after magazine from his pouches, single-handedly taking a deadly toll on the enemy. The Pakistani attack had been effectively stalled, and they were unable to make any progress towards the defences. Finally they gave up and firing blindly in the direction of where they thought the LMG was, beat a hasty retreat.

This courageous action against all odds cost Nb Sub Sarup Singh his life, but he saved the company position from falling. He was awarded the Sena Medal for this exceptionally brave act.

The Pioneer Commando
Major Megh Singh
– Meghdoot Force

In military history, there are numerous instances when small, irregular forces have carried out daring and unconventional operations with spectacular and often disproportionate results. The exploits of Lawrence of Arabia are well known, as are those of the Chindits Force, the special British Indian force formed in 1943 and led by Maj Gen Orde Wingate in Burma. Based on these and similar experiences, many armed forces have raised special forces battalions, which are military units specially trained and equipped to perform unconventional missions in enemy territories.

However, even until 1965, the Indian Army did not have any such special forces battalions. One person who was convinced about the need to have such a force for carrying out covert operations was Maj Megh Singh. He knew the difference such a unit could make by operating deep behind enemy lines, since he himself had been part of such an irregular force during World War II. Unfortunately, he was not in a position to do much about his convictions. Maj Megh Singh was a staff officer in the Western Command Headquarters under Gen Harbakhsh Singh.

He had been the second-in-command of 3rd Battalion the Brigade of Guards (3 Guards) where he had run into trouble. As a result, he had not been promoted to the rank of lieutenant colonel and when the war had broken out, he was awaiting approval of his application for premature retirement. But the hostilities changed everything. He had soldiering in his blood so there was no question of him walking out when a full fledged confrontation was on. Yet, he thought, what good was he sitting in the Command Headquarters, so far away from the action? The fact that he was performing an important function as a staff officer who looked after the training of young soldiers at the Command Headquarters and thus contributing to the war effort, was of little consolation. He longed to be in the thick of battle. More than anything else, he longed to redeem himself.

Brooding over what he could do to play a more meaningful role in the war, he thought of raising a special operations force, which would operate behind enemy lines and support the actions of the main forces. He decided to approach the Army Commander with his idea. Gen Harbakhsh listened to the experienced Major carefully and felt that there was a great deal of merit in what he was suggesting. Such a unit would be of tremendous use in the rugged mountainous terrain of Jammu and Kashmir. A small team could sneak into territories held by the enemy and wreak havoc by destroying a bridge here, targeting an enemy camp there, or blowing up some vital ammunition dump. The pay-offs would be far more in proportion to the efforts vis-à-vis a conventional attack to capture a similar bridge or ammo dump. The psychological impact on the enemy of such a force operating deep behind them would also be significant – it would keep them constantly on their toes. So he readily agreed. 'You get me results, and I promise, I will personally pin the rank of lieutenant colonel on your shoulders,' General Harbakhsh told him, even though Maj Megh Singh had not once mentioned his stalled promotion or expressed a desire to win any reward at all.

The Army Commander gave Maj Megh Singh a virtual carte blanche to select the men and equipment for his force, which was christened the 'Meghdoot Force' after its founder. He selected some of the fittest and most enthusiastic men from his own battalion, 3 Guards, and from 3rd Battalion the Rajput Regiment (3 Rajput). He personally screened each man before accepting him into the force, knowing very well that while operating behind enemy lines, he couldn't afford to have a single weak link in the chain.

Gen Harbakhsh asked Maj Megh Singh to report to XV Corps under Gen Katoch and take orders from him for the deployment of his force. On 1 September, the Meghdoot Force was officially in business. It was allocated to 93 Infantry Brigade, which had been tasked to capture important features between Poonch and the Haji Pir pass to link up with Brig Bakshi's 68 Infantry Brigade after they had captured the pass. The Brigade Commander also suggested that Maj Singh should incorporate the commando platoons of the infantry battalions in their operations. This addition greatly enhanced the fire power available to this small force.

The first task assigned to this highly unorthodox force was to penetrate enemy lines and blow up an important bridge on the road between Dwarandi and Bandigopalpur. The mavericks of the Meghdoot Force, charged up on getting a chance to prove themselves, infiltrated 7 miles into enemy-held territory and blew up their target in a highly risky operation. This caused severe disruption of the move of reinforcements to the forward posts held by Pakistani forces, and also made the task of enemy forces withdrawing from them more difficult.

The Brigade Commander was justifiably pleased with the success of this operation and his increased confidence in the Meghdoot Force led him to entrust another important task to them. While 2 Sikh and 3 Dogra were to attack Raja and Chand Tekri respectively, there were two subsidiary enemy pickets that would interfere in these operations. The Meghdoot Force was tasked to attack and capture these pickets – Neza Pir and Aridhok – in conjunction with the larger operation. The successful and simultaneous capture of Neza Pir and Aridhok on 6–7 September helped speed up the operations of 93 Brigade and limit the number of casualties that otherwise would have been high.

Thrilled with their success, the men were ready for more. Their next target was an enemy ammunition dump at Kahuta, 8 miles behind enemy lines. The unit successfully infiltrated, ensuring that they reached their objective undetected, only to find that it had been vacated by the enemy. However, they found that 3 Dogra, which was attempting to link up with 68 Infantry Brigade after capturing Chand Tekri, was held up by the enemy at the Kahuta bridge. In an audacious manoeuvre, the Meghdoot Force compelled the enemy to vacate this bridge. Subsequently, it was this force which actually carried out the link up south of the Haji Pir pass on 10 September, thereby officially completing the capture of the Haji Pir bulge.

By then, the focus of attention within Jammu and Kashmir had shifted to the Chhamb sector and since this is where the action was, the Meghdoot Force was also asked to operate there. The unit carried out a number of harassing raids, spreading chaos and confusion amongst the enemy ranks. On 19 September, elements of the Meghdoot Force quietly slipped through the forward lines and attacked Thil, 4 kilometres inside the Kalidhar sector, inflicting severe casualties. Three days later at 0200 hours, they struck again at the enemy logistics base at Nathal. The Pakistani troops were completely surprised – they suffered heavy casualties and the dump was completely destroyed. On the way back, Maj Megh Singh's daredevils attacked the enemy post at Thuggi. A fierce hand-to-hand fight ensued and the Pakistani troops were severely mauled. Maj Megh Singh was, however, wounded in this encounter.

During one of his visits to the area, Gen Harbakhsh sent for Maj Singh and asked him for an update on his operations. When the Major narrated some of the actions undertaken by his force, the Corps Commander was visibly sceptical. 'I'm not casting any aspersions, but I have no way of confirming or verifying that the Meghdoot Force has actually done all that the Major is claiming,' the Gen says later. Maj Megh Singh did not comment on this very public put down, preferring to wait for his opportunity to prove what he said. The next time the Army Commander visited the sector and was briefed in the operations room, Maj Megh Singh provided irrefutable, if macabre, proof of the success of his latest operation, leaving the assembled Generals and staff officers speechless.

In the fitness of things, Gen Harbakhsh personally pinned the stars of a lieutenant colonel on the shoulders of Maj Megh Singh on 16 September. He was also subsequently awarded the Vir Chakra (VrC). Apart from redeeming his honour and earning well-deserved glory for himself and his band of hardy warriors, Lt Col Megh Singh had also demonstrated that a small well-trained and highly motivated force could be an invaluable asset to the Commander, often being able to undertake tasks that much larger conventional forces would find impossible. It was largely as a consequence of the success of the Meghdoot Force that the Indian Army decided to raise special forces battalions.

Lt Col Megh Singh was deservedly chosen to raise 9 Para (Commando) (now 9 Para [SF]), which he commanded as its first CO. His letter of resignation long forgotten, Lt Col Megh Singh went on to successfully command the 18th (Commando) BSF Battalion during the 1971 war, where his role with the Mukti Bahini was highly appreciated.

In 1973, Col Megh Singh retired and settled down in his village, Kharia Mithapur near Jodhpur. He devoted his time and energies to the problems of farmers in that region, and for many years remained the state president of the Rajasthan Kisan Union. He passed away in 2010 at the age of eighty-eight.

Map Legends

–x–x–	Area captured
◯	Area of deployment
⊔	Armoured squadron
⊔	Armoured troop
———	Canal
–x–x–x–	Ceasefire line
⟶	Enemy
⟶	Indian thrust
⬡	Infantry division
— — —	International boundary
⟶	Main thrusts
⨯⨯⨯	Mines
⟶	Own
▫	Pill box
+++	Railway line
～～	River
～ —	Roads
———	Roads
⊟	Tank

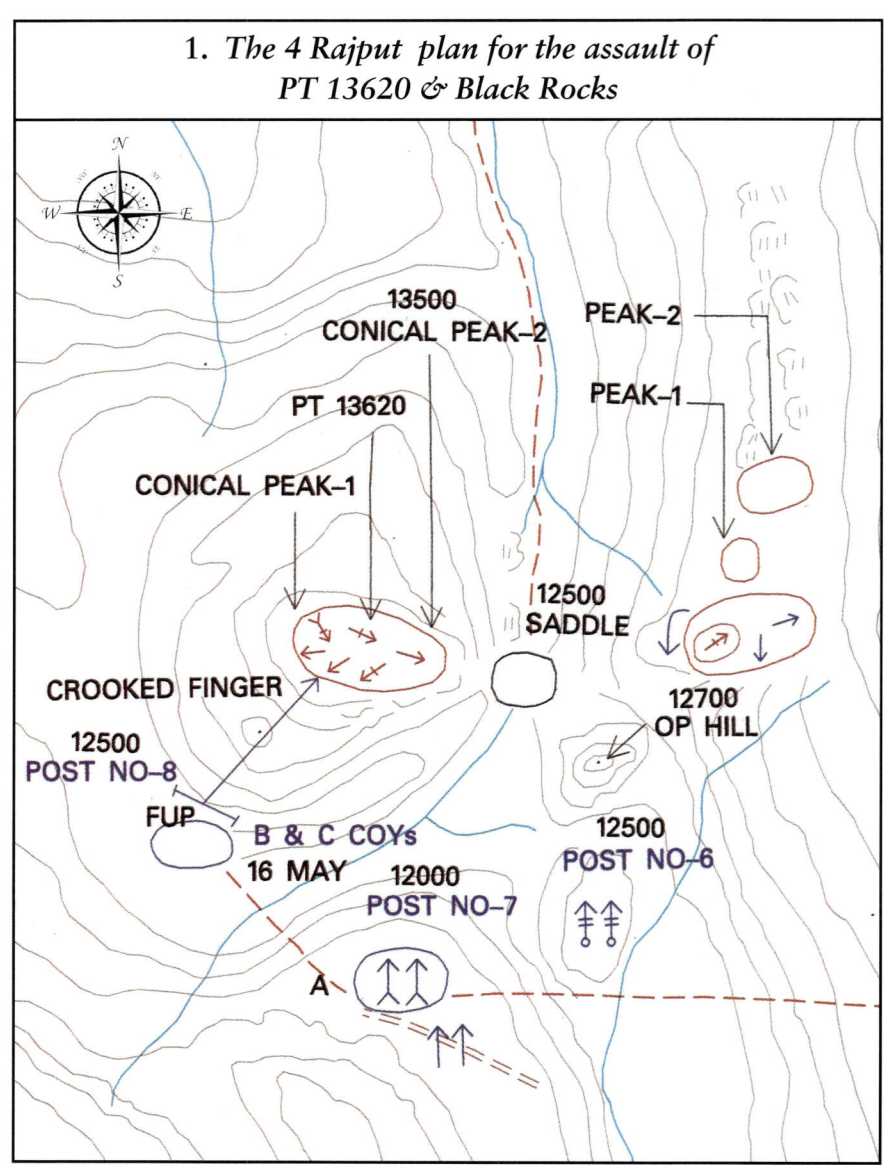

1. *The 4 Rajput plan for the assault of PT 13620 & Black Rocks*

N W E S

PEAK–2

PEAK–1

13500
CONICAL PEAK–2

PT 13620

CONICAL PEAK–1

12500
SADDLE

CROOKED FINGER

12700
OP HILL

12500
POST NO–8

FUP

B & C COYs

12500
POST NO–6

16 MAY

12000
POST NO–7

A

Satellite view of Point 13620 and Black Rocks

Black Rocks

Pt 13620

Kargil

Kargil 194103

Image © 2015 DigitalGlobe   Image © 2015 CNES/Astrium   Image Landsat

2. *Haji Pir Operation Bakshi*

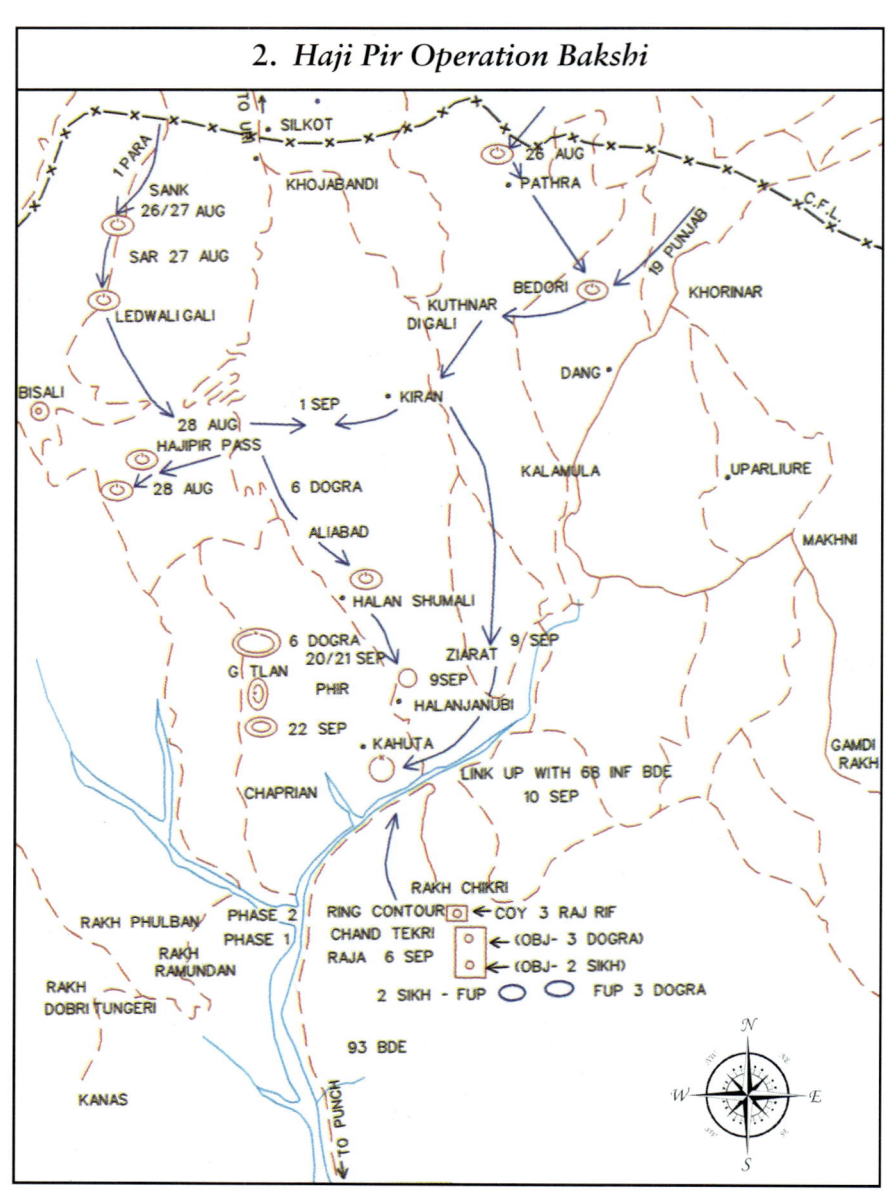

TO URI

SILKOT

1 PARA

26 AUG

PATHRA

KHOJABANDI

SANK
26/27 AUG

C.F.L.

SAR 27 AUG

19 PUNJAB

BEDORI

KHORINAR

LEDWALI GALI

KUTHNAR
DIGALI

BISALI

DANG

1 SEP

KIRAN

28 AUG
HAJIPIR PASS

KALAMULA

UPARLIURE

28 AUG

6 DOGRA

ALIABAD

MAKHNI

HALAN SHUMALI

6 DOGRA
20/21 SEP

ZIARAT

9 SEP

GITLAN

PHIR

9 SEP

HALANJANUBI

22 SEP

KAHUTA

GAMDI
RAKH

CHAPRIAN

LINK UP WITH 68 INF BDE
10 SEP

RAKH CHIKRI

RAKH PHULBAN

PHASE 2

PHASE 1

RING CONTOUR ← COY 3 RAJ RIF

CHAND TEKRI

← (OBJ- 3 DOGRA)

RAKH
RAMUNDAN

RAJA 6 SEP

← (OBJ- 2 SIKH)

RAKH
DOBRI TUNGERI

2 SIKH - FUP

FUP 3 DOGRA

93 BDE

N

KANAS

W   E

TO PUNCH

S

Satellite view of Haji Pir

Rel

Pirkot

Naraji

Moshia

Noori

Nar Sher Ali Khan

Gikote

Asnniji

Gavalata

Moriyan

Isham

Nawaian Rundan

Now Pora

Palangi

Hajipur Pass

Forward Kahuta

Bandi Brahmanan

Sahora

Balkote

Ghar Kote

Manchi Karand Lagama

Nambla

Dulli

Boonga

Bemman

N H
1A

© 2015 Google   US Dept of State Geographer   Image © 2015 DigitalGlobe   Image © CNES/Astrium

3. Operation Faulad
93 Brigade assault on Raja and Rani

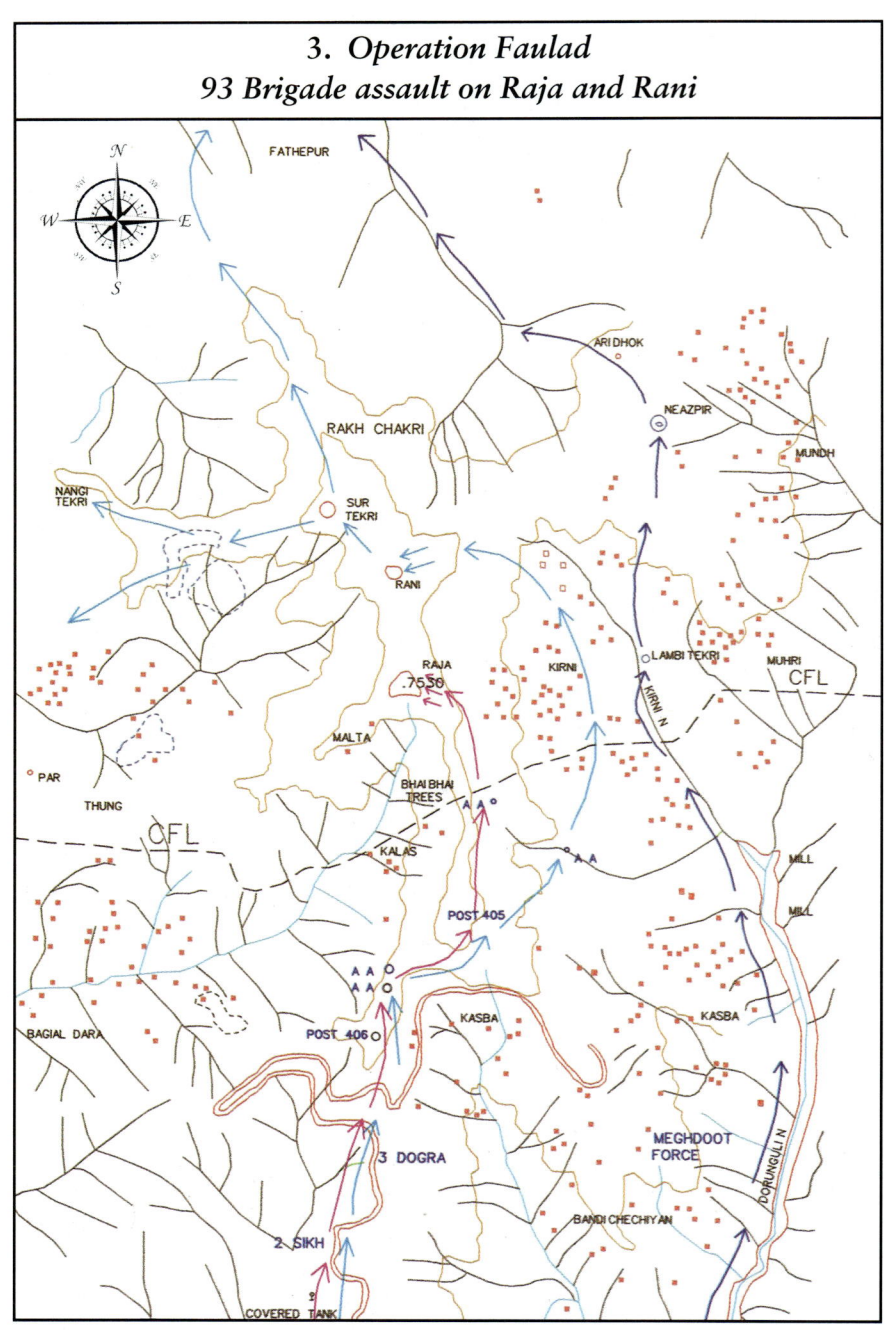

Satellite view of Chhamb

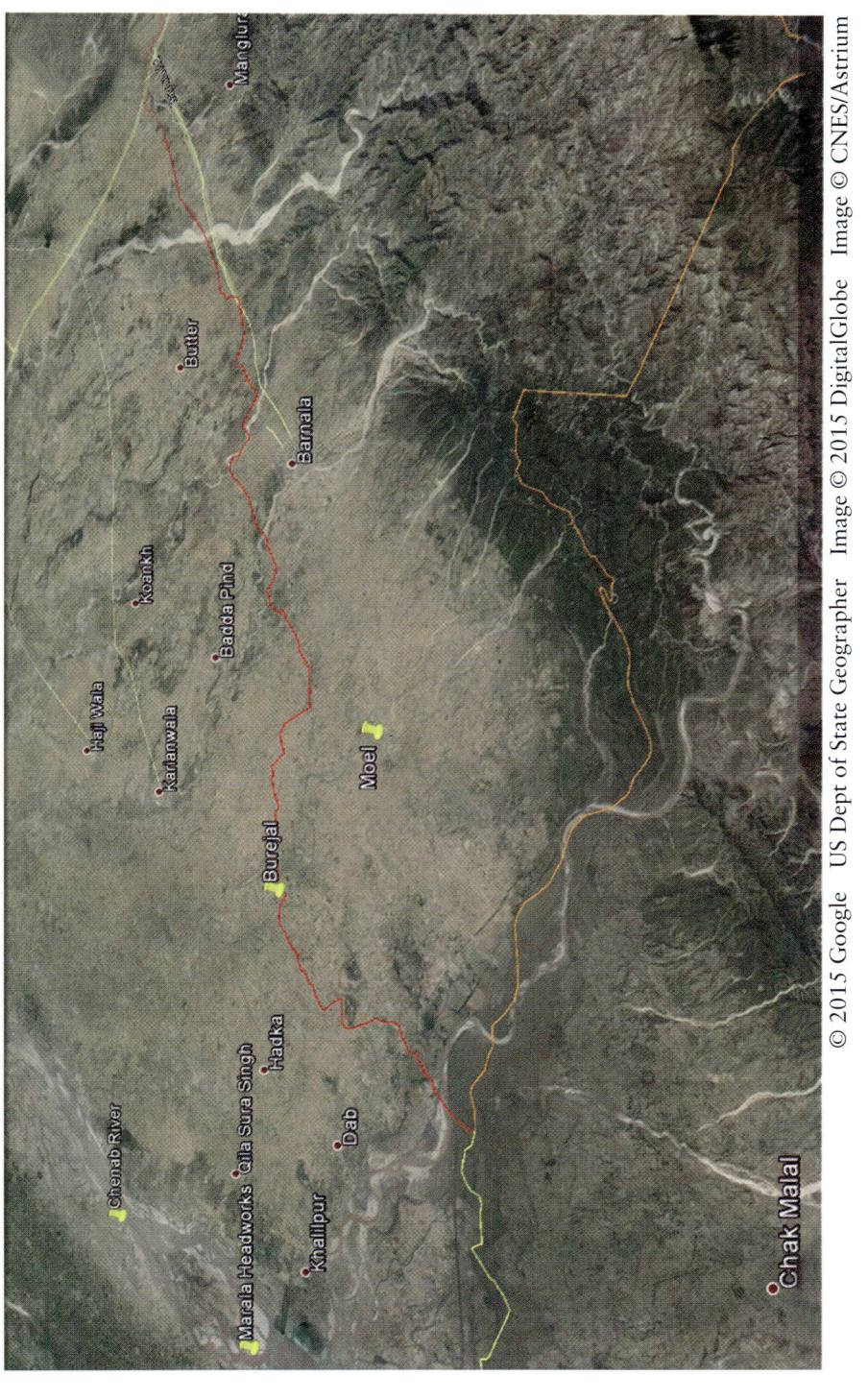

© 2015 Google   US Dept of State Geographer   Image © 2015 DigitalGlobe   Image © CNES/Astrium

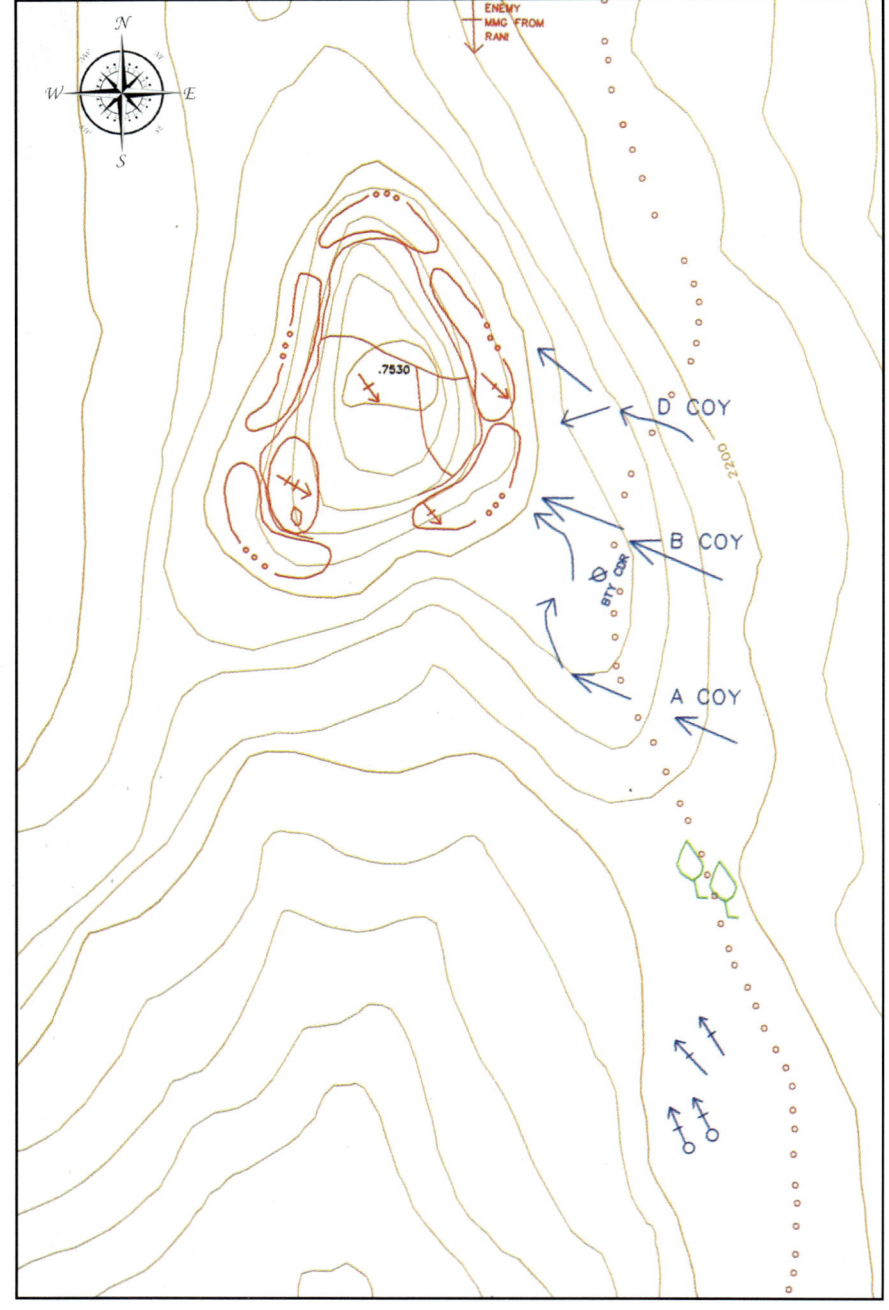

4. 2 Sikh attack on the Raja Post
6 September 1965

N

W E

S

ENEMY
MMG FROM
RANI

.7530

D COY

B COY

BTY CDR

A COY

2 000

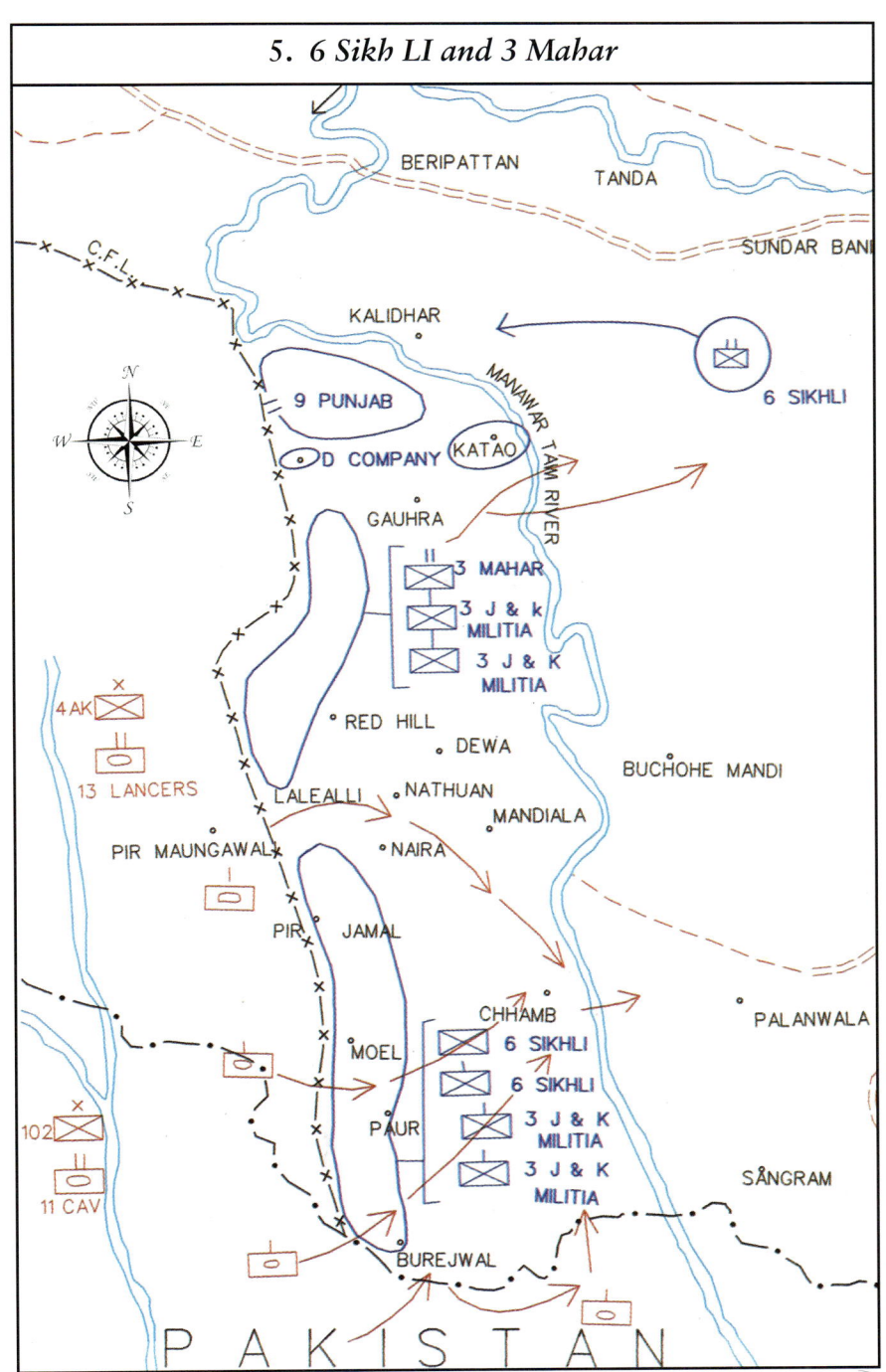

5. 6 Sikh LI and 3 Mahar

BERIPATTAN
TANDA
SUNDAR BANI

C.F.L.

KALIDHAR

6 SIKHLI

9 PUNJAB

D COMPANY   KATAO

GAUHRA

3 MAHAR

3 J & k
MILITIA

3 J & K
MILITIA

4 AK

13 LANCERS

RED HILL

DEWA

BUCHOHE MANDI

LALEALLI   NATHUAN

MANDIALA

PIR MAUNGAWAL   NAIRA

PIR   JAMAL

CHHAMB

PALANWALA

MOEL   6 SIKHLI

6 SIKHLI

PAUR   3 J & K
MILITIA

102   3 J & K
MILITIA   SANGRAM

11 CAV

BUREJWAL

P A K I S T A N

6. 54 Infantry Brigade (3 Jat), 6 September 1965

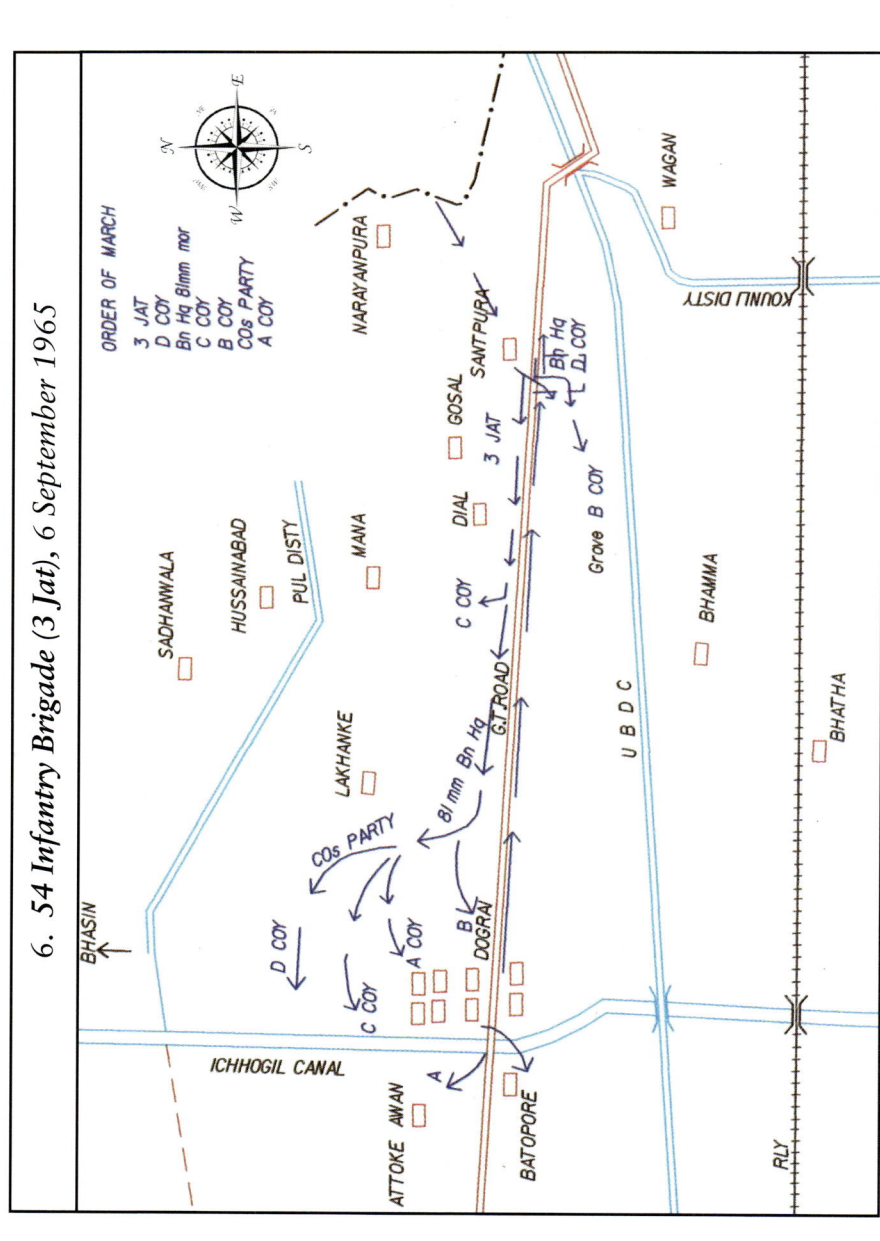

ORDER OF MARCH

3 JAT
D COY
Bn Hq 81mm mor
C COY
B COY
COs PARTY
A COY

7. 3 Jat, Dograi
22 September 1965

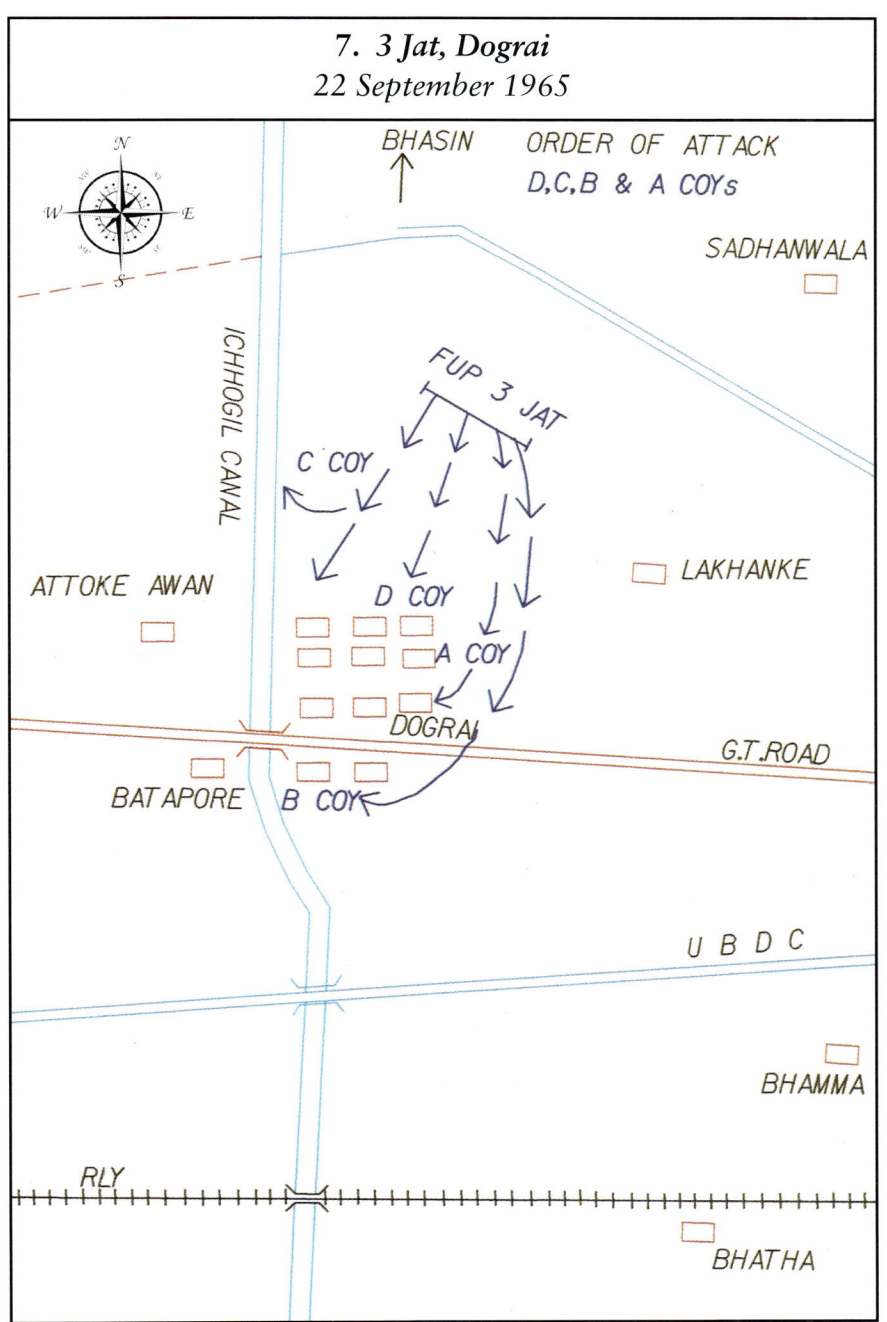

BHASIN

ORDER OF ATTACK
D,C,B & A COYs

SADHANWALA

ICHHOGIL CANAL

FUP 3 JAT

C COY

ATTOKE AWAN

D COY

A COY

LAKHANKE

DOGRAI

G.T.ROAD

BATAPORE B COY

U B D C

BHAMMA

RLY

BHATHA

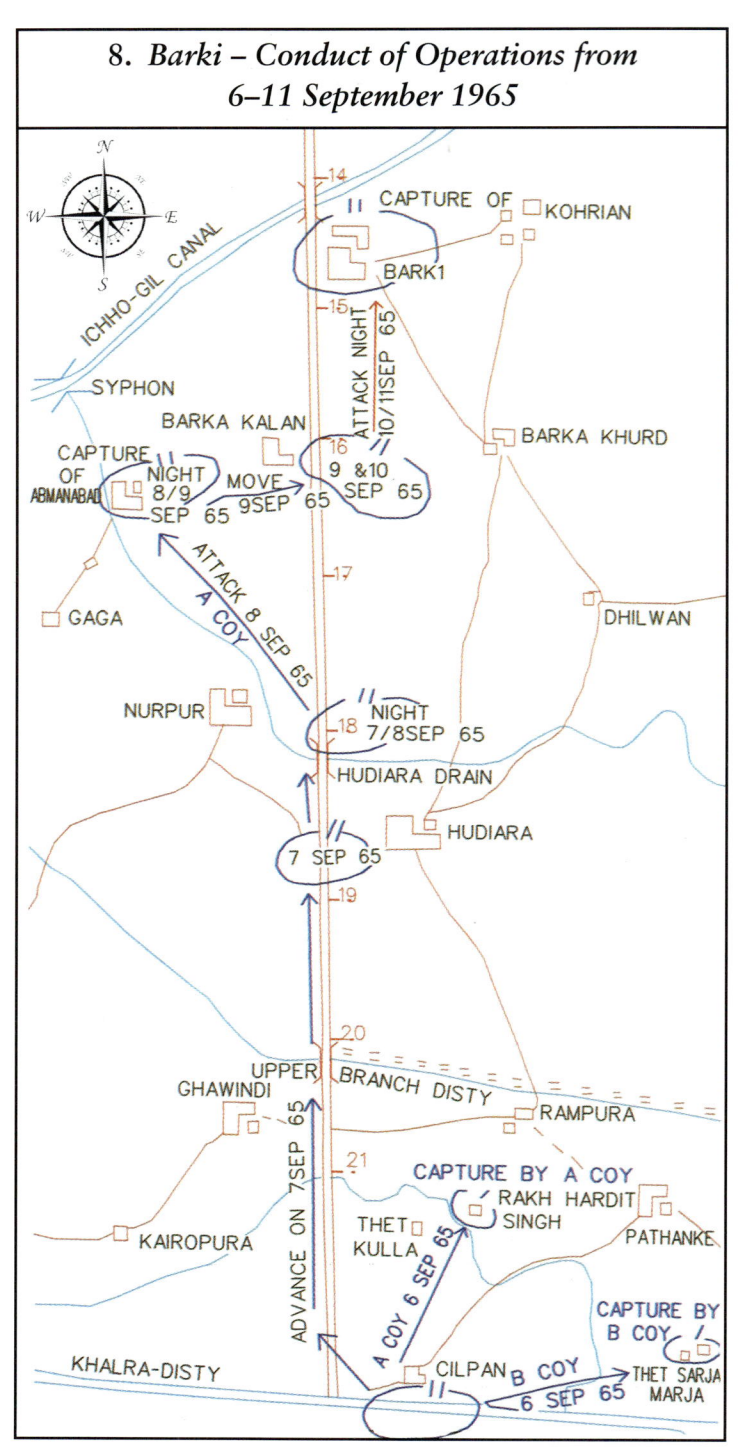

8. Barki – Conduct of Operations from 6–11 September 1965

ICHHO-GIL CANAL

CAPTURE OF

KOHRIAN

BARKI

SYPHON

BARKA KALAN

BARKA KHURD

CAPTURE OF ABMANABAD

NIGHT 8/9 SEP 65

MOVE 9SEP 65

9 &10 SEP 65

ATTACK NIGHT 10/11SEP 65

ATTACK 8 SEP 65

A COY

GAGA

DHILWAN

NURPUR

NIGHT 7/8SEP 65

HUDIARA DRAIN

HUDIARA

7 SEP 65

UPPER BRANCH DISTY

GHAWINDI

RAMPURA

ADVANCE ON 7SEP 65

CAPTURE BY A COY

RAKH HARDIT SINGH

THET KULLA

PATHANKE

A COY 6 SEP 65

KAIROPURA

CAPTURE BY B COY

CILPAN

B COY

THET SARJA MARJA

6 SEP 65

KHALRA-DISTY

9. *Battle of Barki Night*
10-11 September 1965

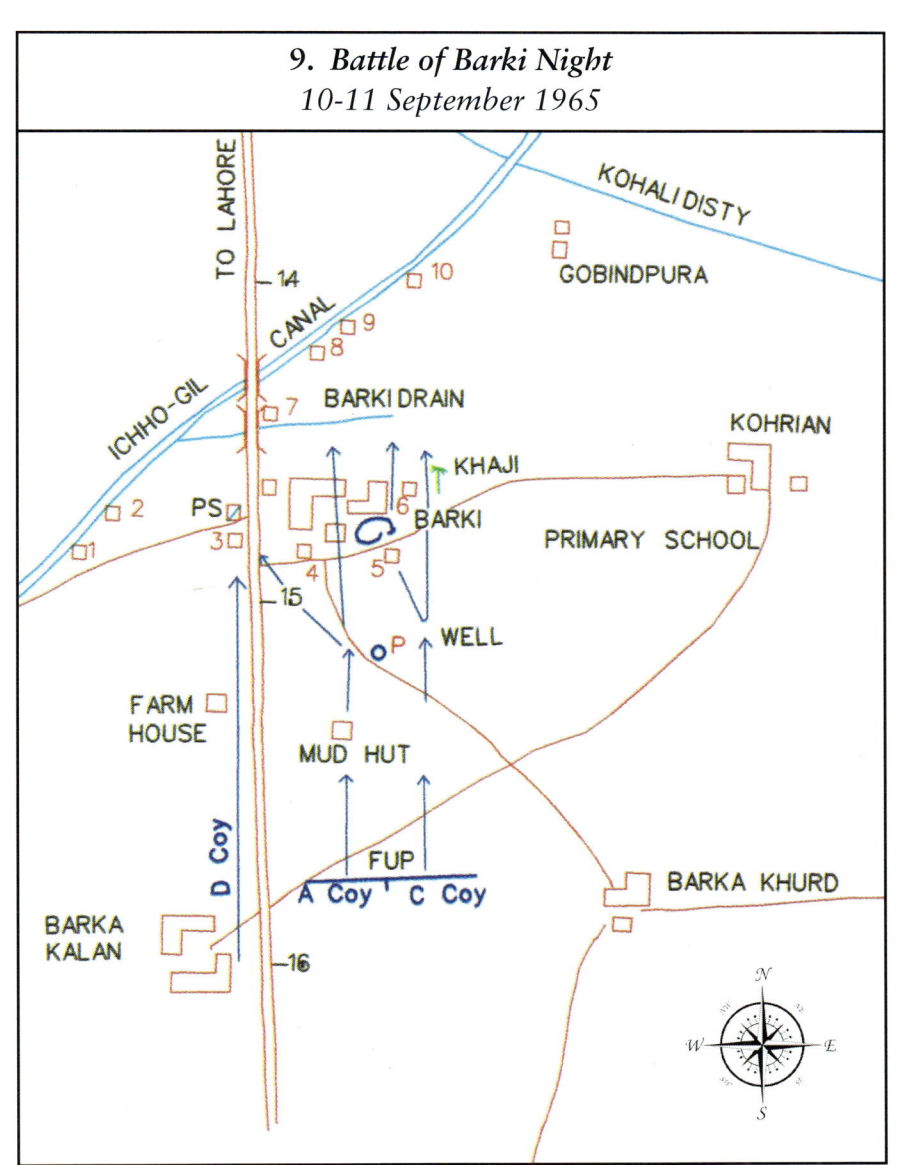

TO LAHORE

KOHALI DISTY

GOBINDPURA

CANAL

ICHHO-GIL

14

10

9

8

BARKI DRAIN

7

KHAJI

KOHRIAN

PS

6

BARKI

PRIMARY SCHOOL

2

3

4

5

1

15

WELL

P

FARM HOUSE

MUD HUT

D Coy

FUP

A Coy   C Coy

BARKA KHURD

BARKA KALAN

16

10. *Battle of Asal Uttar,* 8–10 September

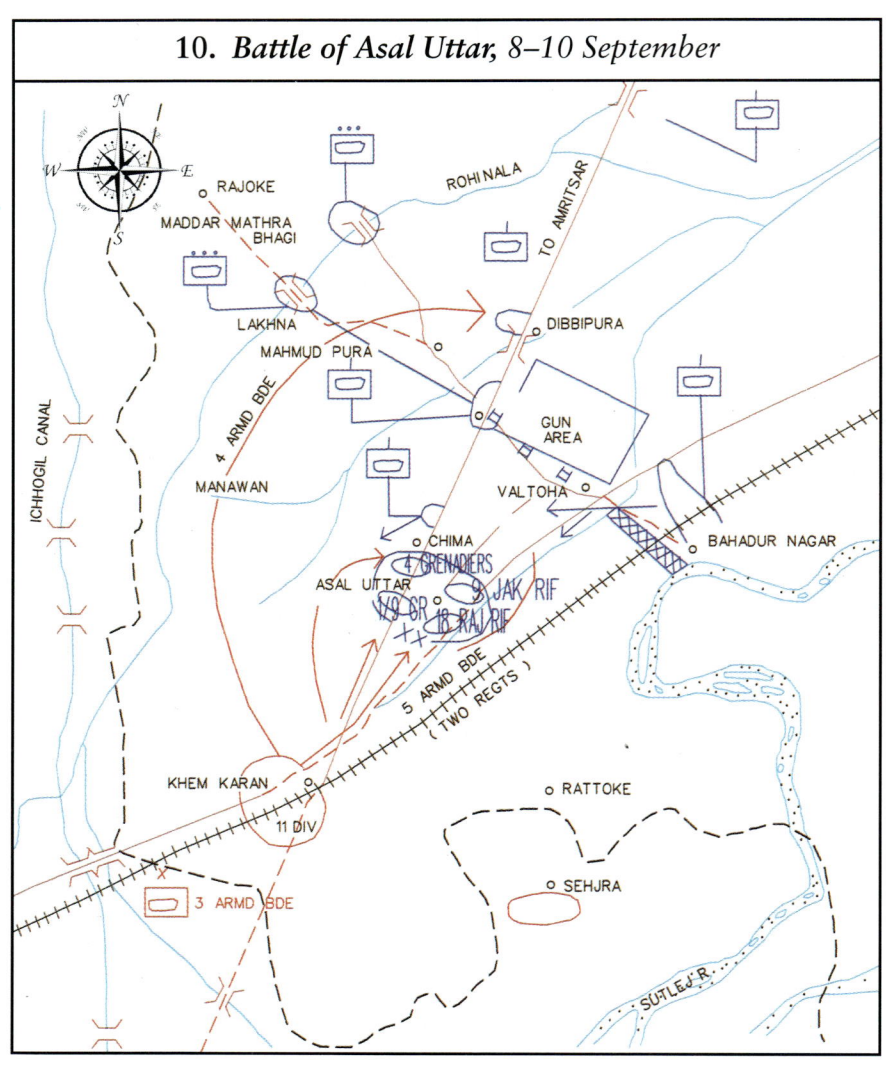

11. 1 Corps Battle – Sialkot Sector, 8–22 September 1965

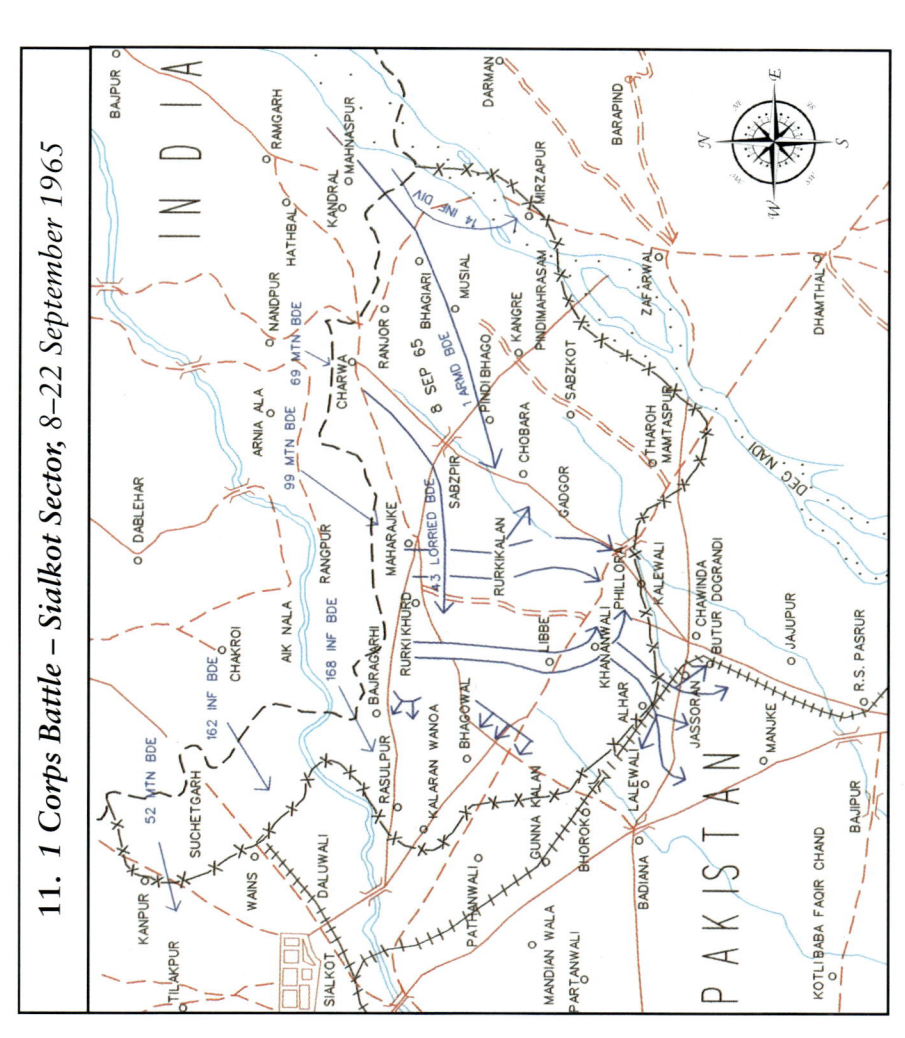

12. *Battle of OP Hill*
2-3 November 1965

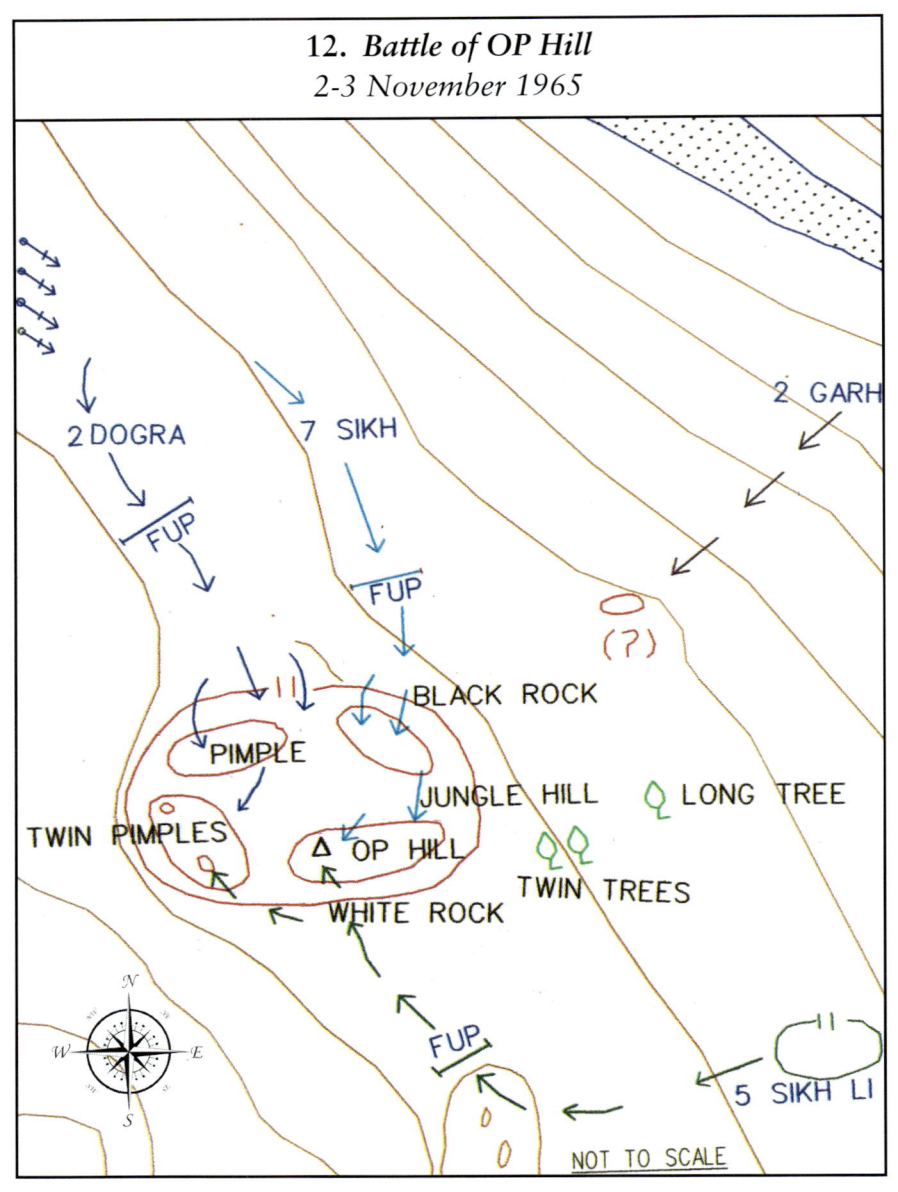

2 DOGRA

7 SIKH

2 GARH

FUP

FUP

(?)

BLACK ROCK

PIMPLE

JUNGLE HILL ☿ LONG TREE

TWIN PIMPLES

△ OP HILL

TWIN TREES

WHITE ROCK

N
W E
S

FUP

5 SIKH LI

NOT TO SCALE

Against All Odds
Major Bhaskar Roy
– Chhamb

The dapper young Maj in perfectly tailored black dungarees was sitting in the office of the Brigade Major (BM) of 191 Infantry Brigade at Jaurian, spiritedly discussing his plan for defending the indefensible. The date was 31 August 1965 and the officer was Maj Bhaskar Roy, the C Squadron Commander from 20 Lancers, whose squadron had been assigned to the brigade defending the Chhamb–Jaurian sector. He shared a degree of bonhomie with the BM, Maj SK Sen, as he belonged to the armoured corps too, and the two had also completed the Defence Services Staff College course together.

Gen Shankar Roychowdhury, former Chief of Army Staff, who was commanding A Squadron of 20 Lancers at that time recalls, 'Bhaskar was six months my senior in Foxtrot Squadron at National Defence Academy (NDA). In fact, I joined the regiment just because he had. I remember him as an excellent athlete and swimmer, with an equally good flair for writing and speaking.' He came from a family of intellectuals and scientists and had studied at Doon School before joining the NDA. Fascinated by stories of the great heroes of Indian epics and military leaders like Alexander and Napoleon from childhood, he chose to join the army instead of taking to science as his family expected. But home and family were far from his mind today as he animatedly tried to put his point across to the BM.

There was no dispute in both their minds that a Pakistani attack on their sector was imminent – even the report from UN observers had indicated a build up of enemy tanks across the border. The point being debated was the direction it would come from. Their area of responsibility shared two different categories of borders with Pakistan – the IB and the CFL. So far all the infiltration had occured through the CFL, as violating this was less serious business than a transgression across the IB, which was tantamount to open war. Maj Bhaskar Roy was convinced that if Pakistan did take the decision to launch its armour into Indian territory regardless, it would be an open act of war in any case. The terrain on either side of the IB was better suited for tank movement and would be the logical choice for any enemy tank commander aiming to make a rapid advance into Indian territory. 'If I was the Pakistani armour commander, I would have certainly taken this approach,' he told his senior.

The AMX-13 tanks of Maj Bhaskar Roy's squadron had been inducted into the sector from Pathankot, where his regiment was located, in April 1965 after the development of hostilities in the Rann of Kutch. The tanks were located near Akhnoor, west of the Chenab River, as the bridge wasn't strong enough for the tanks to make the crossing. However, when things started heating up in August with large-scale infiltrations, they were ferried across the river and harboured closer to the border at Sakrana, near Col Nandagopal's unit, 6 Sikh LI. Maj Bhaskar Roy had carried out an extensive reconnaissance of the entire sector between the Chenab and the border, and this is what led him to the conclusions he was discussing with the BM. Maj Bhaskar had, during his recce, identified suitable positions for deployment of his tank troops along different approaches that the enemy could take. The squadron had also rehearsed occupying these positions both by day and by night, albeit in vehicles and on foot as taking the tanks so far forward would have attracted enemy attention and possibly given away the defensive plans.

Finishing his coffee, Maj Bhaskar Roy bid Maj Sen farewell and returned to his squadron harbour. He had an uneasy feeling that the day of reckoning for his men and machines was now at hand. On reaching, he went around the tanks and spoke to his men. One of the tanks was being repaired, and its engine had been removed. 'By when will it be done?' he asked the mechanics and was told that it would take another day or two. Urging the technicians and crew to speed up the repairs, he made his way from tank to tank, chatting and joking with the crews.

It didn't take very long for Maj Bhaskar Roy's premonition to come true. At dawn the following day, the Pakistani artillery opened up with all guns blazing, literally. That morning the squadron harbour received its fair share of the Pakistani offerings from across the border. Fortunately, both men and tanks escaped unscathed. Maj Bhaskar Roy contacted the Brigade Headquarters and was told that forward troops had reported enemy tank noises and movement from several different places. He asked for and got permission to deploy his troops as planned. The positions had been selected to cover enemy tank approaches from the IB as well as from the CFL, and were located astride the area where the two met.

Maj Bhaskar Roy's appreciation and instincts proved right, and the first enemy armoured assault came in the area of Burejal–Bhusa, with the Pakistani tanks crossing the IB with impunity. The Indian tank crews waited in their tanks, watching the monstrous Patton tanks approaching. Maj Bhaskar counted the dust trails which indicated individual tank positions and estimated this to be one squadron. The crews, including Maj Bhaskar, had read and heard about the mighty Patton tanks – pride of the Pakistani armoured corps. They had also seen grainy black and white pictures during training on recognition of enemy tanks. But to see the mythical beast in real life advancing towards them in all its menacing glory, sent shivers of thrill mixed with fear, down their spines. The advancing M48 Pattons weighed 45 tonnes, with a 90 mm tank gun, and was protected by armour that was 120mm thick. The lighter AMX-13 of the Indian Army, in comparison, weighed a mere 13 tonnes, had a 75 mm gun and was shielded by relatively weak 40 mm armour.

As they were to learn later, they were not only outclassed by superior equipment, but were also vastly outnumbered – Pakistan had thrown in two full regiments into this 'Grand Slam' against the solitary squadron. Maj Agha Humayun Amin, a Pakistani analyst, describes the relative situation as follows:

Pakistani armour enjoyed a marked qualitative and quantitative superiority over Indian armour in this operation. There were two Pakistani Patton regiments against one Indian light tank squadron in the battle. The single Indian AMX-13 squadron defending the area possessed relatively effective firepower (in terms of armour penetration) but was far inferior to the five Pakistani Patton squadrons in terms of protection (armour thickness) and was further dispersed since its area of responsibility was more than even that of one tank regiment. Thus while too wide an area of responsibility nullified the chances of its concentrated employment, poor armour protection gravely increased its vulnerability and seriously reduced its ability to manoeuvre or even jockey.[3]

Yet, at this critical juncture, the tank crews of C Squadron put all thoughts of inferiority out of their minds and focused on halting the enemy tanks as best as they could. Hidden in their well-concealed positions, they waited, allowing the enemy tanks to close into their own shorter effective firing range. Then, on the pre-arranged signal, which was Maj Bhaskar Roy's own tank firing first, the AMXs let loose with all their might. Maj Bhaskar may not have realised it then, but this was the very first tank versus tank battle that the army of independent India had ever undertaken.

Using classic armoured tactics, the defending AMXs fired at a selected Patton and quickly reversed to 'jockey' into another firing position and engage another tank. In this way, they quickly destroyed three enemy tanks, three RCL guns and an ammunition vehicle, temporarily immobilizing the enemy advance. In this encounter, a shell from an enemy tank hit Maj Bhaskar's tank,

[3] 'Handling of Armour in Indo-Pak War', http://www.defencejournal. com/2000/aug/corps.htm, accessed on 9 June 2015.

and a splinter ricocheted, striking him in the chest. Fortunately for him, a silver cigarette case presented by his father, which he was carrying in his breast pocket, blocked the shard and saved his life – possibly a rare instance where someone's life was saved due to the habit of smoking! However, his gunner was not so fortunate, and was killed by another splinter.

Very soon, reports came in of enemy squadrons advancing along multiple thrusts to the north of their location. One troop was detached to take care of the enemy to the immediate north. Maj Bhaskar Roy used his tanks boldly, repulsing three attacks. Even the tank left behind in the harbour without its engine, fired when the enemy came closer to its position and managed to knock out one tank. But the strength was not in their favour at all and it became clear that the handful of tanks could not stem the multiple streams of advancing armour.

Undaunted, the squadron contested the enemy armour as best as they could, delaying the Pakistanis by falling back after each engagement and occupying new positions to take them on again. In this way, the tiny and rapidly depleting force prevented their adversaries from getting a free run. It is quite possible that without this opposition, the Pakistani tanks would have managed to bypass the infantry positions and reach the Akhnoor bridge within a couple of hours, while it was still thinly guarded. The consequences would have been disastrous enough to change the entire course of the war even before it had started.

Meanwhile, back in Delhi, momentous decisions were being taken, the most significant amongst them was to employ the Indian Air Force in support of the ground troops in Chhamb. This was a clear signal that as far as India was concerned, it was an all-out war. Pakistani tanks crossing over the IB had left no room for ambiguity. Interestingly, the air force was never brought into play throughout the 1962 operations, and this decision at such an early stage spoke of the changed political dispensation. The IAF lost no time and later that evening sorties were airborne over the Chhamb sector.

However, any jubilation that the ground forces may have felt on seeing Indian aircraft operating overhead soon changed into dismay when they realised that the air force did not seem to have any means of telling friend from foe. With no strike controllers on ground and no communication with the ground forces, they carried out several attacks on friendly troops. Among the targets mistakenly engaged were Indian vehicles carrying almost the entire artillery and tank ammunition in the sector, three AMX tanks, and one armoured recovery vehicle.

By nighfall, the situation in the entire sector was rather grim. At 2100 hours, the Brigade was ordered to withdraw the bulk of its units to Akhnoor. Maj Bhaskar Roy's squadron was left with only three operational tanks and these, too, were of little use without ammunition. They were also ordered to fall back across the Munawar Tawi River and position themselves at the Troti heights near the Chenab. As the tank crews carried out essential maintenance of the depleted fleet despite exhaustion from a hard battle, Maj Bhaskar looked back at the day with mixed feelings. He felt a deep sense of loss for his men who had died fighting the enemy in the best traditions of the regiment. He also felt regret for the loss of his tanks, each one of which to him was as much of a living being as the men who manned it. Yet he had the satisfaction that his squadron had done its very best given the tremendous odds stacked against them, and felt a deep sense of pride in the way his men had fought. He knew that if given a chance again, they would certainly avenge the retreat.

By the next day, the rest of 20 Lancers had started arriving in Akhnoor from Pathankot and the three surviving tanks from C Squadron were grouped with A Squadron. The regiment had several encounters with the Pakistani tanks over the next few days, before the Indian offensive in Lahore compelled Pakistan to pull out its armour from this sector on 6 September.

For his stellar role in preventing the fall of Akhnoor, and the courage and leadership displayed by him against tremendous odds, Maj Bhaskar Roy was awarded the MVC. In a cruel twist of irony, this brave heart who cheated death several times on the battlefield on that fateful day, succumbed to a road accident barely two years later.

The three stories that follow are told in the words of Maj Bhaskar Roy himself. He had penned these for the magazine of his alma mater, the Doon School, before his unfortunate and untimely death. The eloquent prose proves that he was as good with words as he was with handling tanks in battle.

Dispatches from Action

Two and a half years ago, we were involved in a short, bitter and rather violent struggle over a piece of territory which a number of us had never seen before. It was, however, a matter of national interest, and there was not one of us who had any doubts as to the reasons for the conflict or, for that matter, its outcome. In any case, there has been a lot of literature written and published on the Indo-Pakistani war of 1965. Authors have dwelt on the history, the reasons, the general strategy and the conclusion of that memorable conflict. The country, in its magnanimity, decorated a number of its citizens for gallantry on the field and recognized generously many who had rendered service beyond the call of duty.

But those who were amongst the 'also ran' – what of them? The servicemen and civilians who fought and worked without hesitation, without a thought for consequences and without – alas – recognition? It is, therefore, my intention to give you – or at least endeavour to do so – a few short ballads on some of these unsung heroes.

Hissam Singh

I was commanding a squadron of light tanks in the Chhamb– Jaurian sector in 1965. My squadron had fourteen tanks, an echelon of ammunition, petrol, and other administrative articles;

and approximately eighty men. Amongst these was a tall, well-built young Rajput named Hissam Singh. Until then, despite my best efforts, Hissam was a bit of a black mark against the squadron. I remember seeing him when he was first standing in front of me in an orderly room, on a charge of assault. He told me, very apologetically, that he had not 'meant' to send the other party to hospital, and anyway, they were good friends. He cheerfully took his punishment of a few days' imprisonment and left me with a feeling of having coming out second in the encounter.

Then there was the time when, just before our Annual Vehicle Inspection, the Squadron Senior JCO reported the squadron ready, with the exception (I should have known) of Hissam Singh. He had not only not prepared his vehicle for inspection, but had returned late in the evening in what can only be described as a 'drunk and disorderly' condition. The inspection team having just arrived, there was no time to deal with the case. I began frantically thinking of excuses to present to the Commanding Officer to explain what was bound to be a bad report on my vehicles. To my utter delight – not to mention amazement – my squadron was given a "Good" report and to my horror, Hissam's tank was adjudged one of the three best in the regiment. I am afraid I disobeyed my Commanding Officer's instructions to congratulate Hissam – the Havildar on the inspection team was his cousin or brother-in-law (Hissam was not very sure which) and they had revived old acquaintances until late the previous evening.

You will recall that on 1 September 1965, Pakistan launched a major armoured attack against Chhamb. Things were rather grim that day and you can well imagine the tension. The infantry battalion in whose general area we were was no better off than us. By about 1:30 in the afternoon I had lost a few tanks and there were very few people who entertained the thought of seeing better days again – or for that matter, any sort of days. In this situation, as if things were not bad enough, my Squadron Senior JCO reported the absence of Sowar Hissam Singh. I must admit I cursed Hissam with some fluency and rounded off by demanding that he be brought to me under arrest, if at all he was apprehended

– which, very frankly, I very much doubted. There was, however, no time to think of anything else but the seventy-odd Pattons which were, to say the very least, making life more than a little uncomfortable.

At about 1:30 in the afternoon, an incongruous sight presented itself. Five feet six inches of the Squadron Senior JCO had attached itself to six feet of Hissam Singh and was leading him to me by the scruff of his neck. While I read the riot act to him, Hissam stood shamefacedly before me. I told him what I thought of him and how he had let down the name of the squadron and the regiment – he humbly asked for 'another chance' and promised that he would never again absent himself.

Just at this moment, the infantry Battalion Commander got through to me on the telephone. He was profuse in his thanks – a post manned by his men had been in danger of being cut off by the enemy and it was so kind of me to have sent one of my men with a lorry to get them out! I put down the telephone with a feel of horror (and a little resentment) and asked Hissam what he had been doing. He confirmed the Battalion Commander's story – 'You see, Sir, the idiots had gone and got themselves stuck and someone had to do something about them.' I asked him why he hadn't told me this earlier and he apologetically mentioned that I hadn't given him a chance. Hissam is still with the Squadron and though I am not, I get reports of his having overstayed leave without permission and of his having been insubordinate. Despite these, I am not sorry for having promoted him in 1965.

Sowar Agar Singh

Hissam was, of course, a tough customer, as I have tried to point out earlier. There was no reason however, for little Agar Singh to go out of his way in contributing to my nervous condition. South of Chhamb, the road – a dirt track, actually – bifurcates, one branch going off towards the International Boundary and the other towards the Cease Fire Line. A little beyond the bifurcation was a natural position, which should have been held with nine tanks. Unfortunately, I could spare only three and these were sent under command of my Squadron Captain accompanied by a fervent prayer to hold the position for just a few hours. I might add that the officer maintained the position until after dusk on 1 September.

Between the position and my Squadron Headquarters was 1500 yards of open meadow. At about 2:30 in the afternoon, two Pakistani Pattons had this meadow under fire. They remained hidden in a thick grove west of Chhamb village and there was nothing we could do to dislodge them. At about the same time a new problem arose: my tanks needed more ammunition. While I could replenish the others who were near the Squadron Headquarters, getting ammunition to my Squadron Captain's troop at the road bifurcation seemed well-nigh impossible. If I was to order each tank to come back 1500 yards to replenish, either or both of two things would happen: the enemy would stream through the gap created in an already extended position, or the returning tank would be destroyed in the open meadow.

The only other alternative was to send an ammunition lorry to the position and thereby risk it being blown up on the way. I decided on the second alternative and looked around for a driver. Of the tanks that had been disabled earlier, a few men had luckily returned. Of these was a tank driver, Sowar Agar Singh. He was about twenty-three years old, short, and never had very much to say for himself. How he spoke up on that day I don't know, but before I knew what had happened, I saw the ammunition lorry moving out from behind its cover. From then on, all that the rest of the Squadron could do was watch – watch with bated breath, with our hearts in our mouth, and all other clichés that you can think of.

Agar Singh drove the vehicle steadily over the open tract of land – not too fast for fear of overturning and not too slow for fear of stopping an enemy shell. A couple of hundred yards before the bifurcation was a dry 'nullah'. Just before he reached the nullah, Agar Singh came under very heavy fire from the Chhamb grove. He definitely had someone on his side other than us, because all that happened was that his lorry collected a few splinter holes. According to him, 'the Pakistani gunners need training...' It was here that this young soldier drew on his animal intelligence and drove his lorry straight into the nullah. The banks acted as hard shoulders that he used as cover against enemy shelling.

It was from there that he drove to the first tank, helped the crew to replenish the ammunition; drove back to the nullah; went to the second tank and again back to the nullah; and having similarly effected replenishment of the third tank, he drove back across the meadow, parked the vehicle under cover, came up to me, saluted smartly, and reported completion of his task! I was given to understand later that his major worry was whether or not he would get his water bottle back – he had given it to the driver of the third tank who, according to Agar, was not a particularly reliable fellow.

'Maaji'

There is in every human being a vague quality I would like to refer to as the quantum of courage. All of us, without exception I think, are afraid of death. It is, as Field Marshal Slim so aptly pointed out, the control of that fear which is important. The strength to control one's fear is derived from many aspects: a soldier properly trained would, under shelling, be able to keep a hold on himself for a much longer period than, for example, a civilian unused to the noise and effects of artillery fire. But if, under those conditions, drawing on whatever his inner strength may be, the civilian were to prove equal to the soldier, then the quantum of courage is great indeed. It is with this in mind that I would like to present the case of an old Dogri lady, without mentioning whom this record would not be complete.

Near Akhnoor is the hamlet of Batera. It is a sleepy little village whose green fields are watered by the Chenab River. I am given to understand that on the banks of the river near those same fields, Mahiwal waited anxiously for Sohni to swim across every night. Those fields have lost none of their beauty and I can still see the waist-high bajra dancing to the breeze. Unfortunately, field artillery was not designed to respect either legend or pastoral homestead and so the bajra remained untended for those twenty-two September days in 1965. Despite enemy shelling in the area, the rear elements of my Squadron had camped near Batera.

Because of that shelling, Batera was devoid of its nightly inhabitants, with one exception. At the edge of the village in a large brick house, there lived an old woman. I first met her late one evening when I was hungry, dirty, and very, very sleepy. I remember being shown a rope cot and just before I sank into oblivion, I heard someone say, 'I don't care if he happens to be your Commander. He's in my house.' I think I must have slept the clock around and the next day, after I'd bathed, I asked for my lunch (I'm afraid I had missed my breakfast). My Squadron Senior JCO, whiskers bristling, informed me that the owner of the house had refused to let him provide for me that day.

At this juncture, the owner of the house arrived – she was dressed in the 'churidar' and 'kameez' so typical of the area and, though a little bent with age, there was strength in the hands that held the thaali of food she had brought for me. She stood by while I ate and it seemed the most natural thing in the world to call her 'Maaji'. As a matter of fact, the whole Squadron called her that, with the exception of the Senior JCO who compromised with just 'aap'. Perhaps a clash of personality, but I found that in the evenings, he would not open our little 'mandir' box, in which we had a small image of Chamunda, without Maaji being around!

I asked her once why she had not left with the others of the village. She considered the question and then explained, 'You see, my dear boy, I have you and my other sons (my Squadron) to protect me. Besides, when my husband died, he left me this house and the land. This land is mine, and I shall die on it.' It was, I think, the most effective lesson in patriotism that I ever had and it brought home to us, in no uncertain terms, why we were there. That land is ours and dying on it did not seem much of a problem.

Whereas we never saw Maaji show fear, we did see her worried – once, and once only. Pakistani shells had landed on the outskirts of the village and a couple of houses were demolished. Maaji asked me whether she should leave. I explained, as gently as I could, that if she really wanted to, I'd have her transported back to Jammu. However, I assured her that, apart from anything else, we were there to look after her and should the situation really become bad, I would myself see that to it that she was evacuated. 'Oh!' she said, 'I'm not worried about that. You see, I have a lot of grain lying in the house and I don't want that destroyed. Do you think you could help me send back half of it? I'll need the other half if I am to stay here.'

I got that arranged and our mascot stayed with us. I next visited Batera after the cease-fire had taken effect. Maaji came out of the house, accompanied by her grandson. Having confirmed that a cease-fire had truly been effected, she promptly asked me to get the grain back. The second thing that she did was to hand me a single rupee note. She had tears in her eyes as she apologized for not being able to give me more. At her request, her grandson wrote her blessings on the note. I met her for the last time in December 1965. She wept when I was leaving and I'm afraid I became a little sentimental too. I cannot recall her but with pride; every time I look at her rupee note framed on my desk, I can see an illiterate old woman who had the greatest quantum of courage it has been my privilege to know.

INDIAN OFFENSIVE TOWARDS LAHORE

Plans to launch an offensive towards Lahore by the Indian XI Corps had been prepared as early as April 1965 in the aftermath of the Pakistani intrusion in the Rann of Kutch. Indian planners had anticipated that the situation may deteriorate, and in April 1965, Operation Ablaze was set in motion. Its aim was to position troops well forward in areas from where the least time would be required to commence war preparations and if necessary, to conduct operations. The Indian planners had (correctly) visualised that a Pakistani threat to Jammu and Kashmir in the North, or even to the Rann or Rajasthan in the South, could be neutralised by an Indian offensive in Punjab. Lahore was an ideal target to be threatened in such an offensive, due to its proximity to the IB and the fact that it was one of Pakistan's most important cities. Indian planners were convinced that a move to threaten Lahore would force Pakistan to pull away its armoured and other offensive forces from other sectors to defend its underbelly. Besides, a speedy operation into Pakistani territory would enable India to capture a sizeable chunk of premium real estate in Pakistan's Punjabi heartland. This would serve as a valuable bargaining token at the end of the war, to force Pakistan to give up any gains it would possibly make in other sectors.

When it was clear that the Pakistani offensive towards Akhnoor was not merely a 'feint', and that the threat of Akhnoor being captured was real, the Indian government gave the army a go-ahead to cross the IB in Punjab. The Indian offensive was to be undertaken by XI Corps towards Lahore, and by I Corps towards Sialkot. Ideally, both these offensives should have been launched at the same time to overwhelm the Pakistani defenders and splitting the reactions of its reserve formations. But while the fighting forces of XI Corps were located much closer to the IB and could assemble for the assault within twenty-four to forty-eight hours of the orders being given, I Corps forces would take a little longer to move into their 'launch pads'. It was not militarily sound to delay XI Corps, since the situation in the Akhnoor sector was critical. Hence it was decided that the offensive towards Lahore would be set into motion by 5–6 September, followed by the I Corps offensive the moment it was ready – but more about that later.

The Western Command directive to XI Corps contained two features. First, the plan involved eliminating all enemy defences East of major water obstacles and second, all three divisions were to operate independently. Limited reserves consisted of one Infantry Brigade and an Independent Armoured Brigade at Corps level.

As anyone who has travelled in Punjab would be aware, the entire area is criss-crossed with numerous canals, distributaries, and minor channels. This is also true for the Pakistani side of the border. While the primary purpose of these waterways is irrigation, Pakistan had very pragmatically planned its largest canal, called the Ichhogil Canal, as a formidable defensive obstacle to protect Lahore and other parts of Punjab. The Ichhogil Canal ran from North to South along the entire sector where XI Corps was to operate, at a distance varying between 2 to 8 kilometres to the West of the IB. It was 90 to 140 feet wide and 10 to 15 feet deep, with concrete pillboxes to serve as strong defences for troops holding it. Bridges on this canal assumed great tactical significance as Indian and enemy tanks could only cross the canal by using them.

It is important to note that the task allotted to XI Corps was to *pose a threat* to Lahore, not actually capture it. The idea was to close in towards Lahore along multiple routes, and force the Pakistanis to react to the threat. In the process, the Corps forces were also capture as much Pakistani territory as they could before the anticipated ceasefire intervened. XI Corps had thus tasked each of its three Infantry Divisions to capture objectives on the Ichhogil

Canal located along the three different approaches to Lahore from the Indian side. The successful capture of these objectives would enable the use of the Ichhogil Canal as the Indian forward line of defence, and also secure the territory between the border and the canal as a prize. The section of the Ichhogil Canal opposite XI Corps was divided into three sectors, with each of its divisions tasked to clear all enemy between the border and the canal within its sector, and secure a foothold on the canal itself in its assigned area.

While planning military operations, the higher Commander gives a broad task to his subordinate Commanders, as mentioned above. The subordinate Commanders then do their own planning about what they need to do for carrying out the assigned task. Accordingly, the three Divisional Commanders had selected their own objectives to be captured on the canal itself. From North to South, 15 Infantry Division had selected the town of Dograi, 7 Infantry Division Barki, and 4 Mountain Division had identified the area of Bedian–Ballanwala as its final objective. Each of the divisions, of course, had also anticipated fighting several battles to clear the enemy deployed ahead of the Ichhogil Canal before they could capture their selected objectives.

For 15 Infantry Division, the main task was to advance along the GT road from Atari to Dograi on the Ichhogil Canal and capture all territory East of the canal south of the Ravi river up to the boundary with 7 Infantry Division in the south. Dograi was a village on the East bank of the Ichhogil Canal. The division commenced the advance on 6 September at 0400 hours and by 1400 hours 3rd Battalion the Jat Regiment (3 Jat) had reached and crossed the Ichhogil Canal (Map 6). However, the details of this action remained unknown to higher Commanders and unfortunately, orders were given to withdraw the troops to close to the IB. For fifteen days there were very limited gains by 15 Division till the decision was taken to attack Dograi on night of 21–22 September. On that night was fought one of the most fierce and intense battles, full of courage and valour.

Follow Me – I Lead
– Lt Col Desmond E Hayde
The Hero of Dograi

The Battle of Dograi does not have any equal in modern military history. In it, one infantry battalion destroyed a well entrenched defending force bigger in size in a bold, audacious and unorthodox attack on the night of 21–22 September 1965. 3 Jat, under the leadership of Lt Col Desmond Hayde, captured Dograi and the area of the Ichhogil Canal adjacent to the village, areas held by the Pakistani 16 Punjab Battalion and sub-units from, 3 Baluch, 30 Tank Destroyer Unit, 23 Cavalry, Reconnaissance and Support (R&S) Elements. After the capture repulsed counter-attacks by 3 Baluch, 12 Punjab and 8 Punjab on 22 September, all in a span of few hours from 0130 hours to 1200 noon. Six tanks were destroyed and six captured. The prisoners of war included the Commanding Officer of the Pakistan 16 Punjab – Lt Col GF Golewalla and Maj H Beg and 106 JCOs and men, besides 305 dead bodies were collected the next day. For the victory 3 Jat paid a heavy price of five officers and fifty-nine men killed, while the wounded included six officers, five JCOs and 142 men. This figure does not include those killed and wounded between 6 and 20 September – these were one officer, one JCO and twenty-three men killed, and three officers, three JCOs and seventy-two men wounded. In real terms, more than 50 per cent of the battalion had sacrificed their lives or were wounded to achieve the unparalleled feat.

On 6 September, 3 Jat had advanced from the IB to Dograi, crossed the bridge over the Ichhogil canal to Batapore on the west bank just a few miles outside Lahore, only to be called back by the brigade headquarters, which was unaware of the achievement of the unit. From 6 September till the ceasefire on 23 September, Col Hayde led his brave battalion, 3 Jat, from the front. Though injured he refused to be cowed down by his minor wounds. His message was simple but daunting, 'Follow me! I Will Lead.'

Born in the UK to an Anglo-Indian family of Irish descent, Col Hayde was among the third batch of officers to pass out of the Indian Military Academy (IMA) after independence. He was commissioned into the Jat Regiment in September 1948 when the battalion was at Zojila pass. There couldn't have been a greater contrast between the typically outspoken, rustic Jat soldier, and this soft-spoken erudite Anglo-Indian officer. But, whether it was on the playground or the battlefield, Lt Col (later Brig) Desmond E Hayde had moulded himself into a Jat and was identified by Jat soldiers as one of them. He developed a strong bond with the simple but the hardy soldiers of his battalion.

Col Hayde took command of his battalion, 3 Jat, in September 1965 when war was imminent. The battalion had arrived on 4 August at its new location in Khasa (near Amritsar) under 15 Infantry Division after spending three years in the high altitude environment of Sikkim. He was the second-in-command of the unit before assuming command, and thus knew the battalion, officers and men thoroughly, this being a great advantage during the operations. He was also fortunate that his predecessor, Lt Col JS Mundy, had insisted on high standards of shooting, physical fitness and night training for every soldier immediately on arrival at the new location. These high standards were to stand the battalion in good stead in war.

On 2 September, as Pakistani tanks had crossed the Munawar Tawi in the Akhnoor sector, 3 Jat got 'warning orders' to be prepared for war. Four days later, on 6 September, the battalion was at war, heading for its first objective across the IB in the thick of night. During these four days, Col Hayde spent time on intelligence collection about the Ichhogil Canal and carrying out reconnaissance dressed in police uniform (to hide the Indian military intentions from the enemy). Col Hayde also took one important decision, since the battalion had young officers who had barely commanded platoons; instead, he decided to put the ample experience of his senior JCOs to good use. It takes a great deal of confidence and self-assurance to ignore conventional military hierarchy and take such a decision, but it was a bold step that subsequent events proved right.

The first task of the war for 3 Jat on 6 September 1965 was to capture the Pakistani villages of Gosal and Dial and secure a firm base for the launch of operations towards Dograi. When the Jats stepped across the IB into Pakistani territory at 0400 hours on 6 September, they became one of the very first Indian troops ever to cross the IB in war. The forward positions were lightly held by Pakistan, since they had not really anticipated a full-fledged Indian attack in this sector. The opposition that the 3 Jat encountered at Gosal–Dial consisted of part of a Baluch company and some mobile R&S elements. In a brief fire fight, the enemy were either killed, captured or sent packing, and by 0700 hours the Jats had secured their first objectives.

These skirmishes were not without some anxious moments for Col Hayde, who was in the thick of fighting. The CO's party was the first to reach Dial while the rifle companies were still in the process clearing Gosal a few hundred metres to the rear. They suddenly came across a lorry carrying a Pakistani Lt, an artillery observation officer and his party, rushing back from the Wagah border outpost, which had been attacked by another battalion. Both parties were equally surprised at seeing the other, and the Lieutenant reacted first, firing at Col Hayde. The shots missed, and the Colonel fired back, making the Pakistani officer drop his pistol. Before the other occupants of the lorry could regain their composure, Col Hayde had already taken the detachment, including the officer, as prisoners of war. Shortly thereafter, Col Hayde came face-to-face with death again when three Pakistani soldiers fleeing from Wagah, suddenly burst out of a patch of dense grass and appeared before him. Recovering from his surprise before they could, Col Hayde lifted his carbine to fire, but the weapon did not fire. Fortunately for Col Hayde his buddy, L/Nk Kunwar Lal reacted with lightening speed to kill the enemy and saved his life.

By 0700 hours, the battalion secured the objectives but could not inform the Brigade Commander due to communication failure. However the Brigade Commander, Brig Rikh, soon arrived to personally take stock of the progress of operations. While the Jats had captured their objectives with minimum casualties and were in high spirits, the neighbouring battalion had faced several reverses and the CO expressed his inability to proceed for its main task, the capture of Dograi. On the Brigade Commander's enquiry, Col Hayde willingly accepted the task to capture Dograi.

After two hours, Col Hayde had assembled his 'O' group to brief them on the newly allotted task. By this time the battalion's vehicles, comprising RCL anti-tank guns mounted on Jeeps, mortars and replenishment of ammunition, had fetched up. It is normal practice for units to go into operations with just the loads carried by the fighting men, including weapons and enough ammunition and survival rations to see them through the immediate fighting. The replenishment vehicles and heavy weapons, called the 'F' (fighting) echelon, are brought up whenever there is a pause in battle. The vehicles had moved from Khasa along the GT road in broad daylight, and would have dispersed under cover on arrival at the battalion location, but they never got the time to do so. Six F86 aircraft of the Pakistan Air Force appeared in the sky and started bombing and strafing with cannon fire, aiming at the F echelon and the 'O' group gathered nearby. The Jats lost most of their RCL guns and mortars along with a number of men in this unfortunate incident. The artillery Forward Observation Officer (FOO) accompanying 3 Jat was also killed. The battalion was thus left without almost all its heavy weapons and its FOO who could have brought down artillery fire when required.

Col Hayde did not let this setback affect his own or his battalion's morale and enthusiasm for advancing to the next objective. He had already seen how unprepared the Pakistani troops were, and realised that the key to success lay in a swift operation to capture Dograi and establish a foothold on the Ichhogil Canal before the enemy had a chance to regain his balance. He, therefore, led the Jats in a bold daylight advance towards the objective. Three tanks of the troop of 14 (Scinde) Horse allotted to them for this operation, moving ahead of the column, were the only means of heavy fire with them.

As they were closing towards Dograi, the battalion came under small arms fire from Dograi. Spreading out, they continued the advance, closing in by moving from cover to cover. It was now that Col Hayde realised that Dograi, marked as a small village in their outdated maps, had in fact mushroomed into a small town, spread along the Eastern bank of the Ichhogil Canal. After a short firefight, the Pakistanis holding this town were seen withdrawing across the canal over a partially damaged bridge.

3 Jat had secured its objective, Dograi, and established themselves on the Eastern bank of the Ichhogil Canal by 1130 hours. Col Hayde took stock of the situation along with his Company Commanders from close to the damaged bridge. They were surprised to see the largish built-up area across the canal, which was not marked on their maps. They later found out that it was the township of Batapore, owing its existence and name to the Bata shoe factory that had come up there since the maps were last updated.

Col Hayde, in a bold and audacious move ordered two companies to cross the partially destroyed bridge and occupy the built-up areas of Batapore and Attoke Awan adjacent to it. Thus, in less than eight hours after the launch of operations, Indian troops were across the most formidable Pakistani obstacle, the Ichhogil Canal – they were well within striking distance of Lahore. Unfortunately, the rapid pace of operations by 3 Jat had outstripped the capability of Commanders up the chain to keep up the momentum. The next logical step would have been for the brigade and division to reinforce this success by rapidly moving in troops to strongly hold the gains. Unfortunately, since the battalion had no rearward communications, the brigade headquarters was not even aware of the spectacular developments on the frontline.

3 Jat was on the far side of a formidable enemy obstacle, without its heavy support weapons, without its artillery FOO, without communications and with no reinforcements in sight. The brave men stood firm against enemy artillery shelling and small arms fire. But when they saw Pakistani tanks moved in for the counter-attack in strength, Col Hayde ordered his two companies to fall back to Dograi on the East side of the canal. Shortly thereafter, Lt Brijendra Singh, the tank troop leader from 14 Horse, informed Col Hayde that his CO had ordered him to fall back to Gosal–Dial, and asked him to convey the same order to the CO of 3 Jat as well. The initiative and leadership displayed by Lt Col Hadye had caused panic in the Pakistan military hierarchy, a golden opportunity to retain a bridgehead across the Ichhogil canal lost due to poor higher direction of war.

Thus on the very first day of the battle, major gains by the gallant Jats led by Col Hayde were frittered away in the fog of war. But that was not the last 3 Jat saw of Dograi or vice versa. The battalion returned to the firm base at Santpura and was deployed there for the next fifteen days. During this time they held steadfastly to their positions, fending off several determined counter-attacks by the enemy. Col Hayde ensured that the battalion carried out aggressive patrolling of no man's land, keeping constant pressure on the enemy.

On 17 September, Brig Niranjan Singh gave the order for the capture of Dograi and Mile 13 on the night of 21–22 September, with one infantry battalion to capture Mile 13; the attack was to commence at 2330 hours on 21 September and 3 Jat was to capture Dograi and the canal area, the attack to commence at 0130 hours on 22 September. Col Hadye foresaw this and with his foresight, began planning for the capture of Dograi on 12 September. On a daily basis, he sent strong patrols to dominate the enemy and find out the weak areas; he and the second-in-command Maj Durjan Singh Shekhawat also ventured in to conduct a personal reconnaissance, often in full view of the enemy, who tried hard to shoot at them but with no effect. The domination by 3 Jat was total – the enemy never came to no man's land and the Jat patrols continued to move at will and, of course, all Commanders became familiar with the area they would traverse on the night of the attack. Each night as 3 Jat patrols dominated the no man's land, the enemy would fire most weapons hoping to destroy the ingressing patrols, thus it became a fire display spectacle as Verey (flare) lights and fire became the order of the day. By now Dograi had been reinforced and with its defences prepared, it was a much tougher nut to crack.

Meanwhile, on 18 September, the battalion was overjoyed to hear on the All India Radio news that Col Hayde had been awarded the Maha Vir Chakra (MVC).

Lt Col Hayde gave his orders for the attack on 21 September at 1700 hours, after he gave the rifle company objectives, timings, routes, a movement plan and artillery fire support. He delved into the basic philosophy of the attack, which was leadership. It converted to first, 'follow your leader' – the sections the Section Commander, the NCOs the Platoon Commander who would in turn follow the Company Commanders. Second, shoot at anything you see or even at any spot that looks dangerous on your way to the objective. Third, once on the objective, settle down fast, get your firing positions and shoot anything that moves, one of the section commanders Nk Siri Ram had already told his section if he was hit or injured, he should be carried forward to the objective; this thought was omnipresent in 3 Jat. The call was 'Follow me!' in different versions; for instance, Maj RS Sandhu used to shout 'Pritam Pritam!' to make his men follow him. The effect was the same, with the unit motivated by one thought, 'We Jats are the leading warrior race of history – this is our big chance!' On 21 September, Col Hayde visited and spoke to practically every man in the trenches where the troops prepared for and rested before the attack. The morale boosting talk was plain and direct – 'This is your big day when you will write history, why fear death if in dying you win the supreme reward of the thereafter.' He emphasised the concept of 'Naam (unit honour), Namak (debt to your country) and Nishan (regimental honour)'. His men rose to the occasion, and the rest is history.

The plan was bold and unorthodox – and brilliant. Why it was brilliant will be explained after the battle is described. Four objectives had been assigned to the four rifle companies to be captured in quick succession; there was no reserve for any company, the objectives were D Company – North East part of Dograi, C Company – North Western part of Dograi, A Company Eastern part of Dograi and B Company the area South of GT road. The CO would follow D Company into attack (Map 7). This is a practice in an advance to contact operation of war; in an attack the CO does not jeopardise the command elements to ensure continuity of command, but Col Hadye was unconventional and he would lead from the front. The attack of the other battalion on Mile 13 never commenced. The attack by 3 Jat was to commence after the success of the first attack, but 3 Jat did not wait. The troops left the forming up place on time with Maj RD Vatsa leading D Company to its objective North-East of Dograi and under Maj S R Yadav off towards the canal and North part of Dograi. The other two rifle companies of the battalion under Maj Asa Ram Tyagi and Maj RS Sandhu, headed for their earmarked objectives. The CO and his party entered the village of Dograi between D and C Companies, and were soon embroiled in the fighting.

Dograi was a built-up area with extensive concrete pillboxes, bunkers and trenches connecting the defences. Houses became fortified areas with overhead cover and protected by sand bags and gunny bags filled with sand, while the higher vantage points became observations areas to direct fire and control the operations. Each road or pathway(gulli in Hindi) became a killing ground for a well-entrenched enemy, the darkness of the night aiding the defender and forcing the attacker to clear each house to avoid being hit from the rear. Fighting in a built-up area is a nightmare for troops when the objective has not been destroyed with artillery fire. The dust and smoke further aggravates the difficulty in identifying friend or foe.

During the next few hours, there was a bitter contest of hand-to-hand fighting. Pillbox by pillbox, the sections and platoons fought, clearing each by sheer grit, raw courage and determination. Each building was either cleared or subdued by fire. Molotov cocktails, pole charges, grenades, rocket launchers, small arms and bayonets were used with great effect. Slowly but surely 3 Jat gained ascendancy and the objectives were captured. Some accounts are in the next chapter. However, resistance continued into the early hours of the night.

All this while Col Hayde was in the mayhem that Dograi was, where differentiating between friend and foe was intuitive and a matter of chance. Since he was not part of the assaulting companies and his moving independently to keep track of the progress of the attack was at his own peril. The unorthodox step was deliberate to ensure his presence to influence the battle if the need ever arose. In one instance he came in contact with Capt Bali and his platoon in the North of Dograi and fratricide was averted merely by recognition of a familiar voice. A second time he escaped death by a whisker when his radio operator was shot at point-blank range by the enemy, while he groped for his glasses, and once more his protection man L/Nk Kunwar Lal came to his rescue by shooting dead the enemy duo who had fired at the CO's party. The presence of the CO inside the battlefield had an electrifying effect on his men, who fought the battle of their lives. The strength of the enemy in the defences was equal to the attacking troops, whereas the ratio of attacking troops is generally three times higher in the plains and should be more in a built-up area. The odds were stacked against the attacker but 3 Jat had turned everything upside down.

Once the companies captured their designated objectives, the CO's third commandment was implemented, which was for the men to settle down fast into their positions and shoot at anything that moves. When the enemy realised they had been defeated, the troops who could get out make a dash for the canal, only to be killed by weapons placed to cover the possible escape routes to the canal. As was expected, the enemy's inevitable counter-attack came in the morning; the counter-attack from the South at 0430 hours by a company of 3 Baluch was defeated by Maj Sandhu and B Company, while the North counter-attack was led by tanks with 12th Battalion the Punjab Regiment (12 Punjab) the infantry component and came at 0700 hours. The attack was preceded by very heavy artillery, mortar and tank fire, and in this barrage, Maj Vatsa and many others were killed. D and C Companies to the North-East and North had suffered the maximum casualties in the assaults at night, the further loss added to the CO's worries. The gravity of the situation was well assessed by Col Hayde and Maj Shekhawat. They personally organised the anti-tank and small arms fire, shouting at the top of their voices as they ordered the troops to relocate to take on the counter-attack. The RCL Gun Platoon Commander Sub Pratap Singh lined up the RCL guns, waited till the tanks were 500 yards away and on his orders four guns fired simultaneously, all four hitting the target – two tanks stood still and the remaining ones fled. Sep Lehna Singh joined the troops of D and C Companies to fire at 12 Punjab lined up for the counter-attack and mortars and artillery joined in to break up the attack. The enemy was beaten back and 3 Jat once again carried the day, personally led by the CO. 14 Horse tanks arrived just in time to help defeat the counter-attack. Another 3 Baluch counter-attack from the South on A Company was defeated by artillery fire and accurate fire from the company defences. After the counter-attack, the CO's party moved to observe the Western side of the Ichhogil Canal for enemy activity. Soon a sniper's bullet missed Col Hayde by a whisker – luck was still with him. Good news followed that 2/Lt Kartar Singh had captured the enemy CO, Lt Col GF Golewalla of 16 Punjab, the unit defending Dograi.

The plan was brilliant for three reasons. Firstly, it was not

The Army Chief visits Dograi

sequential – had it been so the enemy could have reinforced the areas under attack from depth areas and stalled the assault. Secondly, the four objectives covered all the approaches to and out of Dograi, the capture of all simultaneously, sealed all reinforcement/exit routes and covered all counter-attack options. The enemy east of Dograi was trapped; though the Mile 13 attack had not succeeded the defenders lay sandwiched and they panicked, abandoning the safety of their defences to be destroyed piecemeal as they tried to escape. Thirdly, the enemy inside Dograi could not reinforce each other nor could they come to the assistance of others by fire. The three leadership directives were tailor-made to implement the plan.

On 22 September 1965, Col Hayde and 3 Jat remembered their first arrival at Dograi on 6 September. A poor decision had brought them back after sixteen days to retake what should never have been given up, the cost for which was not borne by those who took the decision, but by the dead and wounded of 3 Jat. The leadership of Col Hayde was the most singular feature in the capture of Dograi on 22 September, while the courage and valour

PM Lal Bahadur Shastri Congratulating Lt Col DE Hayde, CO 3 Jat

The 3rd Jat Regiment at Dograi

A soldier guards a captured pill box

of the men of 3 Jat had exceeded the expectation of Generals. On 23 September the ceasefire closed the battle, the vanquished collected 300 dead bodies and loaded them in trucks to take them West of the Ichhogil Canal. And there stood Lt Col DE Hayde with the world below his feet – he had achieved what others only dream. For him, the sorrow of losing brave officers, JCOs and men was matched by the joy of victory for the nation and the regiment, the happiness of ending the war on a victorious note and the pride of leading the finest men into battle.

After the war, 3 Jat received numerous visitors including the Chief of the Army Staff General JN Chaudhuri, Defence Minister YB Chavan and Prime Minister Lal Bahadur Shastri.

Lt Col Desmond Hayde rose to the rank of Brigadier before retirement; thereafter he was closely involved in the welfare of ex-servicemen and social service. He donated the land and house he had inherited in Kotdwara, Uttarakhand, for a school called Heritage Academy which is being run in his memory. He breathed his last on 18 September 2013 at his chosen retirement abode, Kotdwara. God bless a great son of India.

We Led the Brave, Gallant and Intrepid – 3 Jat
Dograi Heroes

The preceding of Lt Col DE Hayde gave an insight into both the battles of Dograi. While he as the CO was the undisputed hero of the battles, in real terms the entire battalion was the epitome of courage and bravery, each man a hero, each man a fighter, each man a saviour and a leader. To write about all the actions is not feasible, but the ones included here have been selected because they changed the course of the attack in more than one way, even though other exploits were as brave or braver. The narration is in the sequence of action on the battleground of Dograi.

Subedar Khazan Singh, B Company

When on 5 September 1965, 3 Jat was moving for operations, a despondent Sub Khazan Singh was in hospital, recovering from a bout of jaundice, feeling frustrated and useless. He remembered standing with his grandfather's sword in his hand as a child, looking in fascination at the armless sleeve of his tunic. Neki Ram, his grandfather, had fought many wars in the North West Frontier Province (NWFP), where he had lost his arm to a tribesman who shot him. His father, Tulsi Ram, had also fought at Kut el Amara in the Second World War and won the Indian Distinguished Service Medal (IDSM). His father's words came back to him now. 'The war will come only once during your lifetime. Make sure you don't stay away from it.' So Sub Khazan Singh 'absconded' from the hospital to join his battalion which was just setting out for operations.

The Bravo Company Commander Capt RS Sandhu was away on a training course and Sub Khazan Singh was the seniormost junior commissioned officer (JCO), therefore on his return, the company was most happy to see him. If any of the officers had questions about how he, who was supposed to be recuperating in the hospital, had suddenly appeared, no one asked them. He was asked to take charge of Bravo Company as its Company Commander in line with Col Hayde's decision to appoint experienced JCOs instead of young officers to lead the companies.

Sub Khazan Singh crossed the IB at the head of his company at 0400 hours on 6 September. The specific objective assigned to B Company was a grove close to Gosal–Dial, extending between the Grand Trunk (GT) road and the Upper Bari Doab Canal (UBDC), which ran parallel to each other in this area. As A Company moved towards its objective, it came under fire from the grove. But when Sub Khazan and B Company reached the grove, they found the troops loitering about as if on a training exercise rather than at war – an officer was even seen washing his face at leisure. It was only one alert sentry manning the machine gun who fired at A Company and then turned his weapon at B Company.

Sub Khazan Singh had just opened his mouth to yell 'Charge!' (he was a rare Jat JCO who spoke English and was not averse to flaunting this skill) when the machine gunner fired a burst. Sub Khazan fell to the ground, struck in the centre of his forehead. The 'loss' of their Company Commander stopped the Jats of B Company on their tracks. Meanwhile, the Pakistanis opened fire with all their weapons. The Jats also took cover and started firing back. Suddenly the 'dead' Sub stood up and charged at the enemy, shouting 'Jat Balwan!', the Jat war cry, his first target directly aimed at the officer. Seeing their Company Commander, B Company also rushed at the enemy trenches and the Pakistani troops from 21 Baluch were soon routed,twenty-one of them killed and seventeen taken prisoners of war.

Once B Company was firmly in possession of its objective, Sub Khazan Singh finally took the time to examine the wound on his forehead where the bullet had struck. Fortunately for him, it had struck his helmet – a couple of centimetres lower and he would have been a dead man. As the Regimental Medical Officer (RMO) was bandaging his forehead, the words of his father came back to him. 'I didn't abscond from the hospital only to be struck down on the very first day,' he thought. He assured the doctor that he was perfectly fine, and just the bandage would be enough to get him back in action. He repeated the same arguments to the CO, who arrived while his wounds were being ministered to.

But all conversation was cut short by the rattling of fire from an enemy aircraft that had spotted the Jats beside the grove. It made repeated passes and seemed to target Sub Khazan Singh in particular – it was probably the white bandage on his head that made him stand out conspicuously. Fortunately, he survived the runs by the belligerent aircraft, and lived to tell the story.

Refusing to even consider any respite due to his wound, Sub Khazan Singh pressed on with his company and the rest of the battalion for the attack on Dograi, which they captured by 1100 hours. The battalion was called back to Gosal–Dial area a few hours later. On 12 September, Lt Raghbir Singh Sandhu re-joined the battalion, and took command of B Company on promotion to the rank of Captain. Sub Khazan Singh cheerfully reverted to being the Senior JCO of the company but continued to be part of domination and reconnaissance patrols in no man's land. During one such patrol, yet another bullet hit Sub Khazan Singh. His guardian angel seemed to be working overtime to protect him, as this time it was on his right arm but not serious enough to evacuate him, thus allowing him to take part in the attack on Dograi on 22 September.

On 22 September, B Company objective was South of the GT road. When the ceasefire was announced the very next day, Sub Khazan Singh finally admitted to the RMO that he had been having regular headaches ever since he had been struck on his helmet. With the fighting over with the ceasefire, he had no objections to the doctor referring him to the hospital in Amritsar. Here it was discovered that the impact of the bullet on the helmet had embedded several pieces of metal deep into his scalp. He was operated upon and these were removed. It was after several days, once his bandages were removed, that someone recognized him as the absconder from that very hospital. By then he had become a minor celebrity in the hospital, having been awarded the Vir Chakra for his dauntless courage and leadership.

Subedar Pale Ram, C Company

The attack on Dograi on 22 September began at 0130 hours with D Company assaulting the North-East area of the village. The enemy had taken defences in depth and created a false front. As soon as the company reached the village lane, fire rained down from well-concealed positions, and then the war cry of 'Jat Balwan!, D Company attack now commenced and hand to hand fighting continued for the next few hours. C Company left the forming up near simultaneous for its objective in the North and West area of the village. North of the village ran the Ichhogil Canal bank, this area had been subjected to artillery fire and in the days preceding the attack had been reconnoitered and no enemy had found hence was not included as part of the company objective, however as C Company began its advance the enemy rained down small arms fire from the canal area in an 'utterly violent, such a witheringly ferocious' attack, to quote Col Hayde. The effect was like a scythe cutting the feet of the men as they fell to the ground – at this stage C Company under Maj SR Yadav was 250 yards from the built-up area. This small arms fire could later prove to be dangerous and deadly to A and B Companies as they were leaving the forming up place at that time. At this precise moment in the noise and din of war, Sub Pale Ram of C Company gave a clarion call, 'All jawans, turn right with me and charge!' urging the men to deal with the source of the small arms from the canal bank. To quote Col Hayde, 'This must undoubtedly rank among the finest infantry charges and the noblest acts of gallantry of all time. And directly towards certain death did he himself charge.' In an act of unmatched daring, bravery, and valour, 108 men turned to follow Sub Pale Ram into the hail of fire.

In the charge Sub Pale Ram had taken six bullets in his chest and stomach, from what must have been a machine gun burst, yet he was found on top of the captured bunkers where such a burst could not have hit him. It is certain that the bullets struck him during his lightning charge to the pillboxes. His body was damaged, but his fighting spirit continued to guide his men till the enemy defences were captured. When his subordinates found him they presumed he was dead, but the man of steel had survived his injuries. On Sub Pale Ram's call for the charge, Capt Hardyal Rai and Sub Jhabu Ram led two platoons of C Company in the direction given and attacked the defences consisting of pillboxes and bunkers closest to the assaulting troops. Capt Kapil Thapa of D Company too heard the call of Sub Pale Ram and turned the platoon he was leading in the same direction and assaulted the depth position. Capt Hardyal, leading the platoon, saw tracer bullets coming his way. Fearlessly, he continued his charge yelling 'Maro maro, mere saath chalo aur maro!' His platoon followed and destroyed the enemy pillboxes, one personally by him and Sep Mohindar. Capt Kapil Thapa and his platoon repeated the actions on a different set of enemy defences, but the brave Capt was killed at the end of the battle, his heroism well recognised later. The three platoons attacked two platoons of 12 Punjab and 18 Baluch (next day there were dead bodies and prisoners of both the units) and in pitched hand-to-hand fighting destroyed them in the next few hours. The price they paid was eighty-one dead or wounded, only twenty-seven men emerging to fight the next battle to beat back the counter-attack in the morning. Sub Pale Ram changed the course of battle by one act of leadership and the three platoons acted in good and blind faith. The split second decision – whether intuitive or calculated – was correct and at the right moment. The enemy had no chance against the ferocious attack led by Sub Pale Ram, who for his daring was awarded the Vir Chakra.

Capt Kapil Thapa, D Company

Leading the depth platoon of D Company tasked to capture North-East Dograi was Capt Kapil Thapa. Both D and C Companies left the forming up place simultaneously – Maj RD Vatsa of D Company led the two forward platoons while Capt Kapil Thapa followed in their wake some distance behind as is the drill. When the assault of D Company and C Company began, enemy artillery and mortar firing landed around the forming up place. In the din of battle, Capt Thapa's platoon drifted to the right and came close to C Company and it was at this juncture that Sub Pale Ram gave his clarion call for a charge to the right. The call of the charge reached the ears of the gallant Captain, adrenalin rushing in him. For Capt Thapa, the call for the charge came from the divine, the shooting and bursting of high explosive shells urging him to go forward to be face-to-face with the enemy. In that instant, he gave the order to follow him and the platoon instead of going to the left turned right and joined the assault of C Company. Whether it was providence or destiny, Capt Thapa found himself embroiled in close combat in enemy pillboxes and bunkers that lay in depth to those being attacked by C Company. The platoon systematically and methodically cleared each pillbox or bunker with Capt Thapa in the forefront. Fighting in the canal and built-up area was slow and protracted, each action being a challenge to eliminate the hidden enemy. One by one the platoon gained ground, bunker by bunker, trench by trench, house by house. The enemy fought from every bunker till the Jats gained ground, bunker by bunker, trench by trench.

It was inevitable that at some stage Capt Thapa's luck would run out. It happened when he saw a man throw a grenade which blew up next to his foot and metal pieces rammed into his body. Injured, he staggered towards the man who was the enemy machine gun Commander, the man shouting at the gunner to aim low along the ground so that bullets would hit Capt Thapa. Instinctively, he shot the Commander. As Capt Thapa fell after being hit by a grenade, Hav Hawa Singh grabbed his arm to help him. He told Hav Hawa Singh to move forward quickly to lead the assault, saying that he would follow. Bleeding and in pain, he continued to move through the trenches with his men, firing as he went and silencing the enemy resistance. Finally, he found another trench with the enemy firing at him, just then his weapon jammed and stopped firing. When he hit the ground in an effort to change the ammunition magazine, two bullets hit Capt Thapa on the helmet, piercing it and his head. By now Capt Thapa's platoon had destroyed the enemy holding the depth defences, and he died after completing his assigned role in the unit's call of duty. A fine soldier had sacrificed his life for the glory of 3 Jat.

Capt Thapa drifted from his company in the confusion of battle, but D Company still captured its objective. The contribution of his platoon in the success of C Company was momentous – it tilted the balance against the Pakistani platoons and the feat is etched in his victory. Capt Kapil Thapa was awarded the MVC for his leadership, bravery and gallantry.

A Jat soldier on sentry duty after capture of Dograi town

Major Asa Ram Tyagi, A Company

It was Maj Asa Ram Tyagi who led A Company to attack the Eastern area of Dograi on 22 September. Before the main task, he was additionally responsible for securing the battalion forming up place and guard the right flank of the unit line of advance, to ensure that other companies commenced the attack without hindrance and interference from enemy action. An additional ad hoc platoon was placed under command. He accomplished the secondary task with perfection, B, C and D companies had exited and now A Company had to form up and assault the objective, which also included the enemy tank harbour at the edge of Dograi. The platoon guarding the right flank under Naib Sub Sardara could not be found when Maj Asa Ram Tyagi sought it to join the attack – not wanting to be delayed he directed Captain Rathi, the battalion mortar officer, to order Sardara's platoon to follow on to Dograi. The ad hoc platoon was tasked to come with the battalion headquarters. The directions to Capt Rathi and the ad hoc platoon given, Maj Tyagi ordered the two platoons of A Company and company headquarters to commence the assault, the call simple but a loud roar, 'Follow me!.'

As soon as A Company cleared the forming up place, the enemy artillery and mortar fire came crashing down – not only did A Company exit in time, but even the battalion headquarters and the regimental medical officers were lucky to escape the barrage by a distance of 200 yards. Maj Tyagi had planned to hit the objective where enemy tanks had to harbour for the night, close to the Eastern part of Dograi. The route to the objective lay across open fields some distance away from the buildings under attack by D Company. As A Company advanced, there was firing all around from small arms, grenades, machine guns, with flares illuminating the battlefield. However Maj Tyagi's objective was still engulfed in darkness. The company closed in and just short of the objective, a bullet hit Maj Tyagi in the back near the shoulder blade and pierced into the other side of his back. Apparently it came from an enemy weapon in the area under attack by D Company. 'Move, move!' bawled Tyagi as the Company Havildar Maj Ram Singh and another jawan helped him move forward at speed. On the move, Maj Tyagi ordered Naib Sub Chottu Ram to get the tanks first, 'Sahib tankon ko pahle marna, tankon ko pahle marna'. By now the entire town of Dograi was on fire, the Jats attacking and the enemy fire in full flow to mow down the attacking troops in the open. The enemy tank crew had also just arrived, as they saw the Jats charging, they dived under the tanks, but from the objective area someone fired in the direction of the company headquarters and one bullet struck Maj Tyagi in the chest. Company Havildar Major Ram Singh gripped Tyagi's arm and continued to advance. From his inner strength came the cry 'Jat Balwan!' and they pounced towards the two tanks. The enemy soldier who was firing at the company headquarters was quickly shot down by Ram Singh as he moved in to overpower the tank crew. The next action is described by Col Hayde:

> Major Rehmat Khan was half way up towards the tank turret when a bullet hit him in the back, he turned and came sliding down and it was as his feet hit the ground that Tyagi's bayonet slid into his stomach and pressing the muzzle of his pistol against Tyagi's body fired two shots. The two majors slid to the ground together, locked in an embrace, and thinking he must save his officer a Pakistani ran up and plunged a knife into Tyagi's side. Ram Singh who was wrestling on the ground with another could not get his bayonet free but turning, he threw himself on the knifer, a stone came into his hand which rose and fell, rose and fell even as Chottu stood on top of the second tank and fired downwards into its dark interior.

A Company now turned its attention to the buildings closest to the road and began the attack, clearing the bunkers. After stiff resistance the enemy crumbled and the objective secured. The severely injured Maj Tyagi refused to be evacuated till the task was accomplished – only then did he relent. Maj Tyagi was taken to a safe place, grievously injured. The decision to first capture the tanks ensured the enemy lost their mobile firepower reaction capability. Till the battle lasted, no reaction was possible and A Company and the battalion could continue the attack without fear of an armoured intervention. He then directed Sub Sube Singh to organise the defences before the enemy reacted from elsewhere. The area to the east at Mile 13 was still held by the enemy and to the South was an open area from where a counter-attack could be launched. A Company followed the third directive of the CO, to settle down quickly and prepare for the counter attack, from this they gained immensely when the enemy counter attacks were launched.

It was terribly dark and confusing amongst the lanes but the CO's party reached where Tyagi lay. Col Hayde comforted Maj Tyagi with an assurance that medical help under the RMO, Capt Timmareddi was at hand. Before Col Hayde moved on to take stock of the situation of B Company, Maj Tyagi told the CO that Zile Singh, who had saved him had been shot at from across the road. His sacrifice to save the Company Commander was a noble act of heroism.

Maj Tyagi's will power and physical tenacity ensured he survived to be evacuated to the military hospital. However, the wounds were too grievous and the brave Maj breathed his last on 25 September, three days after sustaining so many gunshot and physical wounds. The courageous soldier was awarded the MVC for his acts of courage.

Major RS Sandhu, B Company

Impatient to take part in the battle, Maj RS Sandhu returned to his unit on 12 September and assumed command of B Company. He got his first chance on 19 September when he was tasked to simulate an attack during the night with two platoons. During this action, Sandhu demonstrated his distinctively innovative mind by a series of unique actions which completely flummoxed the enemy, causing them to fire wildly and senselessly, not only divulging their positions but also wasting resources as not a single Indian soldier was struck. The actions by Sandhu were so successful that in captured Pakistan documents the action was recorded as a successful defence of A Company 12 Punjab (Pakistan) against an Indian attack lasting four hours.

Capt RS Sandhu implemented the 'Follow me!' dictum by verbal directions and physical indications. First he would shout 'Pritam Pritam!' to draw the attention of his troops to follow him and second, he had tied a white ribbon (pheeta) to the back of his turban for the troops to identify him, telling them, 'Now you have these two things, the pheeta and my voice and you must keep close to them.'

On the heels of C Company, Capt RS Sandhu led his company to the objective which lay furtherest from the forming up place, past the pond on the Eastern edge of Dograi to the platoon of 3 Baluch holding the built-up area south of the GT road and guarding the crossing over the Ichhogil Canal. The bridge had been blown up on 6 September and was now a rope bridge crossing. As B Company skirted the village it drew fire; fortunately, it was not effective fire. One person hit was Nk Siri Ram mentioned in Col Hayde's account – he had directed his section take him forward if he was hit so his section complied and propelled him towards the objective. B Company hit the objective square. First, Nb Sub Ram Phal's platoon hit the first lane with a section on each side and surprised the defenders, threw grenades and overwhelmed them with ease. Soon they reached the end of the lane, which opened to the south and Jallo. Here they established two machine gun positions, one on each side of the rooftop. The other two platoons followed the Company Commander into the buildings on either side of the road towards the canal, where a machine gun from a pillbox was firing onto both sides of the road. To silence it, Lance Naik Arjun Ram left his machine gun and with a lighted petrol bottle in one hand and a pistol in the other, charged at the pillbox. In one sweep he threw the bottle at the enemy, caught hold of the machine gun, turned it away and pumped the pistol bullets into the enemy. He held onto the gun and in support, Sep Gokul

Ram ran to lob a number of grenades into the pillbox. The third platoon under Nb Sub Arjan Singh cleared the next lane and a four-courtyard complex. Capt Sandhu's unorthodox approach of leading his platoons directly to the rear of the objectives helped surprise the Baluch platoon and resistance collapsed – the crossing point over the Ichhogil Canal was now firmly with 3 Jat.

The Pakistan Brigade Commander ordered the CO of 3 Baluch to help 16 Punjab when he learnt the Indians had reached Jallo Mor. Capt Sandhu was busy organising his company to defeat the inevitable counter-attack, but he had barely done so when he saw the enemy emerging along the track of the Ichhogil Canal. The time 0430 hours, the day 22 September. The B Company weapons were well placed to inflict casualties as many men fell to the ground; some ran away, but only a few reached B Company, including Maj Karim Khan who was killed by Capt Sandhu close to the reorganised defences. Sub Khazan Singh took part in the assaults of B Company and the defeat of the counter-attack. His zeal had not left him – he was running around distributing ammunition, giving pep talks to the tired soldiers and of course, ensuring the readiness of weapons. The enemy launched one more counter-attack on A and B Companies from the south on the night of 22–23 September. Both companies did a commendable task, the attack was defeated and the next morning, they counted sixty-five dead bodies of 8 Punjab. Capt Sandhu, the cool and gritty leader, basked in a sense of achievement and triumph as the ceasefire came into force.

Sep Lehna Singh

Finally, we must recount the bravery and cool headedness of Sep Lehna Singh, who accounted for at least thirty enemy soldiers but the numbers could be close to fifty. This simple soldier chose to position his light machine gun at a point from where he had a 360-degree vantage view of the canal and area to the North of Dograi. After 3 Jat had captured Dograi, the enemy panicked and made efforts to get away by crossing the canal. Lehna Singh killed at least thirty men making an effort to swim across the water.

Later, when 12 Punjab assembled for a counter-attack North of Dograi along with armour, he caused havoc amongst the infantry. How many he hit is not known, but the overall fire directed by the remnants of C and D Companies and himself was the cause of the counter-attack failing on 22 September at 0700 hours. Sep Lehna Singh's singlehanded contribution was recognised by the VrC awarded to him. An illiterate and simple man had become an unsung hero by his astute sense of commitment and common sense.

The battalion won three MVCs, four VrCs, seven Sena Medals, eight twelve Mention in Despatches and eight Commendation Cards. This was the zenith of bravery, determination, fortitude, grit, gallantry, heroism, leadership, purpose, resolve, valour and willpower of 3 Jat.

Tricolour proudly hoisted atop a pill box at Dograi
Jats do the nation proud

The Maharaja of Patiala with CO 3 Jat Lt Col DE Hayde, MVC

Maharaja Patiala and Brig Niranjan Singh with CO and other ranks pose
in front of the captured Pak patton tank

Lt Col Hayde with 3 Jat victors

Inspecting the destroyed bridge

BARKI

In a parallel and simultaneous operation to the south of 15 Infantry Division, 7 Infantry Division was tasked to advance along the Bhikiwind–Khalra–Barki road and capture all Pakistani territory up to the Ichhogil Canal in the section allotted to it. Barki was a prominent town almost in the centre of its allotted area on the canal, and the division was asked specifically to capture this town and the bridge near it.

Maj Gen HK Sibbal, GOC 7 Infantry Division, planned to carry out the attack in two phases. In Phase I, 48 Infantry Brigade supported by tanks of CIH less one troop was to advance from Khalra to Barki and capture it, along with the adjacent bridge over the Ichhogil Canal, by last light on 6 September. Simultaneously, 17 Rajput, with the remaining troop of CIH, was to cross the border along Wan–Bedian axis and secure Bedian by last light on 6 September. In Phase II, 65 Infantry Brigade Group was to 'mop up' the enemy in the area up to the Ichhogil Canal and destroy all the bridges in the divisional area of responsibility.

Of the three divisions in XI Corps, 7 Infantry Division was the most successful in carrying out its allotted tasks. Crossing the IB well before dawn, the troops of the division were able to capture their initial objectives of Hudiara and Nurpur by that evening. Two more villages en route to Barki – Barka Kalan and Barka Khurd were captured on 7 and 8 September. Barki itself was captured by the morning of 11 September in a fiercely fought and intense battle where the enemy fired as many as 2500 artillery shells in a short span of forty-five minutes.

After this most of the action shifted towards the South, to the 4 Mountain Division sector as we will see later. But first, let's take a look at some of the battles and people who fought them in detail.

Selfless Service

Subedar Ajit Singh – Barki

The tall, slim JCO was instructing the jawans of his platoon on the intricacies of the newly issued 7.62 mm self-loading rifle. Picking up the rifle by the tip of its barrel and expertly swinging it around with one hand, he pointed out the features which made this modern weapon different from the .303 bolt action rifle that the soldiers had been using so far. The JCO, Sub Ajit Singh, was a qualified weapons instructor, and an acknowledged marksman. His prowess with weapons at the shooting range was matched by his skill at wielding the hockey stick in the play field. He was one of the best backs the battalion's hockey team had seen for a long time. He took pride in the fact that no opponent could dribble the ball past him.

The date was 3 September 1965 and the battalion, 4th Battalion the Sikh Regiment (4 Sikh), had reached their new location, Ferozepur, less than a month ago. The new rifles had been issued to them on arrival, and were state-of-the-art compared to the ancient .303 rifles the men were used to. Besides being lighter, they could be fired repeatedly without having to be 'cocked'[1] between rounds.

---

[1] The old .303 rifle was 'bolt action' meaning that after firing a round, it had to be 'cocked' – physically moving the 'cocking handle' behind to eject the spent cartridge and load the new round. In the self-loading rifle, this happens automatically, using the backward pressure of the gases from the fired round. Thus all the firer has to do is keep pressing the trigger.

But with war ominously looming in the horizon, it was a matter of urgency to make sure the men were proficient in handling the weapons they would use if war actually broke out, and Sub Ajit Singh was doing his bit.

The impromptu class was interrupted by a runner carrying orders for everyone to gather at the gurudwara as the CO wanted to address the battalion. Sub Ajit Singh knew the significance of this. He had heard how Pakistani infiltrators had streamed into Jammu and Kashmir, heard of the exploits of Maj Ranjit Singh Dyal and the capture of Haji Pir, and also of the massive Pakistani attack in the Chhamb sector. His instinct told him that it wouldn't be too long before they were called to war. And the CO's words proved him right. The CO, Lt Col Anant Singh, who had just returned from the Brigade Headquarters, said:

> *The paltan (battalion) has been placed on four hours' notice for war. Another opportunity is likely to come by to achieve glory. In this war, God willing, we shall capture back the places from where he had been thrown out during the partition. Remember the deeds of the Saragarhi heroes and the gallant martyrs of the 1962 operations, be prepared for sacrifices and to perform deeds of valour and dedication for our beloved country.*

The mention of Saragarhi sent a surge of pride through every man present. The CO was referring to the battle of Saragarhi fought in 1897 by twenty-one soldiers of the battalion, then known as 36 Sikh, in the village of Saragarhi in Afghanistan. This small detachment was attacked by a force of 10,000 Afghan tribesmen, and they stood their ground till the last man was alive. In fact, the battalion was to celebrate the anniversary of this battle in another nine days had war not intervened.

Events moved very fast, as they do in times of war. On 6 September, Sub Ajit Singh found himself crossing the IB along with his platoon as part of A Company (Map 8). The company had been given the task of clearing a border outpost called Rakh Hardit Singh. These outposts are manned by paramilitary forces during peace time, and are reinforced by regular troops when war is imminent. This hadn't happened so far at this post, and they took the Pakistani Rangers occupying the post completely by surprise. The Rangers were quite literally caught with their pants down – some of them were seen running away in their underwear.

Maj Shamsher Singh Manhas, the Company Commander, gathered his company, commended them on their success and told them to be ready for the next task. The next day was relatively uneventful, but on the 8th, the company was ordered to clear the enemy from village Brahmanabad, along with D Company under Lt Kanwaljit Singh. The enemy soldiers did not seem to have much appetite for a fight, and as the Sikhs closed in towards the village, the Pakistani resistance quickly collapsed. However, artillery shells exploding all around them soon put an end to any thoughts of celebrating their victory. The withdrawing enemy had called for fire support and the Sikhs, who were in the process of reorganising their defences and digging new ones, were vulnerable to fire.

Expecting a Pakistani counter-attack to re-capture the lost village, the Sikhs were ordered to move up beyond the village after last light and be deployed by morning, ready to meet the attack. They could only dig shallow trenches in the limited time available, just enough to protect them from enemy artillery fire, provided they remained confined to them. As the sun rose, Sub Ajit Singh saw his men getting thirstier and thirstier. Intermittent artillery shelling made moving around difficult. But the resourceful Sikhs made best use of the sugarcane fields around their positions. Taking turns at slipping into the fields, they could quench their thirst with the juicy sugarcane and also remain undetected by the enemy.

That night they learnt that the battalion had been given the task of capturing Barki, a village located near the Ichhogil Canal, just a kilometre ahead of their present position. This was a matter of honour for the battalion, as Maj Shamsher explained to Sub Ajit and the rest of the company, 'Barki is the main objective of the division, and we have been chosen to capture it.' Ajit Singh remembered the CO's words, and vowed to live up to the name of the defenders of Saragarhi.

Barki's formidable defences are described by Gen Harbakhsh Singh in his book *War Despatches* as follows:

The bastion of Barki was a tough nut to crack. The enemy had deployed one company in Barki village and two companies on the east bank of the Ichhogil Canal. In addition there was a company of reconnaissance and support battalion in this area and the whole position was ringed round with accurately surveyed defensive fire tasks. A few tanks were also spotted in the area. The defences were elaborately prepared and based on cement-concrete pill boxes which were sited to cover all approaches to the village and cunningly camouflaged to resemble mud huts. Each pill box was 15 feet square with 3 feet thick concrete walls and an equally thick roof. A team of three men equipped with automatic weapons manned each of these strong points. The pill boxes were sell stocked for sustained operations and sited with care for mutual support. Extensive tunnelling within the village permitted speedy uninterrupted movement between these defence works, even during periods of intense shelling... In brief, Barki was a virtual fortress bristling with automatic weapons and well supported by armour and artillery. It challenged the best in any unit.

And 4 Sikh was a unit up to that challenge. According to the plan made by the CO, three companies – A, C, and D – would participate in the attack while B Company would be in reserve. The village of Barki was spread on both sides of the Bhikkiwind–Barki–Lahore road. While the majority of the inhabitants were spread to the right of the road, the village police station and a few other houses were located on the left. A small drain, called the Barki drain, ran ahead of the village on both sides of the road, and the Ichhogil Canal flowed a little distance away behind the village. A and C Companies were to attack on the right of the road, and D Company on the left. Tanks from Central India Horse (CIH) would also be part of the attacking force, moving ahead of D Company and firing at any interfering objectives (Map 9). By 1950 hours, A and C Companies were ready in their FUP, and were already under artillery fire. D Company had been left behind to guide the tanks up to the FUP. Unfortunately, the tanks were not fetched up on time and D Company had to run to catch up with the other two assaulting companies.

The enemy had been expecting the attack on Barki and had sufficient time to prepare their defences – positions had been cleverly concealed amongst the houses of the village, fortified as bunkers. The enemy had dug trenches to augment the positions in the houses, and some troops were also deployed along the banks of the Ichhogil Canal. The assaulting Sikhs thus came under fire from three directions, and it became difficult for the commanders to pinpoint the enemy's exact position. The Sikhs continued their advance undaunted. Cries of 'Bole So Nihal!' and the customary response of 'Sat Sri Akal!' punctuated the din of gunfire and artillery shells exploding all around. The progress was slow, but steady, as they moved forward from cover to cover, firing as they advanced.

Sub Ajit Singh's platoon was part of A Company which was on the left, and C Company was to its right. Since the tanks, which were to have made their attack easier were delayed the Company Commanders requested for additional fire from the mortars. When the attacking troops were just about 400 yards from the mud huts of the village, which were spewing fire, the assault almost stalled. The heavy volume of fire made movement impossible and Sub Ajit Singh saw men around him being hit. Seeing his men dying around him infuriated the usually affable and patient Ajit Singh. Something seemed to snap in his head. He then zeroed in on the source of the deadly fire which was taking this heavy toll and holding up their advance.

Accurate machine gun fire from a particularly well situated pill box was the source of their trouble. Sub Ajit Singh suddenly rose from his position and his battle cry ringing loud and clear, charged head-on for the pill box. He was hit in the chest by a machine gun burst from within as he reached the pillbox, but that didn't stop him. He threw a grenade inside, instantly killing the machine gun crew, before he collapsed in a heap just outside the pillbox.

Before his platoon and rest of the company could even realise it, Ajit Singh had eliminated the impediment to their advance, paying for it with his life. His daring act galvanised the entire company, they stood and rushed forward. Soon the objective was filled with swarms of men in olive greens, rushing at the Pakistani bunkers with no concern for their own safety. The Pakistanis could not stand before this resolute charge, and their forward troops were killed or abandoned their positions and ran.

It took another hour and several more resolute attacks to clear the rest of the village, but by 2130 hours, Barki was captured. It was one of the most fiercely fought battles of the war, with almost 2,500 artillery shells fired by the enemy within a span of forty-five minutes. Maj Aziz Bhatti, who had been tasked with the formidable defences with two companies plus, was later awarded Pakistan's highest gallantry award, Nisan-I-Haidar, posthumously.

But the lasting image in everyone's mind was Sub Ajit Singh's daredevil charge that turned the tide of the battle. He had truly lived up to the traditions set by his predecessors at Saragarhi almost seventy years back. His bravery was acknowledged by the award of the MVC.

Indian troops at Barki Police Station

Going Alone
Lieutenant Kanwaljit Singh – Barki

About the time A and C Companies of 4 Sikh were advancing for their attack on Barki, D Company, under its officiating Company Commander – young Lt Kanwaljit Singh, was waiting for the tanks that were to accompany them. They had been ordered to join up with the tanks and move behind them in civilian trucks loaded with wooden planks (colloquially called 'sleepers'). They were to lower these planks on the Barki drain to help tanks get over it. After facilitating the crossing over by the tanks, they were to form up on the left of the Bhikkiwind–Barki–Lahore road and attack the Barki police station. The tanks were supposed to lead, firing on enemy targets both sides of the road, thus making the task of the attacking infantry easier. Lt Kanwaljit waited as the clock ticked past the assigned time for their attack, with the tanks nowhere in sight.

They had been waiting since 1930 hours, and when there was still no sign of the tanks by 2000 hours, the Company Commander asked the Adjutant whether he should continue waiting or go ahead with the planned attack. They received orders to go ahead without the tanks, and D Company moved in towards the police station. Soon after their assault had begun, they could hear the tanks rumbling up behind them, and shortly thereafter the tanks opened fire on the objective that A and C Companies were assaulting on the right of the road. Since the assaulting troops were also in the line of tank fire, the tank Commander was contacted and asked to switch fire to the left of the road, towards the police station, where the attack was yet to go in.

D Company soon shook off the confusion caused by the delayed arrival of the tanks and organised itself to attack the police station. Very soon, cries of 'Bole So Nihal!' and 'Sat Sri Akal!' filled the air as the gutsy Sikhs rushed for their objective. By now A and C Companies had already captured their objectives on the right of the road, and it did not take D Company long to overcome the resistance at the police station and capture it too. The enemy could be seen running helter-skelter, and some of them even jumped into the Ichhogil Canal and tried to swim across to escape the wrath of the deadly Sikhs.

The enemy had, meanwhile, brought up its tanks on the far bank of the Ichhogil Canal, and were firing on the Sikhs with deadly effect. One of our own tanks advancing to deal with this menace had its track blown up by an anti-tank mine. Apparently, the enemy had hurriedly scattered these mines while retreating. The other tanks moved up and engaged the enemy tanks across the canal, which soon withdrew.

4 Sikh found the eastern bank of the Ichhogil Canal virtually unheld by the enemy, and they seized this opportunity to occupy it forthwith.

The capture of Barki was hailed as a masterpiece battalion attack. In the action, 4 Sikh had 39 killed and 121 wounded. Dr S. Radhakrishnan, President of India, visited Barki after the cease fire, had tea with the troops, and complimented the battalion for its sacrifices and victory.

Lt Kanwaljit Singh atop of pill box

Barki's zero

An Army Marches on Its Stomach
Subedar Major Kul Bahadur Thapa

The Subedar Major (SM or Sub Maj) in an infantry battalion is the seniormost JCO and often the person with the longest service – even more than the CO. During the British Raj, one of his key roles was to advise the CO, who was British, on matters relating to the customs, welfare, and morale of the troops. With the coming of independence the cultural gap between the officers and men wasn't much of a factor, but the SM continues to be an institution as important as the CO. Every soldier who joins a unit looks up to the SM, aspiring to reach that position one day. The CO consults the SM on all major matters, and the advice rendered by him is generally a major factor in decision-making.

In battle, he plays a supporting role, located behind the fighting troops along with the administrative support elements. His main responsibilities are administration including taking care of the arrangements for last rites or rearward dispatch of the mortal remains of own soldiers and enemy personnel who die, and also handling the prisoners of war till they are given over to higher authorities. So the only enemy he probably comes face-to-face are prisoners or dead. Rarely does he get a chance to be close to the actual firing line, or face any real danger, except possibly enemy artillery shelling on the rear areas. But Sub Maj Kul Bahadur Thapa of 6/8 Gorkha Rifles was different.

A veteran of World War II, he had been wounded several times and still carried scars of many German bullets to show for it. He had been captured twice and escaped both times from the German Prisoners of War camps. After independence, he had been transferred from his original battalion 2nd Battalion 8th Gorkha Rifles (2/8 GR) to 6th Battalion 8 Gorkha Rifles (6/8 GR) in 1956 as a Hav. He rose to become the SM in his new battalion, and accompanied it to war. His only regret was that he was expected to sit out this war, playing an administrative role. The dauntless old man actually wished that he could be a Sub instead, and be in active battle with one of the companies.

The battalion was in the thick of fighting in the 7 Infantry Division sector. It was launched along the Khalra–Barki axis along with 4 Sikh, whose exploits we followed in the preceeding chapter. The initial objectives allotted to it were the border posts of Ghawindi and Khalra. Unlike most border posts, which are held thinly by Rangers, the intelligence on Khalra was that it had been reinforced by a platoon of regular troops. The fight to capture it, therefore, was not easy and B Company, tasked to capture it, fought a tough battle, losing their Company Commander, Capt RC Bakshi in the firefight before they could capture the post. He was subsequently awarded the VrC for this action.

While 4 Sikh went on to capture Barki, 6/8 GR assisted in clearing the enemy pockets within the villages between the IB and the Ichhogil Canal. During which time they captured the villages Hudiara, Gaga, and Padhana. It also made two attempts to capture a village called Jahman and the bridge close to it. The battalion was constantly on the move in this short period of intense fighting. During this time, Sub Maj Thapa took his responsibility of keeping up the morale of the men very seriously.

He knew that nothing boosts up the spirit of the men like a hot meal after they have had to subsist on survival rations for the duration of approach marches and battles. So he took it upon himself to ensure the delivery of hot meals to the men whenever they had a respite, even though it was not strictly part of his charter of duties. Driving a Jeep himself, he delivered the meals carried in a trailer tirelessly under shelling and air attacks. He managed to round up sixty goats and as a result, all men at all meals had hot mutton. And how the Gorkhas loved it!

On one of his forays forward into the battle area, he was busy driving his Jeep, navigating through the pitch black night while trying to deliver some food to the forward troops. He couldn't risk switching on the lights, as that would certainly attract a bullet from the enemy, or maybe even from an overzealous sentry from own side. So he was relying on the faint starlight to show him the way as he zig-zagged through the fields and trees. Suddenly, his jeep came to a jarring halt and the SM felt every bone in his body being quivered. He thought he had driven into a brick wall, and after making sure all his bones were intact, jumped out of the jeep to see the obstacle that had appeared out of nowhere in the night. It turned out to be a tank, fortunately an Indian one, halted there for the night. The crew, alerted by the loud crash, now faced the bewildered JCO with their weapons ready.

When the two sides had recognised each other as friends not foes, and ascertained that no major damage had been done to man or machine, they had a hearty laugh. The tank crew offered the SM a cup of tea before allowing him to go on his way.

This minor incident never stopped his frequent journeys to the front. Unmindful of the dangers lurking in the battlefield and of exhaustion from lack of sleep, the doughty JCO made trip after trip, keeping up the morale of the fighting troops. The only reward for his efforts was a sense of gratification in going beyond his duty and the all-round respect of troops and offices alike that he earned.

KHEM KARAN

In 1965, Khem Karan and Asal Uttar – two nondescript border villages in Punjab –became household names in India. In fact they even found mention in faraway Detroit, USA, where the American Patton tanks, which met their nemesis here, were designed. It was around these two villages that some of the fiercest tank battles since the Second World War were fought, and it was here that the 'Graveyard of Pattons' came to be.

The area was under 4 Mountain Division, the southernmost of the three divisions of XI Corps. It was in this sector that Pakistan was expected to launch its offensive into Indian Punjab in accordance with the appreciations of the Indian commanders. The alignment of the canals and existence of the road network made this area the most suited for Pakistan to rapidly advance along the Beas river deep into Indian territory, cutting off the entire Amritsar sector from the rest of the country. So when XI Corps launched its offensive towards Lahore with 15 and 7 Infantry Divisions, 4 Mountain Division was also tasked to cross the IB and advance up to the line of the Ichhogil Canal, clearing any enemy it found on its way. It was to then occupy a defended sector within Pakistani territory to contain any enemy offensive towards this sector.

Like in the15 and 7 Infantry Division sectors to its North, 4 Mountain Division met with little enemy resistance initially. Commencing operations on the early morning of 6 September, 9 Jammu and Kashmir Rifles (JAK Rif) and 13th Battalion the Dogra Regiment (13 Dogra) of the division quickly overcame initial resistance and captured their objectives by that afternoon. But neither the division, nor its battalions, had been prepared for the strong enemy reaction. Pakistani forces had actually planned their own offensive, led by their 1 Armoured Division, in this sector – and the attacking forces of 4 Mountain Division were simply brushed aside by the strong Pakistani counter-attacks.

On the night of 6 September, Indian battalions were evicted from the positions they had gained during the days of fighting by these resolute counter-attacks, supported strongly by enemy artillery and tanks. The situation was grim by the 7th morning, and it was abundantly clear that Indian forces were in no position to undertake any further offensive in this sector, as Pakistan was planning its own thrust into Indian territory from here. The GOC of 4 Mountain Division sought and received permission to regroup his depleted and retreating forces to occupy a defensive area around the village of Asal Uttar to halt the anticipated Pakistani thrust.

This was a timely decision, because barely had the defensive positions been prepared than the Pakistani offensive commenced on the morning of 8 September. The first push from the enemy came as a strong 'Recce in Force' by Pakistani forces comprising of two squadrons of Chaffee tanks and one squadron of Pattons at 1000 hours that morning. This was repulsed by the Indian squadron of 9 (Deccan) Horse (Map 10).

The Corps Commander assessed the situation and decided to release his armoured reserve, 2 (Independent) Armoured Brigade, which was placed under the command of 4 Mountain Division to deal with what obviously was a major attack by Pakistan, using its 1 Armoured Division.

The next two days saw repeated attempts by the armoured thrusts of the Pakistani Armoured Division to break through towards its objectives in the depth. The steadfast actions by the Indian infantry prevented it from overrunning the defences and manoeuvring of the Indian armour denied them the opportunity to bypass these defences. Skilful deployment of tanks by Indian armour Commanders led to trapping enemy tanks and destroying them in large numbers.

By 10 September, the Pakistani offensive had run out of steam. It had suffered the loss of seventy-five tanks to the resolute action by Indian tanks and infantry anti-tank weapons. The Pakistani 1 Armoured Division reportedly pulled back to Kasur. Apart from the heavy tank losses it had suffered, another reason for this pull back was that the Indian offensive into Sialkot sector by I Corps had made significant progress and was posing a menacing threat. Pakistani plans of an offensive towards Beas were thus put paid. However, Pakistani troops were still in possession of Indian territory around Khem Karan, which had to be re-captured.

Plans were made to launch a counter-attack to throw out this enemy incursion. Additional units were allotted to 4 Mountain Division for this action, which included 4 Sikh; it had already fought a tough battle for the successful capture of Barki. The first counter-attack was launched on 11–12 September, but because of the underestimation of the enemy forces present in Khem Karan and around and also the presence of the remnants of the enemy armour, this failed with heavy costs in terms of casualties and prisoners. Another – stronger – attempt was made on 22 September, but this did not make much headway, and operations were suspended with the ceasefire on 23 September. These sixteen days had witnessed very heavy fighting, and superhuman feats of heroism.

Daring Beyond Duty

Company Quarter Master Havildar Abdul Hamid – Khem Karan

In an Infantry Company, the Company Quarter Master Havildar (CQMH) is responsible for the logistics – rations, clothing, and other necessities troops need to keep fighting. An essential but not very glamorous job when there's a war going on, because it keeps you away from the battle itself. Abdul Hamid, the newly appointed CQMH of C Company, 4th Battalion the Grenadiers (4 Grenadiers), was therefore only too happy when he was ordered to return to the role he had previously played – that of a 106mm RCL anti-tank gun detachment commander. This was in order, because he was one of the most experienced RCL gunners in the battalion, having spent five of his nine years of service in the anti-tank detachment. Preferring the glory and adventure of a soldier's life over his family profession of tailoring, he had joined the army in 1954. He was a veteran of the 1962 war, and had witnessed many of his close friends and comrades falling to the Chinese onslaught at Namka Chu. Abdul Hamid himself was one of the few who succeeded in making a fighting breakaway and survive the battle. Now was his chance to prove himself in another war, and he was glad he wasn't going to spend it supplying rations.

The battalion, 4 Grenadiers, had been part of the 4 Mountain Division offensive and had been successful in securing the Theh Pannu Bridge, its objective, on 6 September. It had even managed to hold on to its objective through heavy enemy shelling and attacks supported by tanks. But then the entire division was ordered to withdraw and establish a defensive sector around village Asal Uttar, as a major Pakistani offensive was anticipated in this area. The C Company was deployed on the road leading from Asal Uttar towards Bhikiwind and onwards to Amritsar, near a small village called Chima. They reached this area on the night of 7 September and spent the night digging trenches in the fields close to the village. The standing sugarcane crop was a great help, because the enemy would not be able to spot them easily from ground or from the air.

Crouching in the shallow trenches which were all they could hurriedly dig during the night, the men of 4 Grenadiers heard the rumbling of what seemed to be a large column of enemy tanks heading in their direction at 0730 hours on 8th September. They could make out some dust at a distance, but could not see the tanks, as visibility was very low. This suited them because it meant that the tanks would not be able to spot them either. Soon the ground started rumbling as artillery shells started landing all around them. Exploding shells spewed deadly shrapnel along with clouds of smoke and dust, restricting the visibility further. In the next few hours the enemy had overrun some positions of 1/9 GR, the forward battalion, and an attack on the Grenadiers' position became imminent.

The C Company was being commanded by Lt HR Janu, a young officer whose enthusiasm and grit made up for the relative lack of experience. Actually, the battalion was in the process of moving to a new location on the Tibet border when the sudden orders to mobilise for war came. As a result, most of the Company Commanders were away to the new location, and throughout the war the companies were led by young officers or senior JCOs. The young Company Commander ordered Abdul Hamid to deploy his RCL detachment on the road leading to Chima village, and asked the rest of the company to hold their fire. He was relying on surprise provided by the concealment of the company in the tall sugarcane fields to allow the tanks to get into their range before discovering their presence. Since the tanks had a much longer firing range, if they spotted the infantry before coming into the shorter range of the latter's weapons, the tanks could engage them with impunity without fear of return fire.

Abdul Hamid and his RCL crew took up a concealed position and waited with growing anticipation as the rumbling steel monsters seemed to grow bigger and bigger in size as they approached. The ground under them trembled and the dust raised by artillery shelling made breathing difficult. It was a different thing to fire during practice on the ranges at empty fuel barrels painted to look like an enemy tank, but this was the first time they were almost face-to-face with an actual steel monster. Unlike the barrels, it could fire back at them, or even close in and crush them to oblivion. The crew was well trained, and knew that it was imperative to hit the tank on the first shot, otherwise the tank crew would spot them and fire back immediately, and they had no protection against the deadly tank fire. And even if they did get a first shot kill, they would need to change their position immediately to avoid being fired upon by the other tanks.

The crew spotted three tanks advancing menacingly through the fields, their guns traversing slightly to the left and right as the gunner sitting inside scanned for threats and targets. Abdul Hamid raised his hand to alert the crew and gave orders for the gunner to engage the leading tank. They waited with bated breath as the RCL fired, and within seconds they saw the flash of its round hitting the enemy tank. Saying a silent prayer, the crew quickly jumped into the jeep and the driver reversed it with practised ease as Abdul Hamid pointed to the next selected firing position. But they did not need to fire again, as the crew of the other two abandoned their tanks and fled on seeing the first one being hit. The Pakistani attack seemed to have been stalled for the time being.

The attack resumed after two hours, led by two troops of tanks. Abdul Hamid and his crew went into action, knocking down another enemy tank with similar effect on the crews of the surviving tanks, who either abandoned their tanks, or withdrew.

A third attack came in around 1430 hours, but this was on the B Company and was beaten back by them. By nightfall the Pakistanis seemed to have had enough for the day, and though they had not been able to capture any of the Grenadiers' posts, they had caused casualties and kept the 'Grinders' on their toes. Abdul Hamid and his crew had quite a successful day – their tally was two enemy tanks destroyed and four abandoned by the crew. They spent a large part of the night tending to and cleaning the gun, getting it ready for what they expected to be another day of hard fighting. The night also gave the engineers an opportunity to plant some scattered anti-tank mines ahead of the defences.

The next day, 9 September, played out to a similar script, with Pakistanis repeatedly trying to rush the Grenadier defences with their tanks leading, and the defenders holding steadfast. Abdul Hamid and his detachment destroyed two more enemy tanks and several more fell prey to the anti-tank mines.

On 10 September there was an air of anticipation settled around the battalion, by now they had realised that this was a major offensive. The battalion came under heavy shelling again in the morning, and they expected the enemy infantry to attack. Every man was manning his trench, weapon cocked and ready. But instead of an infantry attack, the Pakistani tanks made yet another attempt at overrunning the defences. A troop of three tanks were spotted moving astride the road while heavy artillery shelling tried to suppress the Indian anti-tank weapons. Undeterred, the irrepressible RCL crew under Abdul Hamid got its fifth and sixth kills, quickly changing their positions after each kill despite the artillery shells raining all around them.

During the third engagement, the intensity of artillery fire was so heavy that it was extremely difficult to man the RCL gun. Abdul Hamid ordered his crew to take cover from the shelling while he operated the gun himself, laying it on the advancing enemy tank. Single-handedly loading and firing the weapon, he got his seventh kill. He did not have the luxury of changing position now, as the following tank had apparently already spotted them, and was

Rasoolan Biwi, wife of CQMH Abdul Hamid,
receiving the PVC from the President S. Radhakrishnan

CQMH Abdul Hamid's RCL jeep displayed at
Grenadiers Regiment Centre

traversing his gun towards them. Abdul Hamid quickly reloaded the gun and took aim at the tank. He fired and so did the tank, almost simultaneously. Abdul Hamid got his eighth tank kill, but paid for it with his life.

The nation recognised his bravery with the award of the highest gallantry award, the Param Vir Chakra (PVC). Even today, a memorial marks the place near the Chima village on the road from Bhikkiwind to where Abdul Hamid fought his epic battle against Pakistani tanks and was martyred. Abdul Hamid's RCL jeep is displayed at the Grenadiers Regimental Centre at Jabalpur in his honour.

The Irreverent Trio

Grenadiers Shafi, Naushad, and Suleiman – Khem Karan

Shortly after Abdul Hamid took his gallant last stand, an incident occurred within his C Company location, which played a major role in turning the tide of the war in this sector. It involved three 'bad hats' of the company, Grenadiers Shafi, Naushad, and Suleiman. The three of them were manning the LMG covering the road along which Abdul Hamid had stopped the enemy tank advance.

When Lt Janu, the Charlie Company Commander had found that one of his LMG crews had abandoned their positions during the previous battles on 7–8 September, he had handed over the charge of this important weapon to the trio, much against the advice of his Senior JCO. With a penchant for getting into trouble and a hearty disregard for discipline, the three were as notorious as they were inseparable. If it wasn't for their turnout, they would get caught for being late, or talking on parade. But that was in peace time, and this was war. Here, courage and a healthy disrespect for the enemy carried premium value. And Lt Janu recognised this.

Shortly after Abdul Hamid's last battle, three jeeps of the Pakistani Recce and Support battalion approached C Company's location along the road. The trio's LMG was deployed to cover this road, and they watched these lucrative targets with baited breath. Since the LMGs were ineffective on the hard steel of the enemy tanks, they had watched in frustration as the RCL guns took these on. Finally, these jeeps represented something they themselves could shoot at. In their enthusiasm, they forgot (or decided to disregard) their Company Commander's injunction not to open fire too soon. The LMG started firing its deadly hail of bullets, and the leading Jeep swerved as the driver was hit. The other inmates were also quickly caught in the sweep of the LMG, as was the second jeep. But before the crew could traverse the LMG to engage the third jeep, it quickly turned around and beat a hasty retreat. The Company Commander, who had been watching this engagement from his command post, rushed to remonstrate the trio for opening fire too soon. Had they waited a little longer, he said, the retreating Jeep would also have been too close to turn around safely.

Suitably chastened and sobered after the dressing down, the trio resumed their vigil over the road. At around 1100 hours, they spotted another column of jeeps coming down the road. This time they held their fire till the leading vehicle was almost next to their trench – and when they saw who the occupants of the Jeep were, they almost jumped out of the trench in amazement. It was a Pakistani Maj Gen (later identified as Maj Gen Nasir Ahmed Khan, GOC of the Pakistani 1 Armoured Division.) The jeep was being driven by a Brig (Brig AR Shamim, Commander 1 Armoured Division Artillery Brigade). One of the trio stood up as the jeep stopped alongside the trench. Assuming the lone soldier to be a straggler, the GOC summoned him to approach the vehicle. When the soldier demurred, the Gen stepped out of his jeep, unbuttoning his holster apparently to shoot him. It was then that his two companions sprung out of the trench and without much ado, shot the Gen. The Brig quickly turned the jeep around in an attempt to escape, but was shot too.

The Pakistani Gen, who had been wounded by the shot, took advantage of the diversion created by the Brig and crawled into the dense sugarcane fields which abounded the area. Before the Grenadiers could start searching for him, very heavy shelling from both Indian and Pakistani artillery commenced, forcing them to dive into their trenches. Shortly thereafter, a message was intercepted on the Pakistani radio network, confirming the GOC's death. '*Bara Imam mar gaya.*' (The big chief is dead.) However, as per some Pakistani authors including Farooq Bajwa, the Gen survived and later even gave testimony about the failed offensive.

At about 1400 hours, the Pakistanis launched a determined attack consisting of eight Patton tanks with infantry mounted on them to recover the body of their Gen. Charlie Company was out of anti-tank ammunition, and the men were not in a position to engage the enemy tanks. They stayed in their trenches and called for artillery fire on their own location to deter the enemy. The Pakistanis managed to locate the body of their GOC and carry it away on their tanks before the artillery shelling commenced. But they did leave behind Brig Shamim's body, which was later recovered by Indian troops.

The offensive by the Pakistani 1 Armoured Division had failed to make much headway in the past three days, and the incapacitation of their GOC was possibly the last straw that forced them to abandon their plans and fall back. The three branded troublemakers thus played a stellar role in pushing back this mighty formation.

GCO 1 Armd Div and the Cdr Artillery of Pakistan were shot down by Gdrs Shafi, Naushad and Suleiman. The Rover managed to turn around but all its occupants barring the driver were shot dead

Blunting the Spearhead
Lieutenant Colonel AS Vaidya – Khem Karan

Lt Col AS Vaidya (later General and COAS) was born on 27 January 1926. He was commissioned on 20 January 1945 into the Royal Deccan Horse and saw action during the Allies' advance to Rangoon in Burma. He commanded the Deccan Horse from 29 August 1964 to 7 September 1967. The regiment was equipped with Sherman Mk IV tanks, ostensibly discarded after the Korean war, maintaining a 76mm gun. As part of 2 (Independent) Armoured Brigade, then an all-Sherman brigade, the regiment had deployed between Jandiala Guru and Tarn Taran during Operation Ablaze from April to June 1965. Being the XI Corps reserve, the regiment had carried out a broad reconnaissance of the entire corps sector. After Operation Ablaze, it moved back to Sangrur in July 1965 but soon afterwards was moved to Ambala and designated as the Army Headquarters reserve.

On 1 September, orders were received placing the regiment under the command of 4 Mountain Division with instructions to be prepared to move at short notice. A message was received the same evening asking the Commandant to report to Headquarters of 4 Mountain Division. Orders for the move were received at 0600 hours on 2 September. The first two tank trains left the same day, and the move to the concentration area near Sarhali Khurd was completed by 3 September.

4 Mountain Division, as the name suggests, was organised and equipped for operations in the mountains. It, therefore, had no

armoured regiment in its order of battle, which is why Deccan Horse was allotted to it at the last minute for its role in the plains. Thus no prior joint training had been conducted between the regiment and the infantry battalions of the division. A bigger problem was that the radio equipment of the division was not compatible with the regiments. These were just some of the problems which had to be overcome due to the exigencies of war.

The divisional offensive was launched on 6 September as described earlier. During this operation, Charlie Squadron of Deccan Horse was allotted to 7 Mountain Brigade for the capture of Theh Pannu and Ballanwala. Alpha Squadron was tasked to support the operations of 62 Mountain Brigade along the Khem Karan–Kasur axis, with orders to cross the Rohi Nala and contact the Ichhogil Canal. Bravo Squadron was the reserve in the Khem Karan area during this operation.

On 7 September, Pakistan moved elements of 1 Armoured Division Reconnaissance Regiment across the Ichhogil Canal and engaged the Western flank of A Squadron, which destroyed two of the enemy tanks, but also lost two tanks.

In the afternoon the division ordered the troops to fall back and hold a defended sector in the general area of Asal Uttar and Chima. A Squadron helped in the extrication of 9 JAK Rifles, which had suffered heavy casualties. The divisional defended sector was occupied with 62 Mountain Brigade in the Khem Karan area with B Squadron in support, and 7 Mountain Brigade in the Chima area with A Squadron in support. C Squadron was guarding the Eastern flank in the Kalia–Sakantra area.

The period between 8 and 10 September saw the heaviest fighting as the Pakistani 1 Armoured Division attempted to overrun the defences and break out to cut off the XI Corps area of operations by seizing the bridges over the Beas and Harike. Pakistan launched its offensive at 0830 hours on 8 September. Under the cover of artillery fire, two squadrons of Chaffe and a squadron of Pattons carried out a recce in force into the division's defences. They approached within 900 metres of the forward defences, and were engaged by the tanks of Deccan Horse. Under effective fire, Pakistani tanks broke into smaller groups and tried to infiltrate the defences by a bold outflanking manoeuvre from the South-east. Using the cover of standing crops, this force was effectively engaged by tanks of Deccan Horse, medium artillery guns in a direct firing role, and the tank-hunting teams of the infantry. Deccan Horse managed to destroy eleven tanks while losing four of its own; three Pakistani tanks were damaged by medium guns and tank-hunting parties. Such heavy losses compelled the break-in force to retreat.

Pakistan repeated attack after attack against Indian prepared defences, both frontally and from the North-west and South-east flanks, in the process suffering heavy casualties. Tactics adopted by them were astonishing – battering ram attacks along the same axis on which they had repeatedly failed earlier. Consequences were evident – for the defences held.

The enemy attacked again on 9 September with armour and built up pressure on the Eastern flank. The defences held firm, inflicting heavy casualties on the enemy. 10 September saw the last – and desperate – attempt to break through. On a mistaken notion that they had broken through, tanks and light vehicles of the Divisional Headquarters came down along the Khem Karan–Bhikkiwind road. This was led by the vehicle of the GOC of 1 Armoured Division himself, along with his Commander, Artillery Brigade, both of whom were shot and killed.

Col Vaidya commanded the regiment under extremely difficult circumstances. The regiment had not trained with 4 Mountain Division, and the offensive of 6 September was launched with great speed after orders for the move from the peace station were issued. It fought against heavy odds – outnumbered, out-gunned, and without any air support or communications with the Division Headquarters, Brigade Headquarters, or the battalions. To overcome the communications problem, Col Vaidya used his ingenuity to locate himself in the Medium Regiment gun area, when otherwise not on the move meeting the Squadron Commanders or visiting the Divisional Headquarters.

Lt Col AS Vaidya, Comdt,
The Deccan Horse with his Crew

Throughout all this action, he displayed exemplary courage without regard to his personal safety. By his calm and mature approach, he was able to organise and motivate his command to outperform itself. The regiment lost twenty-one tanks (almost half its authorised strength) and can proudly lay claim to destroying thirty-six to forty enemy tanks. It had fifty-one personnel casualties – killed, wounded, and missing in action. Col Vaidya was awarded the MVC for his leadership and courage. He went on to receive the same award once again in the 1971 war in the Shakargarh sector while commanding an armoured brigade. He rose to become the COAS.

Abandoned M47 Pattons near Mahamudpura

Lt Col Salim Caleb
– Khem Karan

About the time the GOC of the Pakistani 1 Armoured Division was driving up for his fateful tryst with the Three Musketeers of 4 Grenadiers, a fierce tank battle was raging between the Centurions of 3rd Cavalry and Pakistani Pattons, to their North-West. The carefully planned trap orchestrated by Lt Col Salim Caleb, Commandant of 3rd Cavalry, had been sprung and the Pakistanis had walked, or rather been driven, into it unsuspectingly.

3rd Cavalry was one of the regiments of 2 Independent Armoured Brigade, which had been the corps' reserves. Though the brigade had been placed under the command of 4 Mountain Division only on the night of 8 September to take on the Pakistani ingress into their sector, 3rd Cavalry had already been located in the vicinity of Bhikkiwind. Once the enemy armour had attacked the forward defences of the division, Col Caleb, who had been commanding the regiment for just over a year, had deployed his regiment to cover the possible approaches Pakistani tanks could take for advancing beyond Khem Karan. While CQMH Abdul Hamid and the rest of 4 Grenadiers was fending off the Pakistani attacks, 3rd Cavalry less A Squadron deployed to block any movement along road the Khem Karan–Bhikkiwind road, and A Squadron under Major SC Vaḍera was similarly deployed astride the Khem Karan–Patti road.

Col Caleb had also established contact with Lt Col AS Vaidya, CO of 9 (Deccan) Horse, whose tanks were deployed ahead to support 4 Grenadiers and 7 Mountain Brigade. Together, they had worked out the plan to deal with the Pakistanis in case they succeeded in breaking through the defences of 7 Mountain Brigade. But the resolute fight put up by the infantry at their defences ensured that such a situation did not arise. When the Pakistani tanks started withdrawing, Col Caleb was quick to appreciate that their route back should be cut off. He sent half of C Squadron under a young troop leader, Lt RP Joshi, to outflank the Pakistanis from the West. Taking six tanks, Lt Joshi rushed towards Bhura Karimpur, but did not run into any Pakistani tanks.

B Squadron had an encounter with the Pakistani tanks near milestone 37.5 on the Khem Karan–Bhikkiwind road, and in the short but sharp engagement, their Centurions got the better of the Pattons. Lt Joseph was peering out of his tank, scanning the sugarcane fields in the far distance to see if he could locate any enemy tanks when he heard a loud bang and could feel his tank shake as it did while firing. Looking down and cursing his gunner for firing without orders, he realised that the shock he had felt was his own tank receiving a hit. A Patton had fired directly at them from about 800 metres, though the damage caused to the tank was not substantial, the Armour Piercing round failing to penetrate the thick armour of its turret. After that, the Centurion crew were never afraid of facing the Pattons, though careful not to present its broadside to the enemy. Before the days fighting was through, B Squadron had knocked out five Pakistani tanks.

That night, Col Caleb studied his map carefully, deciding how he would deploy his regiment for the next day's battle. It was quite clear that the Pakistanis would make a determined bid to break through despite the setbacks and losses they had suffered that day. He was quite confident that the enemy would not be able to penetrate the infantry defences at Asal Uttar and Chima, as the actions that day had demonstrated. His own job was to ensure that they did not succeed in outflanking these positions and getting through the undefended gaps in the areas of Mahmudpura and Dibbipura.

He had carried out an extensive recce of the area during the day, and came to the conclusion that the widespread sugarcane fields would serve as good hiding places for his tanks. His plan was to conceal his squadrons in two semi-circular 'horse-shoes' in this area, and allow the enemy tanks to come as close as possible before giving the Pakistanis a taste of the devastating firepower of the Centurions. Any enemy tanks trying to outflank the Indian infantry defences were bound to head for the trap he planned to lay.

Next morning the Pakistani attack came as anticipated. While CQMH Abdul Hamid was fending off any attempts to break through the defences around Chima, Col Caleb's tanks were lying in wait to the north. The first lot of tanks that tried to bypass ran into C Squadron which formed the southern horse-shoe. They waited, hidden in the sugarcane fields, allowing the first Pakistani squadron to come closer. Then, almost in unison they opened a deadly barrage of fire, knocking out 4 Pattons within minutes. The second squadron tried to avoid these tanks by swinging West and going around them in a wide circle, only to run into the northern 'horse-shoe' formed by A Squadron.

The Pakistani armoured thrust had thus come up against an impenetrable wall of Indian defences and tanks. It was possibly this failure to make any headway that irked the Pakistani GOC 1 Armoured Division, prompting him to come forward and see for himself what was holding up his advance, when he ran into the men from 4 Grenadiers. But Col Caleb and his squadrons towards the North were yet unaware of those goings on. They were fully occupied in dealing with the waves of Patton tanks that were advancing towards them, with the enemy artillery raining shells on the Indian tanks. In fact, artillery from both the sides was pounding the battlefield. The Pakistani tanks crossed over the small water channel marked on the map as Khem Karan minor with ease, as it was dry. The Indian tanks were well concealed and spread out to cover the entire area, and could pick out the advancing Pakistani tanks one by one. The battle raged for over three hours, with Indian tanks jockeying and changing positions repeatedly to engage the Pakistanis. By now water had started flowing through

Pakistani Patton tanks abandoned by their Crews

Stopped in its tracks: A Patton tank destroyed by Indian troops

the minor the Pakistani tanks had crossed, and the damage caused to its sides due to this crossing resulted in inundating the ground behind them. As a result, when they tried to reverse to manoeuvre out of the killing ground, they got bogged down.

By nightfall, Indian tanks withdrew to a night harbour, while the Pakistani tanks that were not destroyed were also unable to move back over the boggy ground. During the night, Col Caleb asked the artillery to continue intermittent firing at the enemy tanks, keeping the crews under pressure and not allowing them any rest.

The next morning, A Squadron under Maj SC Vadera engaged the enemy tanks near Mahmudpura again, with half the squadron engaging them from front while the other half outflanked them from the right. Under heavy tank and machine gun fire from two directions, and with little scope for manoeuvres due to the boggy ground, the Pakistani tank crews started abandoning their tanks. Some were mowed down by the incessant fire, while others ran for safety to the cover of sugarcane fields. They fled, leaving their tank engines running and wireless sets on.

A party of men from 1st Battalion the Dogra Regiment (1 Dogra) under Lt PJS Mehta of 3rd Cavalry were sent to comb the sugarcane fields and capture the Pakistani crews. The prisoners they brought back included Lt Col Mohammad Nazir, the CO of Pakistani's 4 Cavalry and three of his officers. The enemy tanks were littered for kilometres around, and were subsequently collected at one place near Bhikkiwind, which earned the well-deserved sobriquet of 'Patton Nagar'. These included quite a few

Captured Pakistani equipment

Curious villagers impecting captured Pakistani tanks at Patton Nagar

Prime Minister Lal Bahadur Shastri at Patton Nagar

fully functional tanks that had been abandoned by their crews. When Prime Minister Lal Bahadur Shastri visited the area after the war, he was awestruck by the sheer number of enemy tanks in various states of disrepair. He remarked, '*Maine to apni zindagi me itni bail-garian bhi tuti hui nahi dekhi.*' (I have never even seen so many damaged bullock carts in my life).

Col Caleb was awarded the MVC, and later as a Major General, raised 31 Armoured Division as its first GOC. This gallant officer passed away on 28 January 2015.

SIALKOT

While Pakistan was already under pressure in the Lahore sector, India launched a second offensive towards another important Pakistani city, Sialkot. The first offensive was, in a sense, limited in its scope. It was launched by XI Corps, essentially a defensive formation, with the primary objective of improving its defensive posture by extending its frontline to the formidable Ichhogil Canal. But the second offensive was by I Corps, the newly raised 'strike' Corps with the primary purpose of capturing enemy territory and destroying the Pakistani war-waging potential.

The offensive was launched on 8 September 1965 and started with 26 Infantry Division to establish a firm base and take the frontline close to Sialkot. 6 Mountain Division attacked the Charwa–Maharajake to establish a firm base for the launch of the armoured division captured it after some fighting. 14 Infantry Division established a bridgehead in the Ikhnal area further to the East. This set the stage for the advance of 1 Armoured Division. It commenced advance on 8 September towards Phillora but enemy action and bad weather hindered its progress (Map 11). The Commander then chose another axis to mount an attack on Phillora on 11 September. While the Armoured Brigade was engaging Pak armour, 43 Lorried Brigade captured Phillora in a spirited action. The Pakistani army lost nearly sixty-one tanks in this battle

1 Armoured Division then proceeded to capture Chawinda on the 14th. By this time Pakistan 6 Armoured Division had entered the battle and assumed responsibility for the defence of the sector, in addition 4 Armoured Brigade from Khem Karan had joined the sector. In all a force of armour greater than the Indian Armoured Division, therefore, the division could make little progress. However, it succeeded in capturing Jassoran and Batur Dograndi on the 16th. Another effort by I Corps to capture Chawinda on

the 18th night met with limited success. The corps, however, succeeded in capturing about 466 sq km of Pakistani territory; also, it destroyed and captured about 180 Pak tanks.

Lieutenant Colonel HL Mehta – Maharajke

As a prelude to the launch of 1 Armoured Division towards Sialkot, 6 Mountain Division was tasked to establish a bridgehead by capturing the villages of Maharajke and Charawa. The objective of Maharajke was allotted to 69 Mountain Brigade, which planned a two-phased attack on the night 7th/8th September to capture it. 3rd Battalion the Madras Regiment (3 Madras) and 9th Battalion the Kumaon Regiment (9 Kumaon) were to capture the right half of the village in phase one, and 4th Battalion the Madras Regiment (4 Madras) was to capture the left half in phase two.

The CO of 4 Madras, Lt Col HL Mehta, had planned the attack with two companies, A and C, leading. The brigade phase one went smoothly, and the objectives were captured by the two battalions. 4 Madras then launched its attack at 0200 hours on 8 September. The going was not as easy as it had been for the first phase. The right half was more strongly defended, and the enemy was warned and alert. Also, the remnants of enemy troops from the left half had moved there, bolstering up the strength. As soon as the two companies crossed the Start Line for the assault, they came under heavy RCL, machine gun and artillery fire.

The fire was of such heavy intensity that the assaulting troops had to take to ground, making even the slightest forward movement impossible. Col Mehta, who was moving closely behind the assaulting companies, launched the reserve company to push through the stalled attack. However, the enemy fire was so intense that even with the increased fore level, the attack didn't progress.

Watching this, Col Mehta turned to his adjutant Lt Ramesh Kumar, who was walking right behind him, and pointing to a cluster of bunker and trenches, told him, 'I want you to clear these.'

Lt Ramesh took a handful of men and crawled closer to the bunker, from within which a MMG was spewing its deadly fire towards the attacking 'Thambis'. On getting closer, he lobbed a grenade into the bunker and charged in from the rear, spraying the insides with his carbine. The adjoining trenches were also cleared after a brief but fierce hand to hand fight. Sub CA Madhavan Nair, who was commanding the signal platoon of the battalion, was also moving closely behind the CO. Inspired by the daring actions of the adjutant, he mustered a section of men from the signal platoon and charged at another MMG bunker. He charged headlong towards the deadly fire and was mowed down, but his ad hoc section put the offending MMG out of action. Soon other officers and JCOs took initiative to identify and clear individual bunkers that were holding up the attack. Lt SK Bose, and Sub PM Gregory personally led charges on enemy positions.

While this helped move things along a little, daylight was approaching fast and the movement was slow because of the tall sugarcane crop. Besides making the movement of the Madrasis slow and difficult, it provided enemy cover from observation and fire. That is why, despite suffering heavy casualties, the enemy had been holding steadfast to his positions. Daylight was approaching, and Col Mehta weighed the options available to him. He came to the decision that he would personally lead the remaining reserve company to clear the remnants of enemy still holding on. While the three companies were still fighting their way towards the objective, Col Mehta led the reserve company for attack from the flank.

The enemy were surprised at being attacked from a fresh direction, and their fire was now divided. With attacks from the two directions fast closing in, the enemy responded by unrestrained firing unmindful of ammunition expenditure. The brave Madrasis made good progress from the flank, their zeal doubled as they were led personally by their CO. Reaching the forward line of trenches, they charged at the enemy trenches yelling fiercely, firing at the enemy and stabbing him with their bayonets. For a short time it was a scene of confused frenzy, with close quarter battle raging all around. Col Mehta kept encouraging the men, shouting instructions and directing them from their very midst.

Maybe it was a stray burst from an automatic, or maybe an observant enemy had realized that this was the man leading and guiding the attacking force – Col Mehta was struck squarely in the chest and he collapsed. We continue to push his men forward till he fell unconscious. The battalion continued in the momentum set up by this daring charge and soon cleared the objective of all the remnant enemy. Col Mehta succumbed to his injuries shortly thereafter, giving the supreme sacrifice to ensure that his battalion carry out the task assigned to it. He was awarded the MVC posthumously. Sub Nambiar and Sub Gregory both got VrCs, as did Sep Kannan, who had bayoneted two enemy soldiers to death before being cut down himself. The battalion suffered heavy casualties in the battle – 1 officer, 1 JCO and 9 ORs killed, 2 officers, 1 JCO and 31 ORs injured. The enemy toll was equally heavy – they fled leaving behind 16 dead, and 1 officer, 1 JCO and 24 ORs were taken prisoner.

Lt Gen Harbaksh Singh, the Army Commander, has this to say about the action in his book 'War Dispatches':

> ... *each task group worked in excellent coordination towards the achievement of their common goal. Leadership was of an exemplary standard.*

Param Vir
Lt Col AB Tarapore
– Sialkot

It was his courage that had got him into the cavalry in the first place. Commissioned at first as a 2Lt into the 7th Hyderabad Infantry in the pre-independence state forces of the Nizam of Hyderabad, young Ardeshir Burzorji Tarapore had actually wanted to join the cavalry instead. The glory and glamour, the dash and elan associated with a cavalry unit and a cavalry officer had always attracted him, even as a young boy. With a stoic acceptance of a situation he had no control over, the young officer worked hard at being good at his job – till the chance came for him to get what he wanted.

The battalion was all spruced up for an inspection by none less than the Commander-in-Chief of the Hyderabad state forces, Maj Gen El-Edros. As inspections are want to in army units, it threw everyone from the junior-most soldier to the Commanding Officer (CO) in a tizzy of activity. Young Tarapore's company was scheduled to conduct grenade firing as part of its routine training that day, and the Commander-in-Chief decided to watch the exercise for himself.

During the demonstration, one young soldier lobbed a grenade, which fell into the firing bay itself. Young Adi Tarapore leapt into the bay, and in a flash grabbed the grenade and threw it towards the target area. His quick thinking and reflexes saved the people who were standing in the vicinity of the bay from possible death and certain injury. The only wound in the entire incident was sustained by Lt Tarapore himself – his chest was peppered with flying shrapnel from the grenade, which had exploded in mid-air. His actions impressed Maj Gen El-Edros, who was witness to the whole scene. He summoned Tarapore to his office after he had recovered from his injuries, wanting to congratulate him personally. When asked if he wanted anything specific as a reward, the young officer thought on his feet, once again, and requested for a transfer to the cavalry. The General, a cavalry officer himself, readily agreed and had him transferred to 1st Hyderabad Imperial Service Lancers. After independence and the subsequent merger of Hyderabad into India, the state forces were also incorporated in the Indian Army, and Tarapore was posted to the 17th Poona Horse. During the Second World War, he served with the regiment in the Middle East. He had risen to command the regiment when the war broke out in 1965.

On 3 September 1965, Col Tarapore was conducting a Tactical Exercise Without Troops (TEWT) for his regiment when he was summoned to the brigade headquarters. The regiment, part of 1 Armoured Brigade of 1 Armoured Division, had been stationed at Kapurthala since May. After the Rann of Kutch affair, the regiment had been mobilised from Babina in April and deployed near Jandiala Guru. Since a no-war no-peace situation prevailed, it was considered better to redeploy it closer to the operational area rather than move it back to Babina. He returned from the brigade headquarters with orders to get the regiment moving for what seemed to be the real thing this time. The writing on the wall was clear, for Pakistani tanks had already entered Indian territory in Chhamb two days earlier. By 5 September, the regiment was deployed in its concentration area near the International Border (IB), and Col Tarapore gave his orders to the regiment for the impending operations on 7 September.

The 1 Armoured Brigade was tasked to advance from Rampur towards Phillora, with a view to securing Phillora, Tharoh and Chawinda. The regiment was to lead the left half of the brigade's advance, with 16 Cavalry moving to its right. The aim was to strike deep into Pakistan, capturing as much territory as possible and destroying any of the enemy's forces that they encountered. Col Tarapore had planned to advance with two squadrons leading, to cover and clear a maximum area, and the third squadron was to be held in reserve.

After giving his orders, Col Tarapore took Maj Niranjan Cheema, one of the Squadron Commanders, aside for a private word. 'Niranjan, listen carefully,' he said, 'If I am killed in battle, my body should be cremated.' With an attention to detail and planning ahead which was typical of him, he wanted no ambiguity on the arrangements if the need arose, as he knew that war afforded no scope for Parsi funeral rites. Whether it was a premonition, or just meticulous planning, he went on to tell Major Niranjan that in the event of his death, he wanted his son to join the army and specifically the regiment when he came of age. He also gave him instructions to hand over his ring and prayer book to his wife. Maj Niranjan didn't know how to react, and tried to reassure the Colonel that such an eventuality wasn't going to arise. 'Niranjan, it is better to plan these things – one never knows,' was his prophetic reply.

17th Poona Horse crossed the IB at 0600 hours on 8 September as planned, moving two squadrons up. The leading tank commanders scanned the horizon for signs of the enemy, looking over the tall sugarcane crops, with the rising sun behind them to assist their observation. They soon ran into a platoon of Pakistani infantry led by a JCO, which was quickly dispatched. An air attack followed swiftly, the enemy aircraft flying low in an attempt to notch kills on the lucrative targets that the advancing tanks offered. Daffadar Guman Singh, manning the .30 Browning machine gun on one of the leading tanks, found this impudence by enemy aircraft galling. This spirited NCO's instincts as a boxer prompted him to hit back. With a loud curse, he stood up on his seat and swung the Browning around, firing burst after burst at the offending Sabre jet. The aircraft responded in kind, but the odds were in favour of the pilot and Guman Singh was hit in the neck by the aircraft's cannon, killing him instantly.

A little further the leading squadrons encountered enemy Pattons, and a brief tank versus tank battle ensued. The 16 Cavalry, advancing to their right had also run into enemy tanks, and the Brigade Commander assessed the situation to be worse than it actually was. In his estimation, which later was found to be incorrect, there were two full regiments opposing the advance. Besides, a squadron of 62 Cavalry, which was to have protected the left flank of the brigade, had got stuck around the IB itself. This vulnerability was exploited by the enemy who attacked the brigade's affiliated medium artillery battery, severely damaging it. In view of all this, the Brigade Commander ordered the regiments to pull back and take up a defensive 'box' near the Sabzpir crossroads. The advance halted for forty-eight hours, a costly mistake which gave the enemy enough time to boost the force levels in the sector.

On 10 September, the Brigade Commander issued fresh orders for the capture of Phillora and advance towards Chawinda. The plan envisaged a bold role for the armoured division, by moving from the assembly area at Rurki Khurd with all three regiments of the brigade coming up. 17th Poona Horse and 4 Horse were to spread out to either side of Phillora and encircle it in a classic pincer movement from the flanks, thus splitting the enemy armour into small groups. These could then be destroyed piecemeal.

The advance commenced as planned at 0600 hours on 11 September, and by 0800 hours, contact had been established with the enemy tanks near Libbe. C Squadron engaged the enemy, strategically closing in with an interesting tactic called the 'Caterpillar'. The leading troops advanced while the two following forces provided covering fire from a static position, keeping the enemy tanks engaged. Once the leading troops reached a suitably covered position, it deployed and the following two troops advanced up to the same line. Then the maneuver was repeated up to the next position. This 'fire-and-move' tactic, imitated the movements of a caterpillar hence the name. Thus overcoming enemy resistance, 17th Poona Horse continued closing in towards Phillora.

By noon, C Squadron of the regiment had cleared Libbe and shortly thereafter launched its attack on Phillora along with 5/9 Gorkha Rifles. While this attack was in progress, B Squadron was covering the approach to Phillora from the North-West, while A Squadron was guarding the Libbe approach. About this time, a counter-attack was initiated against C Squadron, and soon A Squadron too was embroiled in this fight. Col Tarapore's tank, which was located close to A Squadron, engaged the enemy and shot up two of the enemy tanks. Leading from the front, he set a personal example by operating with the cupola of his tank open, despite enemy shelling, as he always insisted his tank commanders do. Shutting down the cupola in battle provided protection, but rendered the commander virtually blind, thereby crippling his ability to direct his own tank and his unit in battle. He was wounded by a shell splinter in this action, but continued fighting undeterred after first aid. The counter-attack was beaten back and Phillora was captured by 1530 hours.

Despite his wound, Col Tarapore led the regiment to capture its next objective, Wazirali, on 14 September. The next major engagement came on 16 September, when the forces were ordered to capture Jassoran and Butur Dograndi to further the overall divisional plan to capture Chawinda. Both these objectives were captured after bitter and heavy fighting by C Squadron. As a result of the fall of these critical positions, the enemy began moving troops from Chawinda to recapture them. C Squadron Commander Capt Ajai Singh saw this developing threat and asked for reinforcements. Col Tarapore ordered the move of A Squadron to reinforce them, and wanting to be in the thick of action once again, decided to join them along with his Adjutant, Capt Surrinder Singh, in their respective tanks.

Soon after, the two squadrons and the two tanks of the regimental headquarters were under extremely heavy tank, anti-tank, and artillery fire. Unconcerned by the lead flying all around him, Col Tarapore dismounted from his tank 'Kooshab' to take a closer look at the infantry positions. He found that there was only one infantry platoon available, which would not be able to hold Butur Dograndi. He, therefore, ordered a regrouping at Jassoran, which was firmly in the control of the Indian forces. Meanwhile, his own tank was hit by an enemy shell, rendering it immobile. It was fortuitous that he had not been in the tank at that time, however his Intelligence Officer Lt Amarjit Bal was injured. Then Col Tarapore's luck ran out in just a couple of hours, when his premonition came true – he was mortally wounded in renewed enemy shelling. Inspired by his leadership, the regiment fiercely attacked the enemy heavy armour, destroying approximately 60 enemy tanks at a cost of only 9 tank casualties, and when he finally succumbed to his injuries the regiment continued to defy the enemy.

The performance of Col Tarapore and his regiment in battle was such that even the enemy grudgingly admired it. Lt Gen Gul Hassan Khan, who was Pakistan's Director, Military Operations during the war and later rose to be its Commander-in-Chief, writes in his memoirs:

> *Two regiments—our 25 Cavalry and India's Poona Horse stand out as the best trained ones. The former was commanded by Colonel Nisar Ahmad and played a stupendous role in stemming the primary enemy offensive led by their Armoured Division in the Sialkot–Shakargarh salient. On the Indian side the Poona Horse was commanded by Colonel Tarapurwala (sic) and he commanded it in textbook fashion. I was told by Nisar that it was quite an education to listen to Tarapurwala's wireless intercepts. He maintained a total grip over his command.*

For the courage and leadership qualities displayed in leading his regiment over these actions, Colonel Tarapore was posthumously awarded the nation's highest gallantry award, the PVC.

Charge to Glory
Lt Col MMS Bakshi
– Phillora

The regiment 4 (Hodson's) Horse formed the second claw of the pincer along with 17th Poona Horse for the capture of Phillora on 11 September. The regiment also commenced its advance at 0600 hours, with C Squadron leading, heading at full speed for their first objective, Rurki Kalan. While nearing its objective, the squadron came under air attack, and the Squadron Commander, Maj CB Desraj Urs was injured in the eye by a shrapnel. Undeterred, this brave officer continued to press forward along with his squadron, agreeing to being evacuated only after his objective was secured.

With the first objective successfully in the bag, the advance towards Phillora was resumed, this time with A and B Squadrons leading. Lt Col MMS Bakshi, the Commandant, was following closely behind on his own tank. His crew included Capt (now Brigadier Retd) Ravi Malhotra, who was the Regimental Signal Officer-cum-Intelligence Officer, and had recently re-joined the regiment after the course he had been attending at Ahmednagar was cut short due to the war.

A Squadron, leading the advance from the left, had several engagements with the enemy tanks and RCL guns, but managed to get the better of the enemy and continue pressing forward its advance towards Phillora. Col Bakshi's tank was keeping up with them and closer to Phillora, the Commandant was on the lookout for a suitable position from where he could exercise command

and control over both the squadrons during the impending battle. He halted his tank near a village called Dulmanwali and stood on his seat to survey the area ahead through his binoculars. He could clearly make out the tree-lined road, which lead from Libbe to Phillora, which he found a useful landmark to orient himself in the otherwise featureless area.

He suddenly caught sight of a couple of enemy Patton tanks which had taken up position facing Libbe, their guns and attention in the opposite direction from Col Bakshi's tank. They were obviously expecting the attack to come in from the direction of Libbe, which had been the last reported location of 1 Armoured Brigade. He quickly counted the tanks, and realised that it was a full squadron against his solitary tank. Both his squadrons were already too far ahead for any timely intervention. Since the enemy tanks had not yet spotted his tank, Col Bakshi had the option of making a hasty exit and re-joining the safety umbrella by taking a wide detour. But running away from a fight went against his very nature.

Without a moment's hesitation, he issued fire orders to his gunner. Capt Malhotra, who was standing in for the operator-cum-loader, loaded an Armour Piercing Discarding Sabot (APDS) round in the gun. The gunner traversed the handwheel, laying the gun on Col Bakshi's directions, the enemy tank looming in his sights. He aligned the dot on the target and fired. The Centurion shook with the recoil as the round left the barrel and found its target with deadly accuracy. Even before the next round could be loaded, the gunner was traversing to lay on the next target indicated by Col Bakshi. The second tank was also destroyed before the enemy awoke to this threat in its rear. Both the enemy tanks had been hit and were going up in flames, much to the delight of the solitary Centurion's crew.

They didn't have long to rejoice, as the enemy now regained balance and responded with fury. The Centurion shuddered twice, and the crew realised that the enemy had scored two hits. But there was no visible damage, and the third enemy tank was also engaged and destroyed. Simultaneously, their own tank was hit again. More dangerously, the turret of their tank got stuck. Between loading rounds, Capt Malhotra had been throwing out the fired cases, his task being made difficult by the fact that he could not locate the leather gloves meant for handling the hot shells, and had to improvise by using cotton waste instead. One of the fired cases which he had missed out got stuck under the turret and jammed it, making traversing and laying the gun impossible.

Realising that without being able to shoot, his tank was a sitting duck for the enemy, he took the outrageously bold decision to charge full speed ahead through the line of enemy tanks to break through and join up with his squadron ahead. As ordered, the driver raced headlong, crossing the burning tanks, and took a right turn to head towards where they expected the squadron to be. Just then the tank was hit again, this time near the engine, and burst into flames. Col Bakshi ordered the crew to abandon the tank, making sure they carried the spare carbine carried by all tanks for such eventualities. Apart from that, all tank crews are armed with just a pistol. As they jumped off and ran, Capt Malhotra discovered that he had left behind his pistol in his holster attached to his belt, which he had taken off as it was obstructing him while loading.

The enemy crew had also abandoned their burning tanks, and were now firing at them from the ground. A running fire fight ensued, with Col Bakshi and his crew rushing towards the cover of a nearby sugarcane field. Col Bakshi fired four shots from his pistol at the chasing Pakistani crew before following the others into the fields. Once inside, they hurriedly moved deeper in to take maximum advantage of the cover, while the enemy crew stood outside firing blindly into the dense sugarcane crop. The beleaguered crew heaved a sigh of relief at being out of the line of sight and fire of the pursuers, but they were not completely safe. Intermittent artillery fire continued in the area, and some of the shells and splinters landed uncomfortably close. At the same time, an air attack raged on the enemy tanks, in which six more tanks were destroyed, but a couple of rockets also landed inside the field, giving some anxious moments to the fugitive crew. The last thing they wanted after safely evading enemy tank fire was to succumb to the fire of their own aircraft.

They remained hidden for almost two hours, but meanwhile the enemy tanks that were still functional moved away, leaving the burnt shells of the ones destroyed behind. Then they were alerted by the fresh noise of tanks, and cautiously peering out of the cover, were relieved to recognise that they were their own. The tank they saw was, in fact, of Maj Giriraj Singh, the 2IC of 17th Poona Horse. As they emerged from the sugarcane fields, the Poona Horse men assumed them to be Pakistanis, as the area was littered with destroyed Pakistani tanks. It was only when they waved their berets and showed the Hodson's Horse badges and shoulder flashes that their rescuers were convinced.

They were safely transported back to their regiment, and Col Bakshi commandeered another tank to re-join the battle. By now the squeeze on Phillora had been completed and the ring of armour around it by tanks of 17 Poona Horse and Hodson's Horse closed in towards the town. The town was subsequently attacked and captured by 43 Lorried Brigade. During the battle for the capture of Phillora, a total of twenty-one enemy tanks were destroyed by Hodson's Horse and six more destroyed in their area by air attacks. The regiment had, in return, lost only one tank, which was the Commandant's. This loss was aptly avenged by the regiment on 14 September when in the battle to seize the important railway station at Alhar, they knocked out and captured the tank of Lt Col Jahanzeb Khan, CO of Pakistan's Guides Cavalry.

Col Bakshi was awarded the MVC for his dauntless courage and gallantry under fire.

Gallant to the Last Breath

Major Bhupinder Singh
– Chawinda

While Col Bakshi and the crew of his solitary tank were engaged with the enemy tanks, B Squadron of Hodson's Horse under Maj Bhupinder Singh had advanced around Rurki Kalan and was proceeding towards the next stop when they came up against fierce enemy opposition in the area of Kotli Khadam. In the ensuing action, they knocked out nine enemy tanks and four RCL guns, without any damage to their own tanks.

On 19 September, the squadron had its next major engagement when as a part of the attack on Chawinda, it was tasked to advance across the Sialkot–Chawinda railway line and advance towards Sodreke to protect the right flank of the attacking force. The squadron had just crossed the railway line when it came under very heavy artillery fire. Taking the raining shells in their stride, Maj Bhupinder ordered his squadron to keep advancing. Soon the enemy tanks appeared and a fierce fire fight ensued.

Maj Bhupinder's tank received a hit from an enemy Patton and caught fire. Valiantly continuing to fight the enemy, they were successful in getting the fire under control even as shells continued to rain upon them. Throughout this action, Maj Bhupinder completely disregarded his personal safety, leading his crew and his squadron with resolute courage.

Their advance was slow but steady, punctuated by intermittent engagements with enemy tanks and RCLs. They also continued to receive unwelcome attention from the enemy artillery. By 1700 hours, they had made good progress when Maj Bhupinder's tank was hit once again, this time by a Cobra anti-tank missile. The tank immediately went up in flames, this time the conflagration being even more daunting than earlier. Even with the fire raging, Maj Bhupinder and his crew continued to engage the enemy. Eventually, Maj Bhupinder was evacuated to the hospital with severe burn injuries. While in the hospital, he fought for his life with the same determination that he had displayed against the enemy.

While he was in the hospital, Prime Minister Lal Bahadur Shastri visited it, and the brave young officer left a lasting impression in his mind. Extracts from the Prime Minister's speech given at Delhi the next day are as follows:

Yesterday, I visited some of our wounded Jawans and officers in the military hospital. They have been badly hurt but I did not see a single tear or even a sad face.... I was very much moved to see another officer, Bhupinder Singh, whose whole body was covered with blood. Even now it is difficult to put a piece of cloth anywhere on his body. He was lying in the bed with his eyes closed. He apologised to me for not being able to stand up to show respect to the Prime Minister who was visiting him. He told me that he had destroyed seven enemy tanks, and that his unit had knocked out thirty-one. He also said that he was sure he would get well again but even if he did not, it did not matter because the country can now hold its head high. I told him how proud the country was of him, how deeply grateful the people of the country were for the way in which the Indian Armed Forces had faced the enemy.

This brief exchange speaks volumes for the man Maj Bhupinder was. A soldier to his last breath, he died on 3 October in the hospital, succumbing to the burns that covered his entire body. He was posthumously awarded the MVC.

Defence Minister YB Chavan inspecting a captured enemy tank

Prime Minister Lal Bahadur Shastri on a captured Pakistani tank
in Sialkot sector

Resolute Cavalier
Major MAR Sheikh

Maj Mohammed Ali Raaz Sheikh was born on 6 March 1931 in a princely family of Mongrol (a small principality of Junagadh State) in Gujarat. It is understood that during the partition of the country in 1947, some members of Major Sheikh's extended family chose to migrate to Pakistan while some stayed behind in India.

After his early education in Rajkot, Maj Sheikh joined the Indian Military Academy, Dehradun. He was commissioned as a Second Lieutenant on 6 June 1954 in the oldest cavalry regiment of the Indian Army – 16 Light Cavalry. This regiment, which was raised in 1776, has a glorious history of nearly 240 years of unbroken military service. Maj Sheikh was a tall, handsome but shy person, with a gentlemanly swagger. He was always elegantly dressed and possessed social graces of an aristocratic extravagance; above all else, he had courage, unlikely to fail in battle.

After a few years of regimental service, Maj Sheikh was posted to the Army Headquarters as ADC to Gen JN Chaudhuri, then COAS. During this tenure, he accompanied the Army Chief on all his official travels within India and overseas while attending to his assigned professional military duties.

When he reverted to regimental duty in 1965, war clouds were already looming in the horizon. Maj Sheikh was given command of A Squadron, which he led into battle against Pakistan in the Sialkot sector where he fought in the battle of Gadgor (now in Pakistan) when 16 Light Cavalry was given the unique honour of

Indian soldiers inspect an abandoned Pakistani tank

The Indian Centurion Tanks were the nemesis of the Pattons

leading the advance of the Indian Army's 1 Armoured Division into Pakistan territory on 8 September 1965.

The regiment, after crossing the IB at first light on 8 September 1965 formed the spearhead of the 1 Armoured Division advance into enemy territory. Moving with lightning speed, brushing aside minor opposition, and without any care for his personal safety, Maj Sheikh led his squadron along with other sub-units of 16 Light Cavalry and hit Gadgor village by around 0900 hours. Here they met with heavy opposition from enemy tanks while PAF Sabre Jets strafed and rocketed the advancing column – but no casualties were suffered till then.

Between 0930 hours and 1430 hours, fierce tank-to-tank engagements ensued in which 16 Light Cavalry, including Maj Sheikh's squadron, destroyed eight enemy Patton tanks, two RCL guns, and some enemy infantry. The enemy, comprising a squadron of Pakistan's 25 Cavalry as it was found later, was located in well-concealed positions around Gadgor village which halted the regiment's advance temporarily.

While B Squadron tanks went on engaging the enemy armour through the Gadgor position up to the outskirts of Phillaura, A Squadron under the command of Maj Sheikh was ordered to outflank the enemy location from the South-west. During this manoeuvre, Maj Sheikh, while leading from the front, was the first to draw enemy tank fire and was mortally wounded.

Unmindful of his personal injuries, Maj Sheikh, who was a determined combat tank Commander, continued leading the advance with speed and momentum, fully realising that this move by his squadron was critical to the success of the regiment's overall advance into enemy territory. During this action, Maj Sheikh was hit in the neck and right shoulder and was severely wounded. Even though he was badly injured, he refused to be exit the battlefield till ordered by the Commandant to be eventually evacuated on 11 September 1965. He succumbed to his injuries on the night of 13–14 September 1965 in the military hospital, Pathankot. For this gallant action, Maj MAR Sheikh was awarded the Vir Chakra for his bravery in battle while facing the enemy.

OP HILL

Assault on OP Hill

The Last Battle

The ceasefire had been in place since 23 September 1965, but peace had far from descended on the Mendhar sector, south of Poonch along the CFL. Frequent artillery shelling by the Pakistanis targeted Indian movement along the road Mendhar – Balnoi, and the battalion base at Balnoi itself. The shelling was aided by, and owed its accuracy to, the observation and correction provided by Pakistanis on a feature fittingly called OP Hill, short for Observation Post Hill. Known locally by the more picturesque name of Chuh-i-Nar, the 5000 feet high feature is located south-west of the Mendhar – Baloni road, about 20 kilometres south-west of Poonch. It covered an approach from the Pakistani side into the Mendhar valley, part of this approach hidden from Indian side of the CFL. The hill had been occupied by Indian troops till 1956, and thereafter lay unoccupied. Unknown to the Indians, the Pakistanis had stealthily occupied it during August 1965, and were using the covered approach to send supplies and ammunition to the infiltrators operating in Jammu and Kashmir.

Pakistanis continued to hold this feature even after ceasefire. When appeals to the United Nations observers failed to have the desired effect of getting the Indian territory under Pakistani occupation vacated, it was decided to launch an attack to re-capture it. A battalion attack was launched for this on 6th October, but could not achieve its objective as the Pakistanis had fortified this position into a complete battalion defended locality, complete with bunkers, automatics, barbed wire and anti-personnel mines. Such a position would require a fully brigade to capture, and the task was entrusted to 120 Infantry Brigade under its newly appointed commander Brig BS Ahluwalia. The three battalions in his brigade were 2nd Battalion the Dogra Regiment (2 Dogra), 5th Battalion the Sikh Light Infantry (5 Sikh LI) and 7th Battalion the Sikh Regiment (7 Sikh). The attack was planned from three directions – 2 Dogra on the right shoulder and 5 Sikh LI on the left shoulder of the feature, approaching it from the north. 7 Sikh would skirt around and launch it's attack from the south, or the rear of the enemy, heading for the gap between the two battalions attacking from the North. The D Day selected was 2 November (Map 12).

Maj RK Mazumdar, the officiating commanding officer, gave D Company under Maj GS Pall the task of leading the battalion assault and capture Black Rocks. C Company under Maj Karam Singh was to then capture Twin Pimple. B Company under Maj SL Kapur was to be in reserve, immediately behind C and D Companies. Leading platoon commander of D Company was Capt Gautam Mubayi, a 22 year old officer whose family had migrated from Lahore to Delhi during partition. Shortly after leaving the FUP, the company was pinned down by heavy enemy fire. Within minutes, the leading section commanders fell prey to this deadly hail of lead that seemed to be raining incessantly all around them. On seeing the attack coming to a halt, Capt Mubayi volunteered to establish a foothold for the rest of the company.

Crawling forward, keeping low to avoid the bullets flying overhead, he reached the barbed wire on the outer perimeter of the enemy defences. Cutting the wires, he continued slithering forward towards the enemy bunker housing the machine gun that was holding up their advance. On reaching close to it, he rose to his full height and, ignoring the enemy fire, charged at the bunker, grenade in hand. He lobbed the grenade at the bunker, and started firing through its opening with his carbine. The grenade found its mark, and its shrapnel within the close confines of the bunker dispatched the enemy inside, silencing the machine gun. But while rushing forward, Capt Mubayi had stepped on a land mine, which blew up in a deafening blast, leaving his left foot in a mangled mass of bleeding flesh. Despite difficulty in walking because of his injury, he continued guiding his platoon through the gap, onwards to the objective. He bluntly refused any suggestion of evacuation, despite steadily losing blood from his injury. Moving forward, directing his men towards the enemy bunkers, he ensured a lodgment for the rest of the company to advance. Suddenly an enemy machine gun opened up from a distant bunker, mortally wounding him. The brave Capt went down fighting on the objective itself, but only after he had completed the task assigned to him.

By now both D and C Companies had suffered heavy casualties, and B Company under Maj SL Kapur was brought forward to reinforce them. In the fierce fighting that ensued, Lt Karnail Singh was killed, cut down by enemy fire while making a passage through the barbed wire. Capt PK Uppal, who had been together with Capt Mubayi through school and academy and had also joined the same unit, also fell to enemy bullets shortly after his childhood friend. The battalion captured the objective, but with very heavy cost. They had lost three officers, one JCOs and 50 ORs. Another five officers, six JCOs and 169 ORs were wounded. Capt Gautam Mubayi was awarded the MVC posthumously for his dauntless courage. Maj RK Mazumdar, Maj Karam Singh and Sep Balbir Singh received the Sena Medal.

On to the left of 2 Dogra, the attack by 5 Sikh LI was also pressed in with similar resolve. The objective allotted to them was called White Rocks. Lt Col Sant Singh, the CO, had planned the operation in great amount of detail and with a lot of foresight. Having assessed the formidability of the enemy positions, he knew that the battle would be a hard fought one. Anticipating the possibility of casualties due to severed limbs, he ordered every man to carry a line bedding – a multipurpose roll of rope that forms a part of a soldier's kit – to apply tourniquet on any severed limbs. This proved useful, saving at least twenty lives. He also got an additional fifty stretchers improvised, and detailed men from the administrative personnel to carry the heavy casualties expected. He also allotted extra radio sets and lines to the companies to ensure continued communication even if there were casualties amongst the radio operators or damage to the sets.

The Sikhs crossed their SL with rousing cries of 'Bole So Nihal Sat Sri Akal' at the appointed hour, and commenced the grueling advance towards their objective. Col Sant writes in his account of the battle:

> *I have yet to witness or even read in history a faster and more determined charge. Officers, JCOs, NCOs and Jawans were suffering heavy casualties due to extensive minefields, heavy concentration of enemy air-burst shells, well-coordinated fire of a large number of automatic weapons and showers of grenades but all eyes were glued on the objective; nobody hesitated, nobody uttered a word of pain. Jawans with severed limbs, those who had only a few minutes to live and those seriously wounded refused to be attended to but instead exhorted their comrades to move on, to annihilate the enemy, to complete the task.*

In an feat coincidentally similar to the one performed by Capt Gautam Mubayi on the other flank, Nk Darshan Singh charged at an enemy machine gun bunker despite having had his left leg blown up by a mine. He too refused evacuation and continued crawling forward exhorting his men to carry on with the charge and clear the way for the rest of the platoon and company. He was wounded by a second mine blast, yet with supreme effort of will and courage, dragged himself forward to an enemy bunker and threw a grenade at it. His entire section had become casualties, yet paving the way for the rest of the battalion to take on its objective. He died shouting to the follow up echelon to come by the route which had been cleared of mines by the charge of his section.

Another unforgettable act of valour on this night was by Sub Piara Singh, one of the platoon commanders. He too led his platoon assault through a minefield, cutting across wire obstacles and charging on enemy bunkers. Though he lost 25 of his men in the charge, he silenced an enemy LMG and went on to destroy an 83 millimetre Rocket Launcher by throwing a grenade into its bunker moments after both his legs had been blown off by the rocket fire. He too succumbed to his injuries shortly afterwards.

Selfless sacrifice by many others besides these two notables ensured the ultimate success in capturing the objective. The battalion lost three JCOs and 36 ORs, with two officers, two JCOs and 130 ORs wounded. Coll Sant and Nk Darshan Singh were awarded the MVC, and Sub Piara Singh the VrC.

7 Sikh attack was to go in after the success of 2 Dogra and they eagerly awaited success signal from the Dogras. When this was not received by 0200 hours, the CO 7 Sikh requested the Brigade Commander to let the battalion go in for phase 2 and 3. The permission was granted and A & B companies left the FUP for assault. The objective had to be attacked frontally against heavy odds and on very steep climb as first phase objective on either side of Jungle Hill, their initial objective, had not been captured.

The move onto the objective, through the ring of enemy artillery and mortar defensive fire tasks, cross fire of MMGs and LMGs from both flanks and over a difficult terrain was slow. Approximately one platoon of B company was incapacitated when enemy artillery shells fell in their midst. Though the enemy's artillery and automatic fire, the brave Sikhs went on. The mines took the roll by way of life, shattering of limbs and mutilating of the human body beyond recognition. However, the brave men reached the forward trenches under the propulsion of super-human will poser ably led by their commanders and made the final rush. A fierce hand to hand fight ensued. The enemy put up very stiff resistance to cause tremendous amount of loss of life. At this stage the difference in defeat and victory was made only by the ferocity of the final assault. This was the moment soldiers longed for and they put in the supreme effort. The enemy's will to resist was shattered and the forward trenches of the Jungle Hill were captured.

At this stage, C Company was moved to help mopping up on Jungle Hill and subsequently to attack OP Hill. By this time, 5 SIKH LI had advanced and captured a part of OP Hill. The remaining portion was captured by the gallant 7 Sikh. The capture of Jungle Hill, a punch in the enemy's guts facilitated the progress of 2 Dogra who captured their objective. The degree of appreciation of the Dogras to the Sikhs was evident when they, having reached their objective, shouted '7 SIKH KI JAI'. Immediately after the capture of objective, the enemy subjected it to intense shelling for nearly seven hours but the spirit of 7 Sikh remained undaunted. The battalion suffered twenty ORs killed and two Officers, four JCOs and forty eight ORs wounded.

The successful capture of OP Hill was the last major operation, though minor skirmishes and clashes, which were seen as par for the course even before the commencement of the war, continued.

Vigil against counter attack

STEADFAST SUPPORT

The soldiers who storm an objective after traversing long distances under enemy fire go into battle carrying with them little more than their personal weapons and courage in large doses. They are supported by the battalion's integral weapons – automatics, mortars and light anti-tank weapons, employed to overcome the enemy's defences and his will to fight. In plains, attacking infantry may be augmented with tanks, providing considerable additional firepower and psychological impact. These are the combat elements which are in the 'show window' of the operation. But in the background, there are others, often unseen, unheard and unsung, who play a big part in victory over a stubborn enemy. The next two stories are about personnel of two of such combat support elements whose actions were in no way less heroic than those in the tales recounted earlier.

Olive Green Pilots

The Pakistani crew of the Patton tanks barely noticed the tiny speck in the sky hovering 3,000 feet above. Their attention was focused on dealing with the Indian AMX tanks which were proving tough nuts to crack. Still unnoticed, the speck grew larger as it closed in, flew over them and then banked to return. Moments later it was back, bringing with it a shower of medium artillery shells directly on to the tanks. For Capt Harcharan Singh Chaudhary, the pilot of the small single-engine Auster Mark IV aircraft, the sortie was turning out to be much more exciting than the air photo runs he had been doing the past few days. As the artillery shells started landing all around the tanks, he spoke rapidly into his radio set, giving corrections to the guns, and ensuring that every round landed where it could cause maximum damage to the enemy.

Capt (now Retd Brig) Chaudhary was part of 2 (Independent) Air Observation Flight, one of four such planes that constituted the army's tiny and nascent aviation arm. Based at Jammu, he used to make regular flights to provide photo reconnaissance missions to the formations deployed in the sector. The number of sorties had tripled in the past one month, after Pakistan had launched Operation Gibraltar. But today, on 1 September 1965, the situation came to a boil when Pakistani forces, including tanks, had crossed the IB. He had been called out to fly a mission in the area of Burejal where an intense tank battle was in progress. From his elevated aerial platform, he could spot targets and pass them on to the artillary batteries, which could then engage them from several kilometres away.

His approach to taking such a sortie was simple. He would fly in search of a target, which were often given away by a trail of dust in the wake of a tank column, or flashes of firing from guns. Once the target was spotted, he would approximate its position by comparing it with known landmarks, and then pass those coordinates back to the guns. He would then fly around the target, heading back for several kilometres before turning around to fly towards the target again. By then the guns would start firing on the target, and he would observe where the shells were falling. If they were off target, he would relay the adjustments required to correct the fire.

Capt Chaudhary was thus engaged when he suddenly spotted four Vampires of the Indian Air Force (IAF) flying above and very close. This came as a surprise, as he had no idea that the air force had been pressed into battle so soon. Within seconds, he also saw Pakistani Sabre jets fly in from the West, and an aerial dog fight between the two sides commenced. Highly vulnerable in his tiny, unarmed aircraft, Capt Chaudhary immediately dove to treetop level, not wanting to become an unintended target in the combat between mighty jets. He returned to base at this low height, taking care to avoid ground fire as well, but not before he saw all the four unfortunate Vampires being shot down.

Over the course of the next few days, he flew numerous sorties over the Chhamb sector while the ground battle raged. Then the scene of action shifted to the Sialkot sector, where Indian forces had launched an offensive into Pakistani territory on 8 September. Here the task was even more risky, as it entailed flying deep into enemy territory, unarmed and defenceless as always. There was the risk of being shot at by aircraft as well as by ground forces. So, although the Auster could fly at a maximum height of about 18,000 feet, pilots like Capt Chaudhary preferred to maintain an altitude of about 3,000 feet. This was low enough to avoid detection by enemy radar and stay out of the way of fighter jets, and high enough to be out of range small arms ground-to-air fire. The only drawback was that objects on the ground appeared as tiny specks from that height, which meant that when a potential target was spotted, he needed to fly lower for a better look.

It was on such an occasion, on 13 September, when flying over Phillora area that he spotted a large column of dust, which meant a large body of vehicles was on the move. On closer inspection, what he had initially taken for soft-skinned vehicles turned out to be a complete squadron of enemy tanks. He immediately radioed back for medium fire, which he didn't have on call on that particular day. This was too lucrative a target to miss, but the lighter field guns that he was controlling wouldn't have done much damage to the tanks. The fire was allotted, and shells soon started landing amongst the tanks, which were in a static semi-circular harbour. The whole area was soon a bedlam of explosions, with the tanks moving helter skelter and shooting at everything in sight.

In this melee, Capt Chaudhary had descended perilously low to closely monitor the falling shells and relay target corrections. Engrossed in this task, he suddenly felt an enormous jolt and the Perspex canopy of his aircraft disappeared. He was thrown back in his seat with the blast of strong wind that hit him, and struggled to keep his aircraft under control despite the aerodynamic challenges of the damage. He felt two more jerks and found that one of his undercarriages had crumpled, along with a large part of the airframe. With great difficulty, he steered the aircraft around and flew in the direction of the base. Although he knew he wouldn't be able to make it all the way back, the longer he flew homewards the greater were his chances of ending up in territory under the control of Indian forces.

Soon it became obvious that the damaged airframe would not be able to take much more punishment, and Capt Chaudhary started looking for a safe place to crash land. He spotted a *bundh* on the ground, and slowly brought the aircraft down, all the skill and expertise at his disposal focused on the delicate and perilous task. He slowly lowered the aircraft and hit the solitary landing gear on the *bundh* to avoid toppling the aircraft completely. As the tortured machine came to a jarring halt, a shaken Capt Chaudhary

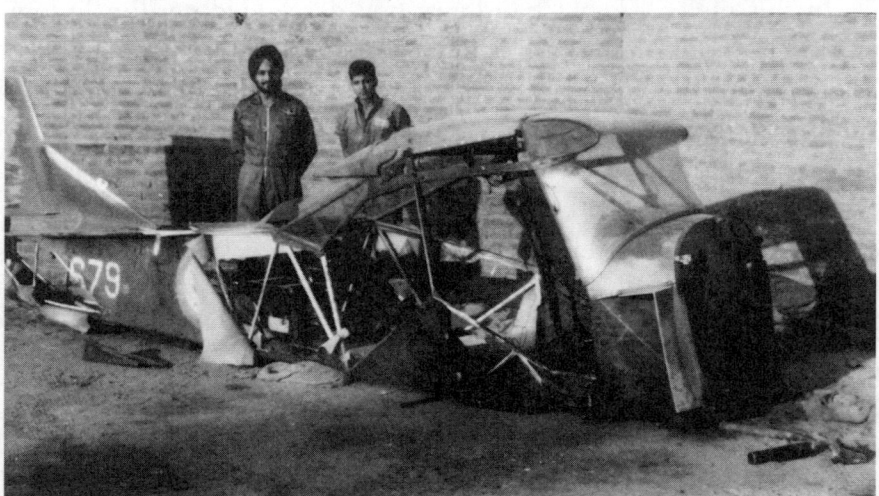

Crashed remnants of Capt Chaudhary's aircraft

undid his harness and jumped clear. He was soon surrounded by Sikh troops from a nearby Indian battalion, who were relishing the prospect of dealing with a captured Pakistani pilot. They were obviously disappointed when Capt Chaudhary removed his helmet and they realised that he was not a Pakistani but as much a Sikh as them. The troops led him to their Company Commander, who arranged his evacuation back to Jammu.

Capt Chaudhary had received a splinter injury in his back, and still carries the piece of metal embedded in his body. The doctor who tended to him preferred to let it be as operating to remove it carried the risk of injuring the spinal cord. With barely a day to recover from his wound, Capt Chaudhary was back in the air, flying almost every day until the end of the war. After the ceasefire he recovered the damaged aircraft from the crash site and brought it back to the squadron base. When, the other pilots saw it they were dumbstruck that he had managed to survive without major injuries.

Capt Chaudhary was mentioned in dispatches for his relentless support to critical operations during different stages of the war.

The Mighty Gunners

Lenin certainly knew what he was saying when he referred to the artillery as the 'God of War'. Like the omnipotent power, the gunners have the means to influence the course of battles through the application of the mighty firepower at their disposal. Artillery guns, along with the bulk of their men, are located far behind the scene of battles, given their ability to fire over very long distances. Since the men manning the guns cannot see the target, they have their eyes and ears in the form of Observation Posts or OPs. Sometimes they are airborne, as in the previous chapter. But most often the OPs are a small detachment consisting of a young officer and a handful of men who are attached to the affiliated infantry or armoured unit and accompany the fighting troops into battle, referred to as Forward Observation Officers (FOOs). They act as the link between the guns and the fighting troops at crucial times when the attacks are going in or an enemy counter-attack is being fought off. Their job is to call for fire and to pass back corrections after observing the falling shells to make sure they hit what they ought to. In addition, the Battery Commander (BC) of the affiliated battery is normally located with the CO of the battalion, and advises him on the artillery fire plan. In the blaze of glory following successful actions, the vital role played by these small but indispensable teams is, at times, overshadowed by the more flamboyant actions. An attempt has, therefore, been made to piece together the stories of a few notable amongst these.

1642 Battery of 164 Field Regiment was in direct support of 1 Para for Operation Bakshi. For the second attack on Sank, the CO 1 Para had decided to ensure a preponderance of artillery fire before his troops assaulted. He had accordingly prepared the fire plan in consultation with the BC, Ma Kesri Singh, which involved the fire not only of the affiliated battery but of the whole regiment. The BC ensured that Sank received the continuous attention of the 25-pounder guns throughout the day. The FOO Capt Naidu, who was accompanying the assaulting troops, kept calling for fire right up to the minute the attack went it, when it had to be lifted, keeping in mind the safety of own troops. Capt Naidu went on along with the 1 Para men under Maj Ranjit Dyal for the assault on the Haji Pir pass, and was responsible for providing accurate and deadly fire support during critical phases of the operation.

For the attack on Raja, 2 Sikh had 75 Patiala Mountain Battery in direct support under Maj Jagdish Singh, the BC. Although the attack was to be launched with three companies simultaneously, Maj Jagdish Singh managed to work out a detailed fire plan to support it all the same. The battalion was in its FAA ready for the attack to commence once the CO arrived after attending the Brigade Commander's orders. When the delay in the CO's arrival caused concern regarding the corresponding delay in launching the attack, Maj Jagdish suggested to the Adjutant that the artillery could start firing on the objective to keep the machine guns from targeting the troops in the FAA. This worked, preventing needless casualties amongst the waiting troops. Soon the CO arrived and though delayed, the attack went in. Maj Jagdish accompanied the CO during the attack, and despite being shot through the shoulder, continued to carry out his task.

In the Haji Pir bulge, 93 Infantry Brigade had been involved in the capture of other prominent features, even after the fall of the pass itself, to consolidate its position and eliminate enemy pockets. One such operation was carried out by 6th Battalion the Dogra Regiment (6 Dogra) on 21 September to capture a feature called 'Gittian'. The CO decided to attack with two companies to simultaneously address two distinct parts of the objective. Maj Darshan Singh Lalli and Maj JP Makkar were the two Company Commanders. The Dogras fought a fierce battle for the capture of their objectives, with Maj Darshan Singh falling to the enemy bullets at a critical juncture of the assault, leaving a young 2LT ZS Chaudhari in command of the company. The stellar role played by the two FOOs from 164 Field Regiment in this battle is described in the Brigade War Diary as follows:

> *The gunners distinguished themselves in this fierce battle. Capt MK Maniwadkar was the FOO with one of the assaulting companies. When he found the infantry company he was supporting had suffered many casualties and that the assault strength had been reduced considerably, he joined the assaulting infantry. The company won the objective but this young officer was killed while assaulting the final objective.*

Capt MD Naidu was the FOO of the other assaulting company... When 2LT Chaudhari found himself with hardly thirty able-bodied men on Tree Hill (his objective), he was a little shaken. The situation became grim when he saw hundreds of Pathans forming up for a counter-attack. Capt Naidu at that time was lying on the Tree Hill after being hit by a MMG burst in his stomach. He was bleeding very badly and could not move about. He realised that the situation was too serious for the young subaltern to handle and he might decide to withdraw under enemy pressure. Capt Naidu called the 2LT and told him not to worry about the large number of Pathans. He said that they were clearly visible to him, and he would bring down accurate artillery fire on them. He did exactly that, and the enemy ran back leaving behind many dead bodies. Meanwhile the reserve company had moved in to reinforce them, and by then Capt Naidu had become unconscious due to loss of blood – but the situation had been saved.

Maj KTM Pillay was the BC of 100 Field Battery of 14 Field Regiment (now 14 Medium Regiment), which was affiliated to 6 Sikh LI for the Kalidhar operations. On 28 September, when the attack on the Budhi Dhah feature was getting stalled, the Brigade Commander spoke to Maj Pillay on the wireless and told him to help out the young Company Commander. Due to the mature and experienced support of Maj Pillay, the objective could finally be captured against all odds. Again, for the final attack on Point 3776 by 6 Sikh LI on 3–4 October, Maj Pillay was the OP who brought down accurate and timely artillery fire to fend off the enemy counter-attack. For his courage, initiative and leadership skills, he was awarded the VrC.

These are just a few instances where accounts of the actions by the gunners are available. Undoubtedly, there were many more such instances where the OP/BC parties went beyond their designated role and actively influenced the course of the battle.

Indian gunners in action

THE COMMANDERS

Battles are undoubtedly won by the grit, determination, initiative and raw courage of the men and junior leadership on ground. And wars are won by the planning, foresight, sagacity and decisiveness of the higher commanders. Their role begins long before the first bullet is fired or the first shell leaves the barrel of an artillery gun, and continues long after the smoke and dust of battle have settled. Like skilful chess players, they manoeuvre the various pieces, represented by their units and formations, into positions where their strengths can be optimally employed against the enemy. Like the grandmaster, they also need to constantly monitor every move of the opponent's, trying to anticipate his game plan, and how can it be check-mated.

It was fortuitous to have two battle wizened, imaginative and assertive leaders at the helm of operations during the war. The next two chapters are about these two commanders who steered the army towards its victorious performance in the war.

At the Helm
General JN Chaudhuri

Affectionately called 'Mucchu' by his friends, who included Lord Mountbatten, Gen Joyonto Nath Chaudhuri was one of the Sandhust-trained King's Commissioned officers of the old school. As the COAS during the war, he played a critical role as the link between the political and military decision-making. His advice to the political leadership was always unambiguous and forthright, just as his orders to the military Commanders were decisive and explicit. Though the war and his position afforded him an opportunity to be flamboyant, seek media attention, and revel in the reflected glory of the men under his command, he preferred to remain discreetly in the background, allowing credit to be assigned where it was due.

Commissioned from Sandhurst in 1928, he had spent a year in a British battalion, as was the norm for Indian officers, before joining 7 Cavalry. He saw active service during World War II, and was conferred the Order of British Empire (OBE) besides also being Mentioned in Dispatches several times. He was transferred to 16 Cavalry, and commanded this regiment during the war itself. At the time of independence, he was amongst the senior-most Indian officers. As GOC of 1 Armoured Division, he led Operation Polo for the liberation of Hyderabad and was appointed the military governor of Hyderabad immediately after its liberation. He commanded XV Corps, an experience that gave him tremendous insight and advantage during the 1965 war. He also served as the Adjutant General and CGS, and was commanding the Southern

Army when the war with China broke out in 1962. He was appointed the COAS when Gen Thapan resigned in the aftermath of the war.

To say that he took over the reins under challenging circumstances would be a gross understatement. It was the biggest crisis that the Indian Army had faced, or has faced ever since. The ignominy of defeat and consequent rock-bottom morale prevailing amongst all ranks of the army had to be set right with as much expediency as handling the crippling shortfall of equipment and manpower. The army had to be reorganised, new units and formations raised, and most importantly, its self-confidence restored. The army's commendable performance barely three years later in the 1965 war is testimony to how well these daunting tasks had been performed.

He took up the task of restructuring the army, after giving a great deal of thought to what ailed the system even before he became the Chief. In his own words:-

> *For some time past I had come to the conclusion that the Indian Army had been organised on the old British war establishment which didn't suit us at all. In fact we had wasted a lot of manpower in raising units which were meant for overseas war, a sort of war we would never fight... I exiled all the superfluous units from our Order of Battle.... So when I finished with the reorganisation of the Indian Army it had a new look. I changed the equipment of the signals so that the telecommunications in the field became much simpler and I put a lot more people into the teeth arms by cutting down the tale (sic).[1]*

Much thought also went into the type of equipment required for different arms, based on the Indian operational conditions, subsequent maintenance capabilities, and requirements. The tougher bit was rebuilding the shattered morale of the troops, and re-building the fighting spirit in them. Gen Chaudhuri made it a

---

[1] General J.N. Chaudhuri: An Autobiography, as Narrated to B.K. Narayan by Joyanto Nath Chaudhuri, Brij Kumar Narayan.

practice to visit as many units as he could and interacting with troops wherever he went.

> *I used to visit the troops at various places and used to tell them that there was a big black mark on our faces which water alone won't wash out and there was only one thing which could wash it out – blood.*[2]

The grit and valour displayed by Indian troops during the 1965 war is testimony to their determination in washing off that mark. The other big change that Gen Chaudhuri sought to bring about was in the doctrine and the thought process of Commanders and troops executing it. The key element of this thought process was an offensive mindset even in defence. While evolving the plans for the defence of the country afresh, he got the government to agree in principle that the moment Pakistani troops came across the IB, the army should be permitted to cross the line into Pakistan. The subsequent offensive actions into the Haji Pir bulge and Punjab as a consequence of Pakistani aggression in Kashmir and Chhamb respectively, could be mounted with rapidity because these had already been thought of and planned for much before the war actually broke out.

The Pakistani military and political leadership – by and large the same thing – was acutely aware of the measures being undertaken on a fast-track basis to modernise and reorganise the Indian Army. The leaders feared that once the army was fully in place, the military balance of power would irrevocably tilt in India's favour. The only chance they had of wresting Kashmir by force was before that, and this led to them precipitating the 1965 war, starting with flexing their muscles in the Rann of Kutch.

While the Kutch operations were on, Gen Chaudhuri received news of a personal tragedy – his father had passed away in Calcutta (now Kolkata). Torn between his filial duty to his deceased father and his responsibility to his position and his country, he took the painful decision of remaining in Delhi rather than go to Calcutta

---

[2] Ibid.

for his father's cremation. As the Kutch affair escalated, he came under a lot of pressure to retaliate. He realised that this would be a grave mistake, as India did not have any airfields in Kutch, and even the land communications were very poor. Besides, the monsoon was due shortly, and rain would have swamped the whole area. Despite coming under severe criticism, he stuck to his decision of not retaliating at Pakistan's time and place of choosing. He was supported by Defence Minister YB Chavan.

That his reservations about retaliation did not stem from any lack of confidence in himself or the army he headed, became evident when he had no such compunctions in taking offensive actions in Kashmir and Punjab later in the year, when Pakistan provoked India again. Throughout the operations in August and September 1965, Gen Chaudhuri provided able and decisive leadership to the army. If it was the blood and guts of soldiers in the field which erected the edifice of victory, it was the planning and decision-making of Gen Chaudhuri and Commanders down the chain which created the blueprint for it.

He was the epitome of a higher Commander, in that he voiced his intent to subordinate Commanders, but allowed them a wide leeway to work out their own plans to fulfil it. Besides allotting resources and satisfying himself about the veracity of the plan, Gen Chaudhuri did not believe in micromanaging the operations. Of course, there were times when he strongly disagreed with a particular course planned by a subordinate, and on such occasions did not hesitate to prevail over such decisions. The example about the difference of opinions between him and Lt Gen Harbakhsh about the direction of launching I Corps into the Sialkot sector cited in the previous chapter is one such occasion when he insisted on following his own plan – and as the success of the operations showed, this bore out his conviction.

Gen Chaudhuri was conferred with the Padma Vibhushan, the country's second highest civilian award for his role in the war. He retired in 1966 and served as India's High Commissioner in Canada.

The Mind Behind the Might
Lieutenant General Harbakhsh Singh

The military leader who planned, directed, and commanded the operations and actions we have talked about so far was Lt Gen Harbakhsh Singh the General Officer Commanding-in-Chief (GOC-in-C) or Army Commander, of the Indian Army's Western Command. Back then, the Northern Command did not exist, and the entire western border from Jammu and Kashmir to Rajasthan came under the Shimla-based Western Command. Thus, the entire action during the 1965 war, except for the skirmishes in the Rann of Kutch, fell under his purview.

Lt Gen Harbakhsh was from the very first course of the Indian Military Academy in 1935. A soldier with near unmatchable operational experience amongst his contemporaries, he had seen action before independence in the NWFP and during World War II, where as a Company Commander in 5 Sikh he had been wounded and captured, surviving three years in a Japanese prisoner of war camp. During the invasion of Kashmir in 1947–48, he served as a deputy and later as the Commander of Infantry Brigades that were involved in major actions, first for the defence of Srinagar and subsequently, to chase out the tribal raiders and Pakistani army personnel who had infiltrated into Indian territory. After commanding 5 Infantry Division, he was the Chief of Staff, Western Command, and also briefly commanded 4 Corps during the 1962 Sino-India war in the absence of Gen BM Kaul, who had fallen ill. He had taken over the command of the Western Army in 1964, just a few months before Pakistan began its misadventures in the Rann of Kutch.

On assumption of his command, Lt Gen Harbakhsh carried out an assessment of the Western Command's operational plans, which for all practical purposes were India's operational plans vis-à-vis Pakistan, and found them to be too defensive for his liking. As he writes in his book, *War Despatches*:

> *Though we had offensive plans of some sort, the bias was primarily on the defensive. This induced in the majority of our commanders an unconscious attitude of defence mindedness.*

He felt that even the Indian defence should be offensive in design and aggressive in nature – and accordingly went about modifying the plans. He significantly altered the manner in which reserves were to be employed. Instead of using them to reinforce threatened areas in the later stages of a defensive battle, the plan envisaged using them in an offensive role Abinitio. He issued his operational instructions in April 1965, in which he gave the bias of defence in the XI Corps zone to the Khem Karan–Bhikkiwind sector as he expected the enemy to launch the main thrust from there. Subsequent events proved his assessment was chillingly accurate.

Another example of his foresight was that he ordered Operation Ablaze, which was essentially the continued deployment of the Armoured Division and other reserve formations closer to their operational areas, instead of returning to their peacetime locations after the de-escalation in the Kutch sector. As a result, India could respond to Pakistan's Operations Gibraltar and Grand Slam launched by Pakistan in a much shorter time frame than if these formations had to be mobilised from the hinterland again. Recognising the importance of maintaining an aggressive posture to keep the offensive spirit of the troops intact, he instructed Brig Ghai, Commander of 121 Infantry Brigade, to capture Point 13620 and Black Rocks in the Kargil sector in May 1965.

In the Jammu and Kashmir sector, he had recommended a change in the deployment and strategy to deal with the Pakistani misadventure across the CFL even before the full magnitude of Operation Gibraltar was realised. His plan called for strong reserves to tackle infiltrators and selectively hold forward positions in strength to prevent infiltration and thwart the capture of important areas. He also proposed taking limited offensive action across the CFL to capture areas which served as launch pads for infiltration.

From the time the large-scale infiltration was discovered on 5 August right up to the ceasefire on 23 September, Lt Gen Harbakhsh was constantly on the move, visiting formations, units, and battlefields. He believed in the old saying 'One look is better than a thousand reports', and his personal presence at the forward formations at critical junctures, such as before the launch of a major operation, ensured that he could give decisions on the spot and speed up operations. Even when he wasn't personally present at a trouble spot, he kept himself constantly updated and took expeditious action whenever necessary. On 13 August, even as the Indian forces were in the process of stemming the tide of infiltrators, he visited Headquarters 68 Infantry Brigade to discuss and finalise the plans for the capture of the Haji Pir pass and bulge. When the Commander of 191 Infantry Brigade, Brigadier BF Master, was killed by Pakistani shelling on 15 August near Jaurian, Lt Gen Harbakhsh immediately instructed the GOC of XV Corps to move the Commander of 162 Infantry Brigade, Brigadier Manmohan Singh, to take over this vital sector immediately. He also ordered the sector to be reinforced by moving 2 Sikh to it from 26 Infantry Division. Even as he was ordering this move, he received a signal from the GOC of XV Corps, recommending that the Haji Pir offensive be called off and the spare troops be used for blocking action against the infiltrators instead. Lt Gen Harbakhsh reacted strongly to this suggested passive course of action, and in his reply made it abundantly clear that it was, 'Essential that enemy is made to react by active operations' and 'Operational plans as discussed must be launched on due date.' He was quite clear on the need to stop reacting to the enemy and wresting the initiative from them.

Reading the various accounts of the war, one gets a sense

Gen Harbakhsh at Haji Pir

that he was the rock that stood unwavering even on occasions when Commanders above or below him had momentary lapses of reason. To his credit, the COAS, Gen JN Chaudhuri, deferred to his advice even at times when he disagreed with him, though he never had occasion to regret doing so. Two instances of such advice are as follows.

On 8 August 1965, when the enormity of Pakistan's grand design in sending in infiltrators became clear to the state government of Jammu and Kashmir, it panicked. The state government requested that the 'Army should take over the state and declare martial law.' Lt Gen Harbakhsh happened to be in Jalandhar along with the Chief when the call from the Defence Secretary to Gen Chaudhuri came through with this news. Lt Gen Harbakhsh strongly advised against such a move for various reasons, all very logical. He felt, and subsequently confirmed by speaking to XV Corps Commander Gen Katoch, that although the infiltrators had managed to reach close to Srinagar, the situation was well under control with army units being rushed in to deal with it. (Lt Gen Harbakhsh had already ordered the move of two battalions to the valley on 6 August – 4 Sikh LI from Kasauli and 2/9 Gorkha Rifles from Jammu, and this timely reinforcement ensured the threat was met before it escalated.) Also, such a move would only give credibility to Pakistani assertions that Kashmir was being held by India by force against the will of its people in the eyes of the international community as well as the people themselves. In hindsight, the summary rejection of overtures of the infiltrators and their Pakistani masters by the people of Kashmir proved the sagacity of his advice. As did the opinion of the United Nations and foreign governments, viewing Pakistan clearly as the aggressor.

The second instance relates to a difference of opinion between Gen Chaudhuri and Lt Gen Harbakhsh on 10 September regarding 4 Mountain Division. The Chief visited Lt Gen Harbakhsh's Headquarters in Ambala to discuss the situation in the Khem Karan–Asal Uttar area which was rather grim, with the Pakistani

1 Armoured Division poised to break through the 4 Mountain Division defences any minute. The Chief was concerned that he had no worthwhile reserves available to commit in case the Pakistanis managed to break through, and they could theoretically have a free run right up to Delhi with hardly any forces to contest them. There was a difference of opinion between the two, and the resulting action exemplifies the leadership qualities of both the Generals. Lt Gen Harbakhsh Singh, convinced of the ability of the troops under his command to stop the Pakistani offensive, was willing to stick his neck out and back this conviction rather than taking the easy way out by agreeing with his boss who felt otherwise. And Gen Chaudhuri had the corresponding confidence in his own subordinate – Lt Gen Harbakhsh – to allow the latter's judgement to prevail over his own.

According to Lt Gen Harbakhsh in his book, *War Dispatches*:

He asked me to consider a readjustment of dispositions should the enemy's 1 Armoured Division break through. I assured him that I was confident of keeping the enemy armoured division in check …. I could see that the Chief was not very reassured with my answer and warned me that the worst might happen, as he knew armour operations better that I did… The argument rested there and the Chief left for Delhi after lunch.

Subsequent events proved Lt Gen Harbakhsh's confidence in his formations well founded, as the Pakistani attack floundered and fizzled out the very next day.

Conversely, Lt Gen Harbakhsh deferred to Gen Chaudhuri's view regarding the launch of I Corps' offensive towards Sialkot. He felt it would be better to launch it via the Indian enclaves of Naina–Kot and Narot involving a crossing of the Ravi while Gen Chaudhuri preferred an offensive along the Samba–Ramgarh direction. In the end, Lt Gen Harbakhsh deferred to the Chief.

Lt Gen Harbakhsh was equally firm and decisive while dealing with his subordinate Commanders. He pushed them when necessary, as he did when the Corps and Division Commanders wanted to countermand his orders for the capture of the Raja and

Rani features in the Haji Pir bulge as part of Operation Faulad. Nor did he hesitate to sack a Commander when he felt that his continuance in command would endanger the chances of success in operations, as he did in numerous cases, including that of the GOC of 15 Infantry Division. It takes a great deal of moral courage to be able to take such decisions and stand by them.

With his maturity and experience, Lt Gen Harbaksh was a Commander who was not given to allowing exaggerated reports of reverses to force him into any kneejerk reactions. After 4 Mountain Division had met with major reversals on 7 and 8 September in the Khem Karan sector, the GOC of XI Corps wrote a letter to Lt Gen Harbakhsh painting an alarming picture about the state of the morale and combat worthiness of the division. Lt Gen Harbakhsh flew down to the Division Headquarters the very next morning and spoke to the GOC. He writes in *War Despatches*:

> *There comes a time in most campaigns when the fate of a battle hangs in the balance and vital issues are at stake. At such crucial junctures unless the commander on the spot asserts himself to dominate the situation, all is lost. That critical stage in battle was then prevailing in the Khem Karan sector and I felt only the highest standard of leadership would save the day.... I discussed the situation with GOC 4 Mountain Division and tried to introduce an atmosphere of calm and confidence in what looked like a very chaotic and confused state of affairs. Fortunately GOC 4 Mountain Division's response was reassuring and self-confident. Within a short space of time he gave all the promise of re-establishing his command and control over the situation. I came away with the feeling that thenceforth 4 Mountain Division would not budge from its position.*

Subsequent events proved him right, as the division stood fast and imposed crippling casualties on the enemy forces, blunting the offensive of the Pakistani 1 Armoured Division and forcing it to withdraw.

Like a skilful conductor harmonising different instruments

in an orchestra to produce melody, he directed the defensive and offensive operations by the three corps – I, XI, and XV – under his command towards ultimate success in battle. His decisive, incisive orders stand out as a common thread running through the conduct of operations across the entire theatre of war.

For his role during the war, he was awarded the Padma Vibhushan, the nation's second highest civilian award. The General passed away on 14 November 1999.

A NATIONAL RESOLVE

People of India

Talking of unsung heroes, there is always a large section of unnamed, faceless people who do not reckon in any counting, who do not figure in any war stories. These are the millions of Indians – ordinary citizens – farmers, merchants, tailors, truck drivers and so on, who did their bit for the nation's war effort. Besides facing the shortages and uncertainties that come with war, they also tried to contribute in their own different ways. Whether it was collection of money for the war effort, feeding of soldiers on their way to the borders, or organizing blood donation camps – the citizens came forward and readily offered all at their disposal to the nation. Thus, a book like this would be incomplete without making at least a small effort to recognise some of the contributions by these unusual heroes. Browsing through the newspapers of this period provides a unique insight into the groundswell of support that the soldiers fighting on the borders enjoyed from the people in cities and villages throughout the country.

The most notable amongst this group of heroes are the people of Jammu and Kashmir. Their steadfast loyalty to India was instrumental in foiling Pakistan's grand design in undertaking Operation Gibraltar. The names of Mohammad Din, a young shepherd from Dara Kassi near Gulmarg and Wazir Mohammad of village Dhabrot near Galauthi are in fact part of the official war history. Mohammad Din was tending to his cattle on 5 August 1965 when he was approached by two armed strangers wearing green salwar kameez uniforms. They offered him a bribe of Rs 400 (a princely sum in those days, especially for a poor man) in exchange for information about the location of Indian troops. While pretending to comply with their request, the young man rushed off and informed the nearest police station. In turn, the army was alerted and the infiltrators were soon dealt with. Wazir Mohammad was made a similar offer by another set of men, and he promptly informed the Indian Army brigade deployed close by. These two men thus played a critical role in uncovering the extent of Pakistani infiltration before they could fully build up their forces.

The basic premise on which Gibraltar was launched was that once the Kashmiri people learned of the Pakistani endeavour to 'liberate' them, they would rise in arms against 'Indian oppression'. Pakistan's operational plans also hinged on the logistic support and shelter the infiltrators would supposedly receive from the Kashmiri people. Their steadfastness and loyalty to India, and in fact, open hostility towards the infiltrators, thus came as a rude shock to the infiltrators and their masters across the border.

There were numerous instances where infiltrators were physically assaulted, apprehended and handed over to the army or police by villagers in different parts of the state. Twenty-year-old Mohan Lal of Jogivan village near Chhamb, along with some companions, tracked down and apprehended two Pakistani raiders. Udey Singh of Kalith village captured an infiltrator along with his rifle and live rounds. He turned out to be a regular soldier of the 2nd Azad Kashmir Battalion. Because of such bold actions by the villagers, the infiltrators could not operate with the kind of freedom they had expected.

As the situation blew up into a full-fledged war, offers of help and support towards the war effort started flooding in from different parts of the country. Mr SL Kirloskar, the chairman of the Federation of Indian Chamber of Commerce (FICCI) appealed to every businessman in every city, town and village to do his duty to the motherland. He stressed the need for the wheels of production to move faster to keep up with the war demands. In Shimla, the Federation of All India Jammu and Kashmir Labour volunteered to depute its entire membership of 5,000 people for any defensive role that the country may find for them.

As all major cities prepared for blackouts and mobilised the civil defence mechanisms, Delhi was divided into ten zones for civil defence. Delhi's Municipal Press Karamchari Union, which was threatening to go on strike for redressal of its grievances shelved the idea and instead all its members decided to contribute a day's pay to the National Defence Fund.

The threat of enemy air raids on towns and cities loomed large. Several towns, especially Ambala bore the brunt of this, when civilian areas and the military hospital were damaged. Blackouts at night was a routine precaution taken in all major cities, including Delhi and Mumbai. But the living were not the only ones who were inconvenienced. As per civil defence measures the burning of funeral pyres was banned between 5 pm and 6 am to avoid presenting a target to enemy aircraft. The annual Ram Leela celebrations at Delhi, one of the highlights of the festive season every year, was also cancelled for similar reasons.

The All India Boy Scouts Association came forward and offered their services in civil defence jobs, as did several other organisations, including the Gram Raksha Dal and former Indian National Army

Civillian trucks drivers who contributed to the war effort

NCC Cadets assisted in maintainance of communications

Euphoria among the civilian population

(INA) soldiers under the leadership of Mohan Singh, an MP at that time and himself a former INA commander. JamAir, the private airlines belonging to the Jam Sahib of Nawanagar offered its aircraft to ferry troops and essential war supplies.

Blood donation camps were held throughout the country, and people donated generously to the National Defence Fund, even going to the extent of offering their family ornaments to the cause of the nation. Young men, eager to fight the enemy, thronged recruitment offices across the country. Truck drivers from across the country offered their services, and were often used to ferry supplies and stores meant for the fighting troops right up to the border. They did so cheerfully and unmindful of the dangers they themselves faced.

An alert civil defence lookout

Alert against sabotage

Politicians from all political parties rallied around the government and Prime Minister Lal Bahadur Shastri, supporting his actions and decisions firmly. Every statement by the Prime Minister or the Defence Minister YB Chavan in the parliament about the progress of operations and exploits of the Indian soldiers met with cheers from members all around. Member after member spoke in the parliament, assuring the government of their unequivocal support in the hour of national crisis.

Apart from the physical contributions of the people of the country, the way they showed their support served as a great morale booster to the soldiers fighting on the front. When they did get a rare opportunity between the fighting to listen to the radio broadcasts and heard of the entire country rallying behind them, it redoubled their resolve to deal with the enemy in a befitting manner.

Bibliography

1. The India-Pakistan War of 1965: A History by SN Prasad and UN Thapliyal
2. 1965 War, the Inside Story: Defence Minister YB Chavan's Diary of India by RD Pradhan
3. War Despatches: Indo-Pak Conflict 1965 by Lt Gen Harbakhash Singh, VrC (Retd)
4. In the Line of Duty: A Soldier Remembers by Lt Gen Harbakhsh Singh, VrC (Retd)
5. Lest We Forget by Capt Amarinder Singh (Retd)
6. Missed Opportunities Indo-Pak War 1965 by Maj Gen Lachhman Singh Lehl, PVSM, VrC (Retd)
7. Behind the Scene: An Analysis of India's Military Operations, 1947–1971 by Maj Gen Jogindar Singh, VSM (Retd)
8. The Crimson Chinar: The Kashmir Conflict: A Politico Military Perspective by Brig Amar Cheema, VSM (Retd)
9. The Red Eagles, A History of Fourth Division of India by KC Praval
10. Saragarhi Battalion: Ashes to Glory by Col Kanwaljit Singh (Retd), Maj HS Ahluwalia (Retd)
11. Living Up to Heritage: History of the Rajput Regiment, 1947–1970, Volume 2 by Mustasad Ahmad
12. The Grenadiers, A Tradition of Valour by RD Palsokar
13. Forefront for Ever: The History of the Mahar Regiment by V Longer
14. Stories of Heroism: PVC & MVC Winners by B Chakravorty
15. The Gallant Dogras: An Illustrated History of the Dogra Regiment by Shankar Prasad

16. While Memory is Fresh by Maj Gen Jagjit Singh (Retd)
17. Role of Tanks in India Pakistan War 1965 by Bhupinder Singh
18. General JN Chaudhuri: An Autobiography, As Narrated to BK Narayan by Joyanto Nath Chaudhuri, Brij Kumar Narayan
19. My Version: India-Pakistan War, 1965 by Gen Mohammed Musa (Retd)
20. Memoirs of Lt Gen Gul Hassan Khan by Lt Gen Gul Hassan Khan (Retd)

The Heroes

Gen JN Chaudhuri
As the Chief of Army Staff during the war, he played a critical role as the link between the political and military decision making.

Lt Gen Harbakhsh Singh
The military leader who planned, directed, and commanded the operations and actions of the 1965 war Lt Gen Harbakhsh Singh was the General Officer Commanding-in-Chief (GOC-in-C) or Army Commander of the Indian Army's Western Command.

Lt Col AB Tarapore
For the gallantry and leadership qualities displayed in leading his regiment in action, Col Tarapore was posthumously awarded the nation's highest gallantry award, the Param Vir Chakra.

CQMH Abdul Hamid
Abdul Hamid, the newly appointed CQMH of C Company, 4 Grenadiers, was ordered to return to the role of a 106mm RCL anti-tank gun detachment commander. With eight tank kills to his credit, he was awarded the highest gallantry award, the Param Vir Chakra.

Lt Col MMS Bakshi
Col Bakshi was awarded the MVC for his dauntless courage and gallantry under fire.

Lt Col Salim Caleb
Lt Col Salim Caleb, Commandant of 3rd Cavalry. Col Caleb was awarded the MVC, and later as a Major General, raised the 31 Armoured Division as its first GOC.

Lt Col Desmond E Hayde
Born in the UK to an Anglo-Indian family of Irish descent, Col Hayde was among the third batch of officers to pass out of the Indian Military Academy (IMA) after independence. Lt Col Hayde took command of his battalion, 3 Jat, in September 1965.

Lt Col NN Khanna
Col Khanna was posthumously awarded the MVC for his exemplary leadership in battle of Raja.

Lt Col PK Nandagopal
Lt Col Pagadala Kuppuswamy Nandagopal personally led two companies of his battalion – C Company under Maj JS Negi and D Company under Major GS Virk – and captured both the features after a tough hand-to-hand fight. Col Nandagopal was awarded the Maha Vir Chakra. He later retired as a Brigadier and settled in Kolar.

Maj Baljit Singh Randhawa
Maj Randhawa, commander of Bravo (B) Company was given the job of capturing Point 13620. Maj Randhawa was posthumously awarded the Maha Vir Chakr (MVC) for his gallant action.

Maj Bhaskar Roy
Maj Bhaskar Roy, the C Squadron Commander from 20 Lancers, whose squadron had been assigned to the brigade defending the Chhamb–Jaurian sector. For his stellar role in preventing the fall of Akhnoor, and the courage and leadership displayed by him against tremendous odds, Maj Bhaskar Roy was awarded the MVC.

Lt Col GS Sangha
Originally commissioned into the Sikh Regiment, Col Sangha had later been transferred to an elite Machine Gun unit of the Mahar Regiment, which he rose to command.

Sub Ajit Singh
JCO, Sub Ajit Singh was a qualified weapons instructor, and an acknowledged marksman. His bravery shown at the battle of Barki was acknowledged by the award of the Maha Vir Chakra.

Lt Col Sampuran Singh
Owing to his personal leadership during both the attacks and the resilience shown by him in turning defeat into victory, Col Sampuran Singh was awarded the MVC. He went on to rise to the rank of a Brigadier.

Capt Kapil Thapa
Capt Thapa led the depth platoon of D Company which was tasked with the capture of North-East Dograi. Capt Kapil Thapa was awarded the MVC for his leadership, bravery and gallantry.

Maj Asa Ram Tyagi
Maj Asa Ram Tyagi led A Company to attack the Eastern area of Dograi on 22 September. The courageous soldier was awarded the MVC for his acts of courage.

Lt Col AS Vaidya
He commanded the Deccan Horse from 29th August 1964 to 07 September 1967. He rose to become the Chief of Army Staff.

About the Author

Lt Col Rohit Agarwal (Retd) is an Armoured Corps officer commissioned into 74 Armoured Regiment in 1989. He took premature retirement from the army in 2010 and now lives in Delhi with his wife and two children. He works as a Learning and Development Consultant and blogs at www.swordarm.in. His earlier books include *Riding the Raisina Tiger* and *Delhi Durbar 1911 – The Complete Story*. Rohit's twitter handle is @ragarwal.